FICTIONS OF THE SEA

Fictions of the Sea: Critical Perspectives on the Ocean in British Literature and Culture

Edited by Bernhard Klein
University of Dortmund

ASHGATE

Published by
Ashgate Publishing Limited
Gower House
Croft Road
Aldershot
Hants GU11 3HR
England

Ashgate Publishing Company
131 Main Street
Burlington, VT Vermont, 05401–5600 USA

Ashgate website: http://www.ashgate.com

British Library Cataloguing in Publication Data
Fictions of the Sea: Critical Perspectives on the Ocean in British Literature and Culture.
    1. English literature—History and criticism. 2. Sea in literature.
    I. Klein, Bernhard
    820.9'36

Library of Congress Cataloging in Publication Data
Fictions of the Sea: Critical Perspectives on the Ocean in British Literature and Culture / edited by Bernhard Klein.
        p.   cm.
    Includes biographical references and index.
    1. English literature—History and criticism. 2. Sea in literature. 3. Sea stories, English—History and criticism. 4. Seafaring life—Great Britain—History. 5. Naval art and science in literature. 6. Seafaring in literature. 7. Sailors in literature.
    I. Klein, Bernhard, 1963–
    PR408.S43F53 2002
    823.009'32162–dc21   2002022345

ISBN 0 7546 0620 1

Printed and bound in Great Britain by MPG Books Ltd, Bodmin, Cornwall

Contents

Notes on Contributors

SUSAN BASSNETT is Pro-Vice-Chancellor at the University of Warwick and Professor in the Centre for British and Comparative Cultural Studies, which she founded in the 1980s. She is the author of over 20 books and her *Translation Studies*, which first appeared in 1980, has become the most important textbook around the world in the expanding field of Translation Studies. Recent books include *Studying British Cultures: An Introduction* (1997), *Constructing Cultures* (1998, written with André Lefevere), and *Postcolonial Translation* (1999, written with Harish Trivedi). She also writes for several national newspapers, and contributes an education column to *The Independent*. Her latest book, a collection of poems and translations, is *Exchanging Lives* (2001).

VALERIE BURTON teaches in the History Department at Memorial University of Newfoundland, Canada. She publishes in British maritime history and, while trained as an economic historian, is now interested in the new economic criticism and its application to historical categories and identities.

TOBIAS DÖRING teaches Literature and Cultural Studies at the English Department of the Freie Universität Berlin, where his current project is 'Performances of Mourning in Early Modern Theatre and Culture'. He has published numerous articles on anglophone and postcolonial writing. His book publications include *Caribbean-English Passages* (2002), *Chinua Achebe und Joyce Cary* (1996) and *Figuren der/des Dritten* (co-edited with Claudia Breger, 1998).

INA HABERMANN is Lecturer in English and Cultural Studies at the University of Erlangen. She has published several articles and reviews on gender and early modern literature. Her book on the staging of slander and gender in early modern England is forthcoming. She is currently working on fiction by women in the early 20th century.

ULRICH KINZEL is Associate Professor for German Literature at the University of Hamburg. His publications include *Zweideutigkeit als System*

(1988), a study on Thomas Mann's *Doctor Faustus*, and *Ethische Projekte* (2000), a study on German literature and governmentality. He is currently working on a project on maritime culture and literary experience.

BERNHARD KLEIN is Lecturer in English and Cultural Studies at the University of Dortmund. His book publications include *Maps and the Writing of Space in Early Modern England and Ireland* (2001), *Literature, Mapping, and the Politics of Space in Early Modern Britain* (co-edited with Andrew Gordon, 2001), and *Common Ground? Crossovers between Cultural Studies and Postcolonial Studies* (co-edited with Jürgen Kramer, 2001). The essay collection *Oceans and Voyagers: Historicizing the Sea as a Transnational Contact Zone* (co-edited with Gesa Mackenthun) is forthcoming. His current project deals with literature and the historical imagination in contemporary Ireland.

JÜRGEN KRAMER is Professor of British Cultural Studies at the University of Dortmund. His main research areas are British Cultural Studies, history of Britain and the British Empire, the sea as a cultural space, transatlantic slavery, literature of the Pacific, cultural memory, anti-colonial resistance, Joseph Conrad, Robert Louis Stevenson. Recent publications include *Cultural and Intercultural Studies* (1990) and *British Cultural Studies* (1997); he is co-editor of the *Journal for the Study of British Cultures* (1994-).

SARAH MOSS holds the Randall MacIver Research Fellowship at Lady Margaret Hall, Oxford, and has recently completed a doctorate on Romanticism, voyaging and the Arctic. She is writing a book called *Scott's Last Biscuit: A Cultural History of Polar Exploration* and is also researching late 18th-century women's writing.

JAMES MULDOON, Professor of History (Emeritus) of Rutgers University, is now an Invited Research Scholar at The John Carter Brown Library at Brown University. His most recent books are *Canon Law, the Expansion of Europe, and World Order* (1998) and *Empire and Order: The Concept of Empire, 800-1800* (1999).

PATRIZIA A. MUSCOGIURI received her first degree in Modern Literature and Languages in Italy and is currently engaged in doctoral research at the University of Salford. Her thesis, entitled *The Sign of the Breaker: Shipwreck, Sea and Language in (Post)modernity*, explores radical inscriptions of sea metaphors in literary and film texts of the 20th century, in particular women's writing. Her research interests include contemporary cinema (1950s to the present) and writers such as S.T.

Coleridge, Joseph Conrad, Virginia Woolf, H.D., Clarice Lispector, Luce Irigaray, Angela Carter and Toni Morrison. She is currently preparing several articles for publication.

CARL PEDERSEN is Associate Professor of American Studies and Director of the Center for American Studies at the University of Southern Denmark. He is President of the Collegium for African American Research (CAAR). His latest publications are *Black Imagination and the Middle Passage* (1999, co-edited with Maria Diedrich and Henry Louis Gates, Jr.) and 'The Tropics in New York: Claude McKay and the New Negro Movement' in Genevieve Fabre and Michel Feith (eds), *Temples for Tomorrow: Looking Back at the Harlem Renaissance* (2001).

ARNOLD SCHMIDT is Associate Professor at the California State University, Stanislaus. He received his BA and MA from the State University of New York at New Paltz, and his PhD from Vanderbilt University, where he wrote a dissertation entitled 'The Romantic Mariner: Sailors, Slaves, and Literary Polemics'. His articles have appeared in such publications as *Nineteenth Century Contexts* and *Wordsworth Circle*, and he contributed several entries to the *Encyclopedia of American Literature of the Sea and the Great Lakes*.

ANNE-JULIA ZWIERLEIN is Assistant Professor at the Centre for British Studies, University of Bamberg. She received her PhD from the University of Münster, and she is the author of *Majestick Milton: British Imperial Expansion and Transformations of* Paradise Lost*, 1667 - 1837* (2001). She has published on early modern science, 18th-century forgeries, and postcolonial concepts of history.

List of Illustrations

Acknowledgements

Most of the essays in this collection were first presented as conference papers at the interdisciplinary symposium *Sea Changes: Historicizing the Ocean, c. 1500 - c. 1900*, held at Greifswald-Wieck, 20-24 July 2000, and convened by Gesa Mackenthun and myself. The great number of excellent papers presented at that meeting that were concerned specifically with Britain and the sea made it appropriate that an entire volume should be devoted to this topic. A second selection of papers from the conference, concerned with transnational explorations of the ocean, is forthcoming under the (current) title *Oceans and Voyagers. Historicizing the Sea as a Transnational Contact Zone.* I am grateful to the Thyssen-Stiftung and to the Deutsche Forschungsgemeinschaft without whose generous financial grants the original conference would not have been possible. Thanks to Jürgen Kramer (Dortmund) and Hartmut Lutz (Greifswald) for their support and encouragement, and to Gesa for being the most reliable of co-organizers. To all contributors to *Fictions of the Sea* I owe a debt of gratitude for their cooperation, for sharing my enthusiasm in the topic, and for not making too much of a mockery of that dreaded term, 'deadline'. Special thanks are due to Martina Iske for her careful and reliable proofreading, and, at Ashgate, to Erika Gaffney for her initial interest in the project and to Kirsten Weißenberg for her expert editorial assistance.

Introduction:
Britain and the Sea

BERNHARD KLEIN

In Barry Unsworth's recent novel *Losing Nelson* (1999), the radiant British naval commander whose victory at Trafalgar 'gave [Britain] supremacy at sea into the twentieth century',[1] is a figure of unrivalled heroic authority in the eyes of the novel's protagonist, the amateur historian Charles Cleasby. Convinced of Nelson's angelic virtues and his status as the 'quintessential hero and quintessential national representative',[2] Cleasby structures his entire life around the rituals of hero worship: moving replica ships across a glass table in his basement, he re-enacts Nelson's major sea battles, always in real time and on the precise date on which they happened; he accumulates what must be the most impressive 'gallery of Nelsoniana'[3] outside the National Maritime Museum; he regularly visits Nelson's 'shrine',[4] the flagship HMS *Victory* at Portsmouth, where he is dismayed by the irreverence of the local guides; and he spends his days writing a biography of the Admiral that will 'revolutionize Nelson studies'[5] and set the record straight on the one incident in his life which has always cast a shadow on an otherwise unblemished career, a dubious act of political scheming at Naples in 1799. Thinking of himself as 'Horatio's other self',[6] a dark shadow to the bright angel, Cleasby's obsession with Nelson grows more and more pathological until he can no longer maintain the pretence of sanity. His occasional typist unwittingly inflicts the first wounds on his fragile psyche when she openly doubts Nelson's heroism and asks impertinent questions about his attitudes to women, but the final blow is dealt by a rival Nelson scholar who confirms Nelson's part in the fraud at Naples and confronts Cleasby with the unwelcome insight that '"[h]eroes are fabricated in the national dream factory. Heroes are not people. ... There are no heroes out there, Mr Cleasby, only fears and dreams and the process of fabrication."'[7]

In this 'tarnished'[8] and cynical age, as Cleasby habitually describes the present from which he feels so entirely alienated, his delusions of heroic

1

grandeur are likely to cause more derision than pity, if they are taken seriously at all. The idea of the spotless hero, or rather the alleged need for this incarnation of national glory, no longer finds much support in the Western world, and has ceased to serve as a viable example of moral rectitude. It is, however, no accident that Cleasby chooses Nelson as his ultimate icon of a bygone age of honour, heroism and national greatness. Nelson was not just a superior military brain and a model patriot, he was first and foremost a sea captain, and the ocean was both his heroic habitat and the foundational site of a vast and evolving political space - the British Empire - that was, to all intents and purposes, an empire of the seas. 'The originating agents of empire', David Armitage contends, 'were the Elizabethan sea-dogs, Gloriana's sailor-heroes who had circumnavigated the globe, singed the King of Spain's beard, swept the oceans of pirates and Catholics, and thereby opened up the sea-routes across which English migrants would travel, and English trade would flow, until Britannia majestically ruled the waves.'[9] Nelson is perhaps the most shining star that ever rose above that sea-borne empire first envisaged in Elizabethan times, and Cleasby's devotion to the greatest of British naval heroes is a sign both of the deep historical affinity between Britain and the sea, and of the ocean's continuing power to evoke fantasies of national and moral supremacy. In the words of Cleasby's antagonist, the sea is indeed a 'national dream factory'.

As a historical topic, the conjunction 'Britain and the Sea' might not stand much in need of explanation. An island people poised just beyond the edge of the European mainland - *toto divisos orbe*, 'wholly cut off from the world', as Virgil thought[10] - would be expected to entertain not only an economic but a deeply affectionate bond with the surrounding sea. Indeed, Cleasby could take comfort in any number of openly nationalist accounts of Britain's patriotic pact with the ocean. Shakespeare famously had John of Gaunt reminisce about a 'sceptred isle' that was 'bound in with the triumphant sea', protected by nature 'Against infection and the hand of war';[11] in this triumphalism he was seconded a few decades later by Edmund Waller, who, speaking in the Long Parliament early in the Civil War, thought that 'God and nature have given us the sea as our best guard against our enemies; and our ships, as our greatest glory above other nations'.[12] In the 18th century, James Thomson elevated the sentiment into the hyperbole that Britannia has been ruling the waves ever since 'Britain first, at Heaven's command, / Arose from out the azure main',[13] and yet a century later, Robert Louis Stevenson added that Britain's relation to the ocean is the natural stuff of literature: 'The sea is our approach and bulwark; it has been the scene of our greatest triumphs and dangers, and we are accustomed in lyrical strains to claim it as our own.'[14] No doubt the Tory historian James

Anthony Froude would have agreed wholeheartedly: 'After their own island, the sea is the natural home of Englishmen'.[15]

Anybody in search of memorable quotations about the sea in British
writing over the last few hundred years is confronted with an embarrass-
ment of riches. Even a cursory glance at the many anthologies of British
sea fiction confirms the wide imaginative range of the literary engagement
with matters maritime,[16] and there can be little doubt that the attempt to
offer a complete coverage of Britain's literature of the sea is bound to fail
in the same manner that Cleasby's Nelson hagiography is eventually abandoned: for his devoted disciple, the Admiral simply stands for so much
more than what could possibly be contained between the covers of a single
book. In calling this collection *Fictions of the Sea*, my intention is thus not
to pretend that it offers a comprehensive survey of British sea fiction.[17]
Knowing that the topic - much as the ocean itself - is boundless, this is a
more modest project: it aims to bring together a series of critical and historically informed readings which encompass a wide but necessarily selec-
tive range of imaginative uses of the sea in British literature and culture.
The term 'fiction' is applied broadly to include not only what is conventionally classified as sea fiction (for instance, novels by Captain Marryat,
Joseph Conrad, Daphne du Maurier, C.S. Forester, Patrick O'Brian), but
also writings which respond to important topics in maritime history (the
rise of the Empire as reflected in 18th-century Milton studies, for instance,
or its decline as echoed in later writers), ideological constructs projected
onto the ocean (for instance, the varying legal conceptions of the sea as a
space either open or closed, or the re-modelling of the public image of the
sailor under the impetus of 19th-century industralization), as well as texts
that engage with wider issues relevant to the historical experience of seafaring: problems of navigation and orientation, piracy, slavery, multi-ethnic
shipboard communities, masculinity, gender relations.

The book covers the period from early modern times to the present, and
literature offers perhaps the best yardstick to assess the changing cultural
conceptions of the sea across the centuries. Alain Corbin's history of the
meaning of the seaside in Western civilization has been among the most
compelling of studies that explore the semantic metamorphoses of an ancient cultural topos,[18] and the shift he traces from a demonic space that was
reviled for its 'barbarity', its chaotic lack of structure (a reminder of unfinished creation) and its imposition of natural and moral limits on the human
world,[19] to a pleasure circuit that signified refined taste, leisure and the
expansiveness of modernity, is reflected in the changing literary representation of the ocean. The negative image of the evil sea and its many associated dangers is traditionally seen to be replaced in the 18th century with an

emerging conception of the ocean - in the contexts of colonization, economic modernization and global trade - as a technically manageable but socially sensitive space, epitomized by the *cause célèbre* of the *Bounty* mutiny.[20] Thus 18th-century accounts present the ocean voyage as a largely pragmatic enterprise,[21] and contemporary nautical drama foregrounds realistic elements of life and work at sea.[22] The Romantic counter-image would re-invent the sea as a realm of unspoiled nature and a refuge from the perceived threats of civilization,[23] yet any actual foray into the timeless maritime expanse of deep cultural longing was to confront man with the extremes of experience - witness Coleridge's *Rime of the Ancient Mariner* or Poe's hyperbolic *Narrative of Arthur Gordon Pym*. 19th-century representations of the sea frequently turn the ocean into a reflector of subjective consciousness or a metaphor of cultural *rites de passage*, often equating the sea-voyage with psychological catharsis or taking the form of a 'moody, metaphysical brooding on the obvious analogue of voyage and life'.[24] The romantic sea adventure tale with its focus on the effects of the ocean on the individual or national psyche properly belongs to the century after the great naval battles of the Napoleonic Wars.

Such generalizations might be crying out for historical contexts but research on sea fiction is still too often conducted in narrowly conceived critical or generic frameworks.[25] This criticism, while often impressively attentive to the textual subtleties of 'writing the ocean', runs the danger not only of losing out of sight the wider cultural contexts of the modern maritime experience, but also of remaining within the imaginative confines of the popular sea adventure tale. In *Lord Jim*, Conrad ridiculed the pretensions of much that is classified under this rubric:

> [Jim] would forget himself, and beforehand live in his mind the sea-life of light literature. He saw himself saving people from sinking ships, cutting away masts in a hurricane, swimming through a surf with a line; or as a lonely castaway, barefooted and half naked, walking on uncovered reefs in search of shellfish to stave off starvation. He confronted savages on tropical shores, quelled mutinies on the high seas, and in a small boat upon the ocean kept up the hearts of despairing men - always an example of devotion to duty, and as unflinching as a hero in a book.[26]

There are, of course, many other ways of writing about the sea, and many other ways of reading the fictions it has generated. Jonathan Raban suggests that '[t]he sea in literature is not a verifiable object, to be described, with varying degrees of success and shades of emphasis, by writers of different periods; it is, rather, the supremely liquid and volatile element, shaping itself newly for every writer and every generation.'[27] There is an element of circularity in this statement but the important point is that fictions of the sea are never limited to any one frame of reference or historically specific perspectival arrangement. The adventure genre that Conrad mimics in his brief ironic sketch has perhaps been a dominant mode in the textual representation of the sea, but it is by no means the only or even the most influential way in which it has been imagined in literature and culture. One aim of the essays in this volume is to foreground the diversity, as well as the politics, of the many different maritime fictions that have shaped ways of thinking about the ocean since the 16th century.

In doing so, this volume follows to some extent the lead of recent innovative studies in maritime history. A number of maritime historians have for some time been involved in re-conceptualizing their field of research as a social and cultural history of seafaring, and a few studies have also begun to bridge the gap between the disciplines of history and literature.[28] In such projects, the sea is no longer discussed merely as an empirical, socio-economic fact or as the imaginative setting for heroic and romantic adventure stories but as a social and cultural space that has been the site of radical changes in human lives and national histories. These insights have also given rise to a number of historical studies on crews and passengers that have both highlighted the ethnically diverse character of many historical shipboard communities[29] and significantly revised our image of the traditional masculine world of the ship.[30] These shifts of focus and emphasis in maritime history have all influenced shape and content of the present volume. Although it is principally concerned with literature, it is decidedly interdisciplinary in approach and method, and considers a broad range of historical evidence: among the textual and visual artefacts examined are early modern legal treatises on marine boundaries, Renaissance and Romantic poetry, 19th and 20th-century novels, paintings, sea songs, recent Hollywood films, as well as a diverse range of historical, critical and philosophical writings. The overall aim of the volume is perhaps best described as the attempt to chart metaphorical and material links between the idea of the sea in the cultural imagination and its significance for the social and political history of Britain, thus offering what I hope is a fresh analysis of the impact of the sea on the formation of British cultural identities.

The twelve essays are arranged in roughly chronological order. The two opening contributions examine significant legal and spatial shifts in the European attitude to the ocean at the beginning of our time frame. In his analysis of the early 17th-century legal debate about the freedom of the oceans, James Muldoon considers the extent to which a contemporary thinking that seemingly responded to the new global context of worldwide travel and trade was in fact still indebted to a legal tradition stretching back to the European Middle Ages. Depending on their national interests, those who engaged in this debate - principally the Dutch, the Portuguese, and the British - defended either the *mare liberum* or the *mare clausum*, but these legal positions were all formulated within a shared intellectual frame of reference, inherited from medieval times. And although, as Muldoon shows, the new international order that emerged from this debate was based on the right of free access to the oceans, ideas similar to those used in the 17th century against the idea of the ocean as a space open to all, and in favour of the papal right to close a sea, resurface in the modern-day demands for sharing the wealth of the sea with all the nations of the world. Conceptual shifts in spatial awareness accompanied such legal reorientations, as Ulrich Kinzel argues in the next essay. The practicalities of oceanic navigation, as opposed to Mediterranean 'coasting', demanded not only a whole new set of technological innovations in seafaring but also resulted in a new moral understanding of the relation between the self and the world. The key word here is 'orientation', a concept that applies equally to a ship transgressing the ancient limits of the world and to the moral economy of the self faced with new forms of contingency. By historicizing the 'oceanic turn' of the 16th century with reference to three discursive aspects of deep-sea voyaging - the art of navigation, the allegory of fortune and the practice of systematic travel observation - Kinzel shows how contemporaries found in the image of the voyager on the open sea a model for the existential condition of modernity.

The following two essays analyse the historical experience of seafaring and long-distance trade as crucial referential frameworks in the literary works of, respectively, Milton and Coleridge. Anne-Julia Zwierlein shows how the poetic ocean in *Paradise Lost* is still largely a symbolic entity, replete with warnings about the material and spiritual dangers of oceanic travel and the luxury goods imported from overseas, even though Milton clearly draws on recent travel accounts and the latest findings of contemporary geographers. In his capacity as a seafarer, Milton's Satan capitalizes on this ambiguity of description: as the prototype of all subsequent human ocean voyagers, he can be recognized as a merchant, an East India Company official, an explorer, and even, perhaps, a slave trader, but ultimately, his epistemological function in the symbolic Christian universe of Milton's poem foregrounds the status of the ocean as the inherently repulsive realm of unformed matter and primeval 'chaos'. It is only in 18th-century re-readings of *Paradise Lost* that the sea is divested of these meanings and Satan's poetic ocean voyage transformed into a sublime comment on British naval achievements, celebrating the global flow of trade and the glory of empire. The realities of 18th-century seafaring enter Coleridge's *Rime of the Ancient Mariner* in quite a different way, as Sarah Moss argues in her contribution. Turning her attention to the play of power on ships in the South Seas and to the influence of early modern voyage narratives on the *Rime*, specifically of John Davis' *Last Voyage of the Worshipfull M. Thomas Cavendish* (1593), Moss rejects recent critical readings of Coleridge's poem which place it in the context of the slave trade. Instead, Moss argues, if the specifically Antarctic setting of the poem is taken seriously - a veritable *terra incognita* in this period, far removed from the slave-trading circuit - the conditions of life at sea and the conditions of life in England which drove men to work at sea offer an equally plausible field for the concerns of a late 18th-century political radical.

In all these essays the ocean and the maritime activities connected with it emerge as intensely political in nature, and this socially inflected understanding of the relation between land and sea only intensifies in the 19th century. The next two essays are concerned with specific local responses to the 'politics' of the ocean; both examine related forms of maritime crime. Arnold Schmidt discusses Sir Walter Scott's novel *The Pirate* (1821) as a text deeply implicated in the colonial imagination of its historical moment. The novel opens on the Shetland and Orkney Islands, at the time colonies of the Scottish mainland, where Scott's characters engage in piracy, wrecking, impressment and smuggling. Thematically, the pirate - both the figure and the novel - foregrounds the close associations between crime and commerce, revealing them as disturbingly similar in nature. Exploring these associations in the light of Scott's image of Regency ethics as a conflict between piratical and bourgeois values, Schmidt reads Scott's novel as a text whose titular pirate serves as a locus of ethical, commercial and political anxieties. Ina Habermann then juxtaposes the philosophical discourse of the 'shipwreck with spectator' - described by Hans Blumenberg as an ancient 'metaphor for existence'[31] - with the social practice of 19th-century shipwrecking on the Cornish coast, popularized by Daphne du Maurier's 1936 novel *Jamaica Inn*, set in 1810. Taking her cue from Shakespeare's *Tempest* (a literary instance of shipwreck tellingly ignored by Blumenberg), Habermann argues that the deeply ambiguous cultural myth of shipwreck only begins to unfold its full existential meaning when philosophical discourse, socio-historical practice and the literary imagination are brought into critical and imaginative proximity.

Two further essays show how the myth of the sea was available for ideological manoeuvres that aimed to mystify political and social realities in the 19th century. Tobias Döring asks how the romance of the sea could be reinvented to sustain the narrative of imperial glory at a time when the 'oceanic sublime' was in fact under attack from various sides - not least from technological innovations that put an end to the heroic age of sail, a contrast Turner suggestively evokes in 'The Fighting "Temeraire"' (1839), the painting Döring uses to open his discussion. Two neglected books from the second half of the 19th century yield interesting, if unexpected answers to this question. Both the Liberal Prime Minister Gladstone in his *Studies on Homer and the Homeric Age* (1858) and the Tory historian Froude in *The English in the West Indies, or The Bow of Ulysses* (1887) turn to the ancient epics of Homer with a view to overcoming modern disenchantments about the sea and the current state of Britain's sea-borne empire. Both authors historicize the ocean in strikingly different ways, and both employ different rhetorical strategies to revitalize the sea as a site of national achievement, but despite their differences, both books are also evidence of the common need to resurrect a - largely mythical - heroic past as an antidote to a decidedly unheroic present. Valerie Burton then considers aspects of the modernization of the mercantile marine in the 19th century within the context of contemporary gender relations. The transition from sail to steam in an age of rapid commercial and imperial expansion radically changed not only the working conditions of sailors but also the cultural forms in which the sailors' male world at sea intersected with the world they shared with women on shore. Focusing in particular on London's Ratcliffe Highway, Burton juxtaposes the social reality of 'sailortown' and the anxieties it caused among moral reformers and political economists with the fictions it generated in the form of sea shanties and seafaring tales. These sailortown legends constructed images of seafaring men as libidinous sailor-heroes whose excessive sexual energies challenged burgeois social norms. Interestingly, such tales of (sexual and economic) 'spending' were couched in an arcane commercial vocabulary that contradicted an economic order where men were ascribed new roles as the responsible sole breadwinners of the nuclear family. These songs, as Burton shows, cannot be explained simply as anachronistic expressions of sea-focused nostalgia; at a deeper level they articulated an imaginative resistance against the imperatives of liberal political economy and its restrictive refashioning of gender relations.

Sea fiction in a more directly literary sense is the topic of the next two essays which both take the modern sea novel as their theme. Jürgen Kramer contrasts Joseph Conrad's real-life experience of multi-ethnic shipboard communities with the literary representation (and obfuscation) of the crews in his novels. It has frequently been argued that the reason why Conrad's fictional crews were more nationally homogenous than their factual counterparts was Conrad's desire to portray his service at sea more English in character than it really was. As Kramer shows, this line of reasoning fails to engage with the far more subtle statements about the mixing of different nationalities on board ship that Conrad incorporates in his novels and tales. In fact, his ironic comments on the forms of cross-cultural contact and the reality of xenophobic nationalism he experienced in his own life and career remain unnoticed when mere statistics are compared. In the double vision that emerges from Kramer's reading, the literary construction of the sea as a multi-ethnic cultural space and its shaping influence on Conrad's seafaring protagonists yields crucial insights into the role of the sea in his own biographical self-fashioning. Susan Bassnett then picks up several thematic strands - heroism at sea, the decline of the British Empire, and in particular the construction of masculinity in maritime fiction - to argue that the popular 19th and 20th-century sea novels by Captain Maryatt, C.S. Forester and Patrick O'Brian all respond to particular cultural conditions of their historical moment. Marryat's world is the heyday of the Empire in the 19th century, Forester's the period of change and uncertainty of World War II and its aftermath, O'Brian's the present moment of devolution, re-evaluation and repositioning, and in each case these historical contexts shape the conceptual possibilities of the fictional re-imagining of heroic life under sail. Thus, although certain representational conventions and plot elements are common to all three sets of novels - exciting naval action, male bonding, individual bravery, etc. - each writer constructs a central protagonist who encodes a very different version of heroic English masculinity, exposing the extent to which writing about Britain's naval past always reflects present-day cultural concerns.

Most recently, the sea has again been the topic of many novels and films, and this recurrence of maritime motifs is examined in terms of its historical significance in the final two essays of the volume. In his survey of fictional and factual accounts of the transatlantic slave trade, Carl Pedersen examines how literature and historiography enter into a dialogue with each other. Concentrating on two recent novels of the Middle Passage - Barry Unsworth's *Sacred Hunger* (1992), which relates the voyage of the *Liverpool Merchant* in 1752, and Fred D'Aguiar's *Feeding the Ghosts* (1997), which recounts the voyage of the *Zong* in 1781 - Pedersen shows how prominent themes of recent slave trade historiography (especially the focus on African agency, the foregrounding of a wider Atlantic context, and the tension between statistical data and accounts of individual experience) have influenced, and been in turn influenced by, the literary imagination. In the final contribution - which moves beyond the national confines of the volume's title - Patrizia Muscogiuri supplements Pedersen's analysis of the 'sea of slavery' constructed in fiction by asking why tales of sea voyages and shipwreck have become such popular topics in contemporary cinema. In her discussion of several recent films, Muscogiuri discovers the reworking of ancient cultural topoi, in particular the concept of the sea voyage as a transgression of man's natural limits and the 'shipwreck with spectator' as a metaphorical rendering of the human condition. More significantly, though, in films such as James Cameron's *Titanic* (1997), Gabriele Salvatores' *Mediterraneo* (1991) and Peter Weir's *The Truman Show* (1998), the shipwreck metaphor absorbs new meanings by effecting a radical break or discontinuity of cultural and social identities, and the discourses which sustain them, thus projecting onto the sea the possibility of a metaphorical escape from the pressures of history.

The time span of these essays is not the result of an arbitrary choice. To begin in the 16th century is to return to the moment of the European 'discovery of the sea', in J.H. Parry's phrase,[32] the moment when Western seafarers 'discovered' that all the seas of the world were really just one vast navigable ocean. It is also the age for which Carl Schmitt has diagnosed a 'space revolution on a planetary scale',[33] resulting in a new world order based on the fundamental distinction between the different spatial entities of land and sea, and leading to a three-hundred-year-long 'British maritime domination of the world'.[34] The loss of that domination in the 20th century clearly haunts Charles Cleasby, and perhaps his desperate efforts to revitalize the memory of Lord Nelson are simply eccentric acts of mourning. Today, the sea no longer affects our lives in quite the same way as it did before the airplane replaced the ship as the principal means of long-distance transport. Our language, however, still bears many traces of an earlier age: we catch our planes at the air*port*, we *log on* to a computer, we *navigate* the web. More importantly, over half a millennium of instrumentalizing the ocean in the service of globalization and imperialism has left visible traces on the present-day world order. The return, then, in current literature and film (even in scholarship), to the sea and to its associated images and symbols, affirms the continuing relevance of the maritime as a shaping fantasy of the cultural imagination as much as it defines the ocean as a deeply historical and radically political space.

Notes

1   Barry Unsworth, *Losing Nelson* (Harmondsworth: Penguin, 1999), 132.
2   *Ibid.*, 103.
3   *Ibid.*, 266.
4   *Ibid.*, 205.
5   *Ibid.*, 276.
6   *Ibid.*, 236.

7 *Ibid.*, 304.

8 *Ibid.*, 108.

9 David Armitage, *The Ideological Origins of the British Empire* (Cambridge: Cambridge University Press, 2000), 100.

10 In *Eclogues*, 1:66.

11 William Shakespeare, *Richard II*, 2.1.40, 44, 61. Quotation to *The Norton Shakespeare*, ed. Stephen Greenblatt *et al.* (New York and London: Norton, 1997).

12 *A Complete Collection of State Trials ... From the Earliest Period to the Year 1783*, ed. T.B. Howell, 21 vols (London: Longman & Co., 1816), vol. 3, col. 1303; quoted in Armitage, *Ideological Origins*, 117.

13 James Thomson, 'Rule, Britannia!', *Complete Poetical Works*, ed. J. Logie Robertson (London *et al.*: Oxford University Press, 1951), 422.

14 Robert Louis Stevenson, 'The English Admirals', *Cornhill* 38 (July 1878), 36; quoted in Cynthia Fansler Behrman, *Victorian Myths of the Sea* (Athens, Ohio: Ohio University Press, 1977), 26.

15 James Anthony Froude, *Oceana; or, England and Her Colonies* (London: Longmans, Green, and Co., 1886), 18.

16 Just for starters, consider these: John Coote (ed.), *The Faber Book of the Sea* (London: Faber, 1989); John Coote (ed.), *The Faber Book of Tales of the Sea* (London: Faber, 1991); Jonathan Raban (ed.), *The Oxford Book of the Sea* (Oxford: Oxford University Press, 1991); and Tony Tanner (ed.), *The Oxford Book of Sea Stories* (Oxford: Oxford University Press, 1994). Despite the universal claims of their titles, all these anthologies deal only, or at least predominantly, with British and American sea fiction.

17 For American sea fiction, this has been Haskell Springer's project in his edited volume *America and the Sea* (Athens: University of Georgia Press, 1995). See also two earlier collections: Richard Astro (ed.), *Literature and the Sea* (Corvallis: Oregon State University Press, 1976); and Patricia Ann Carlson (ed.), *Literature and Lore of the Sea* (Amsterdam: Rodopi, 1986).

18 See Alain Corbin, *The Lure of the Sea. The Discovery of the Seaside in the Western World, 1750-1840* [French original 1988], trans. Jocelyn Phelps (Cambridge: Polity Press, 1994).

19 Many of these meanings are traced in Hans Blumenberg's suggestive little book *Shipwreck with Spectator. Paradigm of a Metaphor for Existence* [German original 1979], trans. Steven Rendall (Cambridge, MA, and London: MIT Press, 1996).

20 For an excellent study on the *Bounty* mutiny and its many cultural and historical meanings, see Greg Dening, *Mr Bligh's Bad Language. Passion, Power and Theatre on the Bounty* (Cambridge: Cambridge University Press, 1992).

21 On the 18th-century sea voyage see Philip Edwards, *The Story of the Voyage. Sea-Narratives in 18th Century England* (Cambridge: Cambridge University Press, 1994); see also his *Sea-Marks. The Metaphorical Voyage, Spenser to Milton* (Liverpool: Liverpool University Press, 1997).

22 See Peter Krahé, *Literarische Seestücke: Darstellungen von Meer und Seefahrt in der englischen Literatur des 18.-20. Jahrhunderts* (Hamburg: Kabel, 1992).

23 See Kirsten Broecheler, *Seereisen in der englischsprachigen Romanliteratur vom 18. bis 20. Jahrhundert* (Frankfurt am Main *et al.*: Lang, 1998), 15.

24 Tony Tanner, 'Introduction', Tanner (ed.), *The Oxford Book of Sea Stories*, xi-xviii, xiv.

25 See, for instance, Broecheler, *Seereisen*; and more recently John Peck, *Maritime Fiction. Sailors and the Sea in British and American Novels, 1719-1917* (Basingstoke: Palgrave, 2001). Both books are exclusively concerned with the novel. By contrast, Iris Lochbaum's recent *Fathoming Metaphors. Meeresbilder in viktorianischer Lyrik* (Trier: Wissenschaftlicher Verlag, 2001) deals exclusively with poetry. Still, these works should be measured against earlier studies on English or British sea fiction which are often little more than extensive compilations of quotes. See, for instance, Ernest Carson Ross, *The Development of the English Sea Novel from Defoe to Conrad* (Ann Arbor: Edwards Bros., 1925); Anne Treneer, *The Sea in English Literature. From Beowulf to Donne* (Liverpool: The University Press of Liverpool; London: Hodder and Stoughton, 1926); Harold Francis Watson, *The Sailor in English Fiction and Drama, 1550-1800* (New York: Columbia University Press, 1931); or Alexander Frederick Falconer, *Shakespeare and the Sea* (London: Constable, 1964).

26 Joseph Conrad, *Lord Jim* [1900] (Harmondsworth: Penguin, 1989), 47.

27 Jonathan Raban, 'Introduction', Raban (ed.), *The Oxford Book of the Sea*, 1-34, 3.

28 In many ways, such studies were pioneered by Marcus Rediker's *Between the Devil and the Deep Blue Sea: Merchant Seaman, Pirates, and the Anglo-American Maritime World, 1700-1750* (Cambridge: Cambridge University Press, 1987). See also Rediker's more recent book, jointly written with Peter Linebaugh, *The Many-Headed Hydra. Sailors, Slaves, Commoners, and the Hidden History of the Revolutionary Atlantic* (Boston: Beacon Press, 2000); and several recent cross-disciplinary collections on maritime history: Colin Howell and Richard Twomey (eds), *Jack Tar in History. Essays in the History of Maritime Life and Labour* (Fredricton, New Brunswick: Acadiensis Press, 1991), Margaret Creighton and Lisa Norling (eds), *Iron Men, Wooden Women. Gender and Seafaring in the Atlantic World, 1700-1920* (Baltimore: Johns Hopkins University Press, 1996); Bernhard Klein and Gesa Mackenthun (eds), *Oceans and Voyagers. Historicizing the Sea as a Transnational Contact Zone* (forthcoming). Greg Dening's excellent work on the Pacific, most notably *Mr Bligh's Bad Language* (see note 20), has also been highly influential in this context.

29 See, for instance, Jeffrey Bolster, *Black Jacks. African American Seamen in the Age of Sail* (Cambridge, MA: Harvard University Press, 1997); and David Chappell, *Double Ghosts: Oceanian Voyagers on Euroamerican Ships* (Armonk, NY: M.E. Sharpe, 1997).

30 See, for instance, recent work on seafaring women such as Suzanne Stark, *Female Tars. Women Aboard Ship in the Age of Sail* (London: Pimlico, 1998); and the essays on gender and seafaring in Creighton and Norling (eds), *Iron Men, Wooden Women*.

31 See Blumenberg, *Shipwreck with Spectator*.

32 See J.H. Parry, *The Discovery of the Sea* (London: Weidenfeld and Nicolson, 1974).

33 Carl Schmitt, *Land and Sea* [German original 1944], trans. Simona Draghici (Washington, DC: Plutarch Press, 1997), 33.

34 *Ibid.*, 26.

1   Who Owns the Sea?

JAMES MULDOON

At first glance, the notion of owning the sea seems silly. How could any nation or group of nations own that vast expanse? Indeed, who would want to do so? Rephrase the question, however, replacing ownership with jurisdiction, asking, 'Who has jurisdiction over the sea and over who sails upon it, and who can exploit its resources?' and the question makes more sense. While again at first glance, the question might still seem silly, in fact, there are several ways to claim jurisdiction over at least part of the sea and a variety of reasons for doing so. After all, nations bordering the sea have always claimed some jurisdiction over the waters adjacent to them. Indeed, any society dependent on sea-borne trade would assert some jurisdiction over the sea if only to protect the sea-lanes that supplied it from pirates. When, for example, the Romans scoured the Mediterranean to eliminate piracy and stationed fleets there to police the sea, they were in effect claiming jurisdiction over the *mare nostrum*.[1] During the Middle Ages, several governments claimed possession of parts of the sea. These precedents for possession of the sea in turn provided much of the basis for the well-known 17th-century debate about whether the sea, especially the Atlantic and Pacific oceans, was open to all who wished to sail there, *mare liberum*, or closed, *mare clausum*, that is, whether navigation and trade could be limited to a specific country or countries.

Furthermore, debate about ownership of or jurisdiction over the sea is not simply an historical issue associated with the 17th century. For the past several decades the nations of the world have been wrestling with two issues involving jurisdiction over the sea. One concerns control of the ocean fisheries; the second concerns the ownership of ore-bearing nodules that litter the seabed. These issues arose because of the increasing number of states, especially the numerous small states created by post-World War II decolonization, that have come to claim a voice in issues involving the sea, often in opposition to the traditional states that dominated international law.[2]

13

Since the early 18th century, states have claimed jurisdiction over a zone extending three miles into the adjoining sea, a distance determined by the Dutch international lawyer Cornelius van Bynkershoek (1673-1743) who noted that three miles was the distance that a cannon could fire.[3] This standard generally applied until 1952 when 'Chile, Peru, and Ecuador proclaimed "sole sovereignty and jurisdiction" over an area of the sea extending not less than 200 nautical miles from their coasts - which seemed to indicate that what they claimed was equivalent to a 200-mile territorial sea.'[4] A major reason for this change was to restrict foreign access to the tuna-fishing grounds, a move that angered the American fishermen who were active in that fishery. Subsequently, however, beginning in 1975 'several developed states ... established their own 200-mile fisheries ... the United States being among the first to do so.'[5] By moving to the 200-mile limit, the United States was responding to pressure exerted by fishermen in New England who were angered at the presence of large Russian and Polish factory fishing ships on the Grand Banks and the other grounds traditionally fished by New Englanders.[6]

The second issue that emerged in recent years to challenge traditional opinions on possession of the sea concerned the existence on the floor of the sea of 'polymetallic nodules' that contained valuable ores that could be extracted.[7] That the ocean floor contained such resources was not a new idea, having been around for about a century. In the 20th century, however, the increased use of metals that exist in very limited supply, magnesium for example, led to greater interest in the ocean where magnesium exists in many of the nodules found there. In 1965, a geologist published a book on these nodules claiming that great wealth lay on the ocean floor, wealth now accessible because of advances in mining technology.[8] This article attracted the attention of the ambassador of Malta to the United Nations, Arvid Pardo, who gave a speech at the United Nations in 1967 'calling for the recognition of the area and the limits of national jurisdiction [over the sea] and its resources as the common heritage of mankind.'[9] Ambassador Pardo's views reached a larger audience when he published them in several articles. His overall theme was the 'intolerable injustice of reserving the plurality of the world's resources for the exclusive benefit of a handful of nations' if the usual rules of international law were applied, that is placing the sea and its bed under the control of those countries that bordered it, leaving the remainder open to any and all others who could exploit it, rules that had been in place for three centuries.[10]

Instead, Pardo proposed a resolution on the future control of the sea that would replace the traditional notion of jurisdiction over the sea with what he saw as a new one that reflected both economic interests and moral values:

> 1. The sea-bed and the ocean floor are a common heritage of mankind and should be used and exploited for peaceful purposes and for the exclusive benefit of mankind as a whole. The needs of poor countries, representing that part of mankind which is in most need of assistance, should receive preferential consideration in the event of financial benefits being derived from the exploitation of the sea-bed and ocean floor for commercial purposes.
> 2. Claims to sovereignty over the sea-bed and ocean floor beyond present national jurisdiction, as presently claimed, should be frozen until a clear definition of the continental shelf is formulated.[11]

In effect, the ambassador was suggesting formal recognition of the corporate nature of human society so that the sea's resources could be employed for the common good of mankind. Pardo's proposal would require reconsidering the meaning of state sovereignty and necessitate conceiving mankind as some kind of corporate whole under the jurisdiction of a supranational authority. Whether or not he realized it, when Ambassador Pardo made his proposal, he was suggesting a morally-based redistributionist world order in which the sovereignty of nation-states would be subordinated to the interests of all mankind under the direction of a universally recognized authority.[12] One observer pointed out that, in effect, Pardo was proposing 'a radical reconsideration of the existing public order of the oceans.'[13] To a medieval historian, however, Pardo's proposal suggests a secularized version of medieval papal and canonistic thinking about the nature of mankind and the possibility of a just world order.[14]

The 'public order of the oceans' that Ambassador Pardo's proposal would overturn was the result of three centuries of legal thought and practice about world order that followed the publication of Hugo Grotius' (1583-1645) *De Jure Belli ac Pacis Libri Tres* in 1625.[15] Even before this book appeared, Grotius had published anonymously his *Mare Liberum*, an argument for the right of free travel across the seas that provided the basic text on the right of all mankind to unimpeded travel and trade across the sea. In the 17th century, his notion of the sea as open to all comers replaced the notion that the sea could be closed, that is the right to travel and to trade with those who lived there could be the monopoly of one nation or a limited number of nations that could exclude any and all others.

Furthermore, Grotius rejected any notion of international oversight of the sea to allocate monopolies and to settle disputes. The countries that he was discussing were, as he pointed out quite forcefully, absolutely autonomous, that is sovereign and thus answerable to no one, a concept fully developed in the late 16th and early 17th centuries.[16] Critics have described Grotius' conception 'of the relationship between man and the state' as 'Hobbesian', a term that might be applied to his conception of inter-state relations as well.[17] Grotius' concept of a world order consisted of a series of sovereign powers in tension with one another. They could not interfere in any way with the universal right to travel and trade freely everywhere, a curious limitation on sovereign power. If taken literally, this would mean there could be no bans on trade with a nation's enemies or no way to prevent the entrance of those who might upset the social order. Grotius, of course, argued that there was no paradox here, because sovereign states could not violate the natural law that authorized free travel. In making this argument, Grotius was attacking those who defended the claim of Pope Alexander VI (1492-1503) to restrict European access to the New World to the Portuguese and the Castilians, thus subordinating national sovereignty to papal universal jurisdiction. The Catholic position was that although all men had the right to travel freely, the spiritual reasons presented in *Inter caetera* and related bulls could justify the subordination of that right to the Church's responsibility to preach the Gospel to all mankind.

Seen in light of the medieval notion of mankind as a single species descended from Adam and Eve, potentially at least forming a corporate whole, subject to the same natural law, and under the headship of the pope who, according to one 13th-century pope, Innocent IV (1243-54), could judge all mankind by that law, Ambassador Pardo's proposal does not appear radically new. While not drawn directly from the medieval tradition, it echoes many of the fundamental themes that Grotius attacked so that Pardo might be seen as a harbinger of a move to reconsider the entire Grotian conception of international order in order to reformulate the law of the sea to the advantage of poor and landlocked states.

The Grotian concept of free travel emerged out of a particular incident that focused the attention of 17th-century lawyers on the question of ownership of the sea. In 1603 a ship belonging to the Dutch East India Company seized a Portuguese ship, the *St Catherine*, in the Straits of Malacca.[18] Some of the shareholders in the Dutch East India Company, pacifist Mennonites, were upset by the seizure of the Portuguese vessel and its subsequent sale as a prize of war. To ease their consciences and to justify the seizure, the Company asked the young Hugo Grotius to write a legal treatise justifying the seizure and, even more important, justifying the Dutch presence in Asia, a presence that was itself a contested legal issue.

The Dutch had made their first permanent settlement in Asian waters in 1598, and, in 1602, they formed the Dutch East India Company, granting it a monopoly of Dutch trade with Asia. These activities brought the Dutch into conflict with the Portuguese who claimed a monopoly of all European trade with Asia.[19] Complicating the issue was the fact that the Dutch were at war with Spain at this point. The King of Spain, Philip III (1598-1621), also ruled Portugal as a result of the election of Philip II (1556-98) as King of Portugal in 1580.[20] He and his successors claimed jurisdiction over all of the lands and seas discovered since 1492 by virtue of Alexander VI's division of the world between Castile and Portugal in 1493.[21] This bull had granted a monopoly of trade with the newly discovered lands in the Americas to the Portuguese and the Castilians. Subsequent negotiations had extended the Line of Demarcation separating the Portuguese zone of control from the Castilian into the Pacific, providing a basis upon which the Portuguese claimed the right to keep the Dutch out of Asian waters.[22] During the winter of 1604-5 Grotius wrote the *De Jure Praedae* in order to demonstrate the legal right of the Dutch to sail in Asian waters, to engage in trade there, and, when appropriate, to seize enemy ships according to the laws of war. This treatise was not, however, published until the 19th century after the long-lost manuscript was discovered in 1864.[23]

Although the seizure of the *St Catherine* by the Dutch in the early 17th century was the occasion for the debate about whether the sea was open or closed, the issue was in fact much older. During the Middle Ages, Venice had claimed possession of the Adriatic and levied tolls on ships that sailed there. The Genoese claimed jurisdiction over the Ligurian Sea.[24] Likewise, the Danish kings claimed jurisdiction over the Baltic.[25] Finally, in the late 16th century James VI (1567-1625) of Scotland and I (1603-25) of England attempted to claim jurisdiction over the seas around Britain, especially over the herring fisheries where there was a strong Dutch presence.[26]

Thus, when Grotius came to write his *Mare Liberum*, he was not dealing with a radically new issue, an issue that had only emerged with the discovery of the New World, but with a long-standing issue, freedom of travel on the sea, that was taking on new significance as Europeans travelled across the Atlantic, the Pacific and the Indian oceans. Europeans now found themselves dealing on a large scale beyond Europe with issues with which they had previously dealt on a small scale within Europe. Thus, the early modern debate about the freedom of the seas was rooted in a legal tradition stretching back to the Middle Ages, as Grotius knew. His *Mare Liberum*, the opening round in the debate about the freedom of the seas, was an analysis of that tradition. As we shall see, he did not simply reject the entire medieval legal tradition in order to replace it with a new one. Rather, he worked within that tradition, employing some arguments he found there, rejecting others, modifying the legal tradition, not rejecting it outright.

In the introduction to the *Mare Liberum*, Grotius set out the issues involved in the debate quite forcefully:

> Between us and the Spaniards the following points are in dispute: can the vast, the boundless sea be the appanage [*accessio*] of one kingdom alone, and it not the greatest? Can any one nation have the right to prevent other nations which so desire, from selling to one another, from bartering with one another, actually from communicating with one another? Can any nation give away what it never owned, or discover what already belonged to some one else? Does a manifest injustice of long standing create a specific right?[27]

The key point in this list is communication. That is, for one nation to prevent any and all the people of other nations from communicating with one another is to violate one of the fundamental aspects of humanity. Following a line of argument that stretched back to Aristotle and was widely repeated in medieval legal literature, Grotius pointed out that God had not divided mankind 'into different species and various divisions, but had willed them to be of one race and to be known by one name' and had given them 'language ... and other means of communication, in order that they all might recognize their natural social bond and kinship.'[28] Furthermore, God 'had drawn up certain laws not graven on tablets of bronze or stone but written in the minds and on the hearts of every individual, where even the unwilling and the refractory must read them.' Consequently, the 'very laws themselves of each and every nation and city flow from that Divine source, and from that source receive their sanctity and their majesty.'[29] The conception of mankind that Grotius outlined here also appeared in the writings of the medieval philosophers and canon lawyers, that is, ultimately, mankind forms a single community and is (or should be) governed according to the universal principles of natural law that all men are able to know. One consequence of this theory was that, according to the medieval canon lawyers, infidel rulers had no right to block the entrance of peaceful Christian travellers, that is missionaries, into their lands.[30]

The elements of this natural order of social life undergirded 'those very laws themselves of each and every nation and city [because they] flow from that Divine source, and from that source receive their sanctity and majesty.'[31] Among the issues with which the law concerns itself is that of property rights. According to Grotius, 'there are some things which every man enjoys in common with all other men, and as there are other things which are distinctly his and belong to no one else, just so has nature willed that some of the things which she has created for the use of mankind remain common to all'.[32] Indeed, this law is so fundamental that 'no king ought to deny [it] to his subjects, and ... no Christian ought to refuse [it] to a non-Christian.'[33]

It was on that basis that Grotius presented 'the following most specific and unimpeachable axiom of the Law of Nations, called a primary rule or first principle, the spirit of which is self-evident and immutable, to wit: Every nation is free to travel to every other nation, and to trade with it.'[34] He pointed out that ancient pagans as well as Christians recognized the right to free peaceful travel everywhere. Therefore, 'the Portuguese, even if they had been sovereigns in those parts to which the Dutch make voyages, would nevertheless be doing them an injury if they should forbid them access to those places and from trading there.'[35] Here again, Grotius was stating a position rooted in the medieval tradition. Pope Innocent IV had argued that infidel rulers had to admit peaceful Christian missionaries to their lands, suggesting a natural right to travel freely in peace everywhere.[36] Subsequently, the Spanish theologian Francisco de Vitoria (1480?-1546) developed Innocent IV's discussion about free travel in his *De Indis*, arguing that missionaries and also merchants possessed the right to travel everywhere freely in peace, a point that Grotius was to make as well.[37]

Having denied that any people could legitimately claim the right to block trade and communication across the sea, Grotius went on to explain why the Portuguese could not claim sovereignty over the East Indies. He offered arguments against Portuguese claims to possess the East Indies by 'title of discovery' (Chapter II), 'by title of war' (IV), 'by title of occupation' (V), 'by title of prescription or custom' (VII and XI), or 'by title of occupation' (IX). Grotius' most important arguments were against two Portuguese claims based on a papal grant. The first was a claim to 'sovereignty over the East Indies by virtue of title based on the Papal Donation' (III). The second argument was that '[n]either the Sea nor the right of navigation thereon belongs to the Portuguese by virtue of title based on the Papal Donation' (VI).

Above all, Grotius argued that the Portuguese claim to possess full jurisdiction over the lands and seas delineated in Alexander VI's (1492-1503) bull *Inter caetera* had no basis in reality. The pope could - and did - legitimately arbitrate a resolution to the conflict between Portugal and Castile that resulted from Columbus' claim to have found a westward route to Asia, because the two parties had requested that he do so.[38] The pope's role in this case was, however, distinct from his spiritual functions. He was acting only as a disinterested party. Furthermore, the papal decision in this matter 'will of course not affect the other peoples of the world' because it only concerned the parties involved.[39] The pope could not, therefore, grant the Indies, East or West, to Portugal and Castile because his power is 'in the spiritual realm only' and he possesses 'no authority over infidel nations, for they do not belong to the Church.' To support this position, Grotius cited 'the opinions of Cajetan and Victoria and the more authoritative of the Theologians and writers on Canon Law.'[40] In other words, Catholic teaching itself was against the claims of the Portuguese in the East Indies.

Turning to the specific issue of access to the sea, Grotius argued that Alexander VI's *Inter caetera* was 'an act of empty ostentation' and not a legitimate exercise of papal authority. After all, 'it is sufficiently well recognized that the Pope is not the temporal lord of the earth, and certainly not of the sea.' Furthermore, 'since neither the sea nor the right of navigating it can become the private property of any man, it follows that it could not have been given by the Pope, nor accepted by the Portuguese.'[41] If the pope claimed the authority to grant jurisdiction over the sea to a Christian ruler, he would be acting in a manner 'repugnant to the law of nature.'[42]

By stressing the universality of the natural law and asserting that the pope could not violate the provisions of that law, Grotius was skirting an issue of great importance in the canonistic tradition. In the mid-13th century, Pope Innocent IV, in his capacity as a canon lawyer, had argued that all mankind was subject to the jurisdiction of the pope. The pope would judge Christians by canon law, Jews by the Law of Moses, and all other people by the natural law known to all men.[43] That being the case, the pope could order a Christian ruler to punish an infidel ruler who was violating the natural law. While Grotius recognized the existence of the natural law, he dispensed with the papal role as universal judge, asserting instead that God, not some human agent, will punish rulers who violate the natural law. Even at this point, Grotius was not as distant from the medieval canonistic tradition as he might appear.

At this point it is important to re-emphasize two points about Grotius' *Mare Liberum*. In the first place, it was a response to a particular situation. In the second place, it was but one chapter in a much larger work. Grotius was not attempting to provide a full analysis of all sides of the debate about freedom of the seas; he was a lawyer writing a brief for his client, the East India Company. One consequence of this narrow focus was that Grotius simply denied that there could be any justification for interfering with travel and trade, a position that he had to know the legal tradition did not support. The same medieval legal tradition he cited to attack Portuguese claims to a monopoly of trade with Asia also contained, for example, a reasonable ban on trade in materials of war with one's enemies.[44] Furthermore, only a few years after writing the *Mare Liberum*, Grotius went to England in a dispute with the English over trade in Asia. The 'Dutch position in Asia rested on sea-power, systematically used to control particular branches of Asian trade', blocking English entry into the lucrative markets that were opening up. As one modern scholar has pointed out, in claiming such a monopoly, 'the Dutch took a leaf out of the Portuguese book.'[45] Such judgments, however, fail to appreciate that Grotius was acting not as a political theorist but as a lawyer, seeking to present the best possible case for his clients out of the legal materials available to him.

The publication of the *Mare Liberum* sparked a debate among the lawyers of several countries about whether access to the sea was open to all. In rejecting the notion of seas open to all, Grotius' critics fell loosely into two categories. The first, those we might term the micro critics, asserted that rulers could claim jurisdiction over the seas adjoining their domains. Such critics included the Scottish writer William Welwood (1578-1622), Professor of Civil Law at the University of Aberdeen, and the English scholar John Selden (1584-1654). Their interest arose from the desire to close the North Sea herring fishery to Dutch fishermen.[46] The second line of criticism, what we might call macro criticism, defended the Portuguese claim to jurisdiction over the entire Indian Ocean. The most important example of this line of criticism was the Portuguese lawyer Serafim de Freitas (1570?-1633) who responded in detail to Grotius, publishing a lengthy defence of the Portuguese overseas empire, justifying the exclusion of other Europeans from the seas claimed by the Portuguese.[47]

The first criticism of Grotius came from Welwood who argued that rulers could legitimately 'reserve their fishing stocks to their own kingdoms.' At the same time he also argued that the 'wider ocean' was a '*mare vastum liberrimum*' and open to all.[48] One consequence of this conclusion was that it enabled the English to insist that the seas in the East Indies were *mare liberum* while at the same time insisting on the right to close the seas around Great Britain itself.[49] Presumably, the Indian Ocean was a '*mare vastum*' and therefore '*liberrimum*' while the domestic fishery was a '*mare clausum*' because it adjoined the king's dominions.

The best-known English response to Grotius' position was Selden's *Mare Clausum*, the very title of which was a direct challenge to Grotius. The theme of his book was the right of King James I to restrict commercial fishing in the waters around the British Isles to his subjects and to others who obtained royal licenses, foreshadowing the claim of some 20th-century states to a 200-mile zone of jurisdiction. His position was that English monarchs had long claimed dominion over the adjoining seas, including dominion over the English Channel, a claim, Selden argued, the French kings had never denied.[50] In claiming 'the dominion of the King of Great Britain over the Irish, western, Scottish, and North seas', Selden was simply extending the king's jurisdiction over the seas in keeping with the extension of his jurisdiction over the constituent kingdoms of the British Isles.

After demonstrating the legitimacy of English claims to dominion over the adjoining seas, Selden turned to claims to the sea arising from the English colonization of the North American coastline. He argued that the 'kings of England' could not only claim the waters adjoining North America, they could also lay 'claim to the western sea from the coast of Ireland to that of North America'.[51] In other words, the North Atlantic was a British '*mare nostrum*'. This would seem to suggest that the English were claiming the kind of jurisdiction over the sea that the Spanish and the Portuguese were claiming. The difference was, however, that while the Iberian nations based their claims to a *mare clausum* on papal authorization, Selden's position rested on effective British control of the coastlines involved.

The work of Welwood and Selden led to the paradoxical conclusion that the sea was both '*liberum*' and '*clausum*', depending on its proximity to a ruler's domain. In this sense, these writers recognized a limited right to 'close' a sea under specific circumstances. What they did not do, being Protestants, was to defend the right of the pope to close a sea. Thus, the second line of attack on Grotius' work was a defence of the right of the pope to restrict navigation on the sea to those licensed to do so. This came from the pen of the Portuguese scholar, Serafim de Freitas, who published a defense of the Portuguese position in 1625. His *De Justo Imperio Lusitanorum Asiatico* presented a full discussion of the legal arguments that would justify a Portuguese monopoly of trade with Asia.[52] While this work, like that of Grotius, was a response to a particular issue, it was more than a narrowly constructed brief. It was a more extensive treatise, drawing on the same legal tradition as had Grotius, but developing the arguments at greater length and in more detail. His goal was to end any further criticism of the Portuguese claim to monopoly of trade with Asia by overwhelming the critics with a massive number of legal citations.[53]

At the beginning of the treatise, Freitas listed the 13 chapters of the *Mare Liberum* and then the 18 chapters of his own book, making the reader well aware of his intention to demolish Grotius' position point by point. Freitas' argument may be reduced to two fundamental conclusions. The first is that the right to travel and trade is not an absolute right and has never been considered as such in spite of what Grotius argued. The second point, a corollary of the first, was that the spiritual responsibilities of the pope might require him to restrict European Christian trade and contact with a particular people in order to achieve a higher goal, the religious conversion of such people.

Freitas pointed out that even the ancient Romans whom Grotius had described as supporting the principle of unhindered travel and trade did in fact prevent communication between tribes that plotted against Rome. Furthermore, he argued that a ruler has the right to forbid his subjects to deal with foreigners under some circumstances.[54]

The core of Freitas' argument was an interesting play on Grotius' use of the theme of a universal human community linked by the ability to communicate. He presented the traditional argument that human beings formed a single species and then concluded that there should be a single head of human society. This would be the pope as successor to Peter to whom Christ entrusted responsibility for mankind.[55] Secular rulers also possessed power ultimately derived from God, but as their power, designed to achieve the good of men in the natural order, was subordinate to the spiritual power which is directed at man's higher good, that is his spiritual good, so too they are subject to the pope as the representative of God in the spiritual order.[56]

Having presented a broad picture of papal power, Freitas went on to respond to two of Grotius' arguments that dealt with papal jurisdiction. The first was that the pope had no jurisdiction over infidels and, therefore, could not legally interfere with communication and trade with them. The second was that the pope could settle quarrels between Portugal and Castile concerning their respective spheres of interest in the newly discovered lands, but such a settlement could not affect the rights of those who were not parties to it. Freitas responded that when the pope granted a monopoly of trade with one of the newly encountered lands to a particular Christian monarch, he was not improperly intervening in the secular order, only fulfilling his responsibility for seeking the conversion of all mankind by insuring that the work be carried out efficaciously.[57] Furthermore, he pointed out that even before the discovery of the New World, the discovery of a water route to Asia, and the publication of *Inter caetera*, popes had been issuing similar bulls authorizing Portuguese and Castilian rulers to have a monopoly of contact with specific regions. For example, Pope Martin V (1417-31) had granted to the Portuguese 'the right to engage in navigation and commerce in Africa and Asia ... on the condition that they support the propagation of the faith, a right that other popes subsequently confirmed.'[58] Throughout the 15th century, popes had indeed authorized the Portuguese, and the Castilians as well, to occupy the islands in the Atlantic: the Canaries, Cape Verde, the Azores and Madeira. These papal bulls, more than 100 from 1420 to the beginning of the 16th century, offered several bases upon which the Iberians could claim possession of these lands.[59] One was that the inhabitants were Muslims and therefore traditional enemies of Christendom.

A second was that the peoples encountered were living at a primitive level and engaging in behaviour that violated the natural law. Finally, these bulls authorized the Portuguese and Castilians to occupy particular islands that were in dispute. According to Freitas, the experience of a century and more of papal authorization of monopolies of contact with various parts of the world meant a century of legal precedents that could not be simply overthrown. In the final analysis, Grotius and Freitas were working within the same intellectual framework, the common legal tradition of Europe, the *ius commune*, but reaching different conclusions.[60] In fact, the debate over the sea was an extension of the medieval debate about the relationship between Church and State. Grotius after all argued that papal grants of monopoly of contact with the newly encountered peoples were an illegal papal intervention into the temporal order, while Freitas argued that the pope's higher goal, the spiritual mission to all mankind, meant that the temporal right of free travel could be subordinated to the higher spiritual goal.

Grotius' line of argument obviously supported the interests of a trading nation. He also seems to assume that the nations that wish to engage in trade would be able to resolve disputes among themselves. Furthermore, he assumed that contact with other societies would be based solely on commercial concerns. As is well known, the Dutch did little to support missionary efforts among the peoples whom they encountered.

Freitas on the other hand, maintained that while there was a right to freedom of travel and of trade, such rights were subordinate to other interests that derived from common humanity. The spiritual good of the peoples of the Americas, Africa, and Asia would be enhanced if the Portuguese and the Castilians did as the papacy required and ensure the success of missionary efforts.

After three centuries, however, the conception of international order contained in the *Mare Liberum*, an order focused on the freedom of every European maritime nation to trade with any other nation, is under reconsideration. Declining fisheries and demands for sharing the wealth of the sea with all the nations of the world as well as an increasing demand for enforcing what some identify as universally recognized standards of behaviour mean Grotius' restriction of international law to the rights to travel and to exploit the sea, along with a refusal to recognize any obligation to convert the peoples of the world to Christian European standards of behaviour, is now under attack from a position similar to that of Freitas. That is, the rights to travel and to trade, and the principle of non-interference in other societies (Grotius' position) must be subordinated to the larger interests of mankind as a whole. Fisheries must be allowed to rebuild, exploitation of the seabed must be controlled, and societies that engage in practices abhorrent to western humanitarian sensibilities must be forced to conform. To a medievalist at least, these current themes in the international political order suggest a return to the world view of the medieval papacy with the Secretary-General of the United Nations acting as pope.

Lest these last words seem too professionally self-serving, let me conclude with an observation from the work of a student of international law, a non-medievalist:

> The subsequent development of the European international society of states [the Grotian world order] was conditioned by its medieval origins. Abstract reasoning and expedient ways of dealing with new problems played their part, as did the revival of the classical tradition. But the distinctive medieval inheritance was especially important. The patterns which evolved later in Europe were shaped by the continuing interaction of reason and experience with men's attempts to defend or alter the ideas and institutions of the Middle Ages. The worldwide expansion of the European international system was itself a continuation of the expansion of medieval Christendom and spread the rules, institutions and values elaborated in Europe over the whole world. Our present global society of states, which is derived from the European system, contains much that is comprehensible only in the light of the medieval heritage and the reaction against it.[61]

Notes

1   Chester G. Starr, *The Roman Imperial Navy 31 B.C. - A.D. 324* (Ithaca, NY: Cornell University Press, 1941; repr. Cambridge: W. Heffer & Sons, 1960), 3-5, 167-98.

2   'In 1859 the British law officers spoke of international law "as it has been hitherto recognized and now subsists by the common consent of Christian nations".' James Crawford, *The Creation of States in International Law* (Oxford: Clarendon, 1979), 13.

3   Cornelius van Bynkershoek, *De dominio maris*, trans. Ralph Van Deman Magoffin (New York: Oxford University Press, 1923), 20-21.

4   Markus Schmidt, *Common Heritage or Common Burden* (Oxford: Clarendon, 1989), 27.

5   *Ibid.*, 30.

6   Bobbie B. Smetherton and Robert M. Smetherton, *Territorial Seas and Inter-American Relations* (New York: Praeger, 1974), 108-12.

7   E.D. Brown, *The International Law of the Sea. Volume I: Introductory Manual* (Aldershot, Hants.; Brookfield, VT: Dartmouth, 1994), 9.

8   John Mero, *The Mineral Resources of the Sea* (New York and Amsterdam: Elsevier, 1965); and 'Whose Is the Bed of the Sea', *Proceedings of the American Society of International Law* 62 (1968), 216-29.

9   Brown, *International Law of the Sea*, vol. 1, 10.

10 Arvid Pardo, 'Who Will Control the Seabed?', *Foreign Affairs* 47 (1968), 123-37, 134.

11   *Ibid.*, 135-6.
12   There is an echo of Lady Barbara Ward's economic views in this proposal; see her *The Rich Nations and the Poor Nations* (New York: Norton, 1962).
13   Brown, *International Law of the Sea*, vol. 1, 10.
14   The notion that modern political thought is often rooted in secularized versions of earlier ecclesiastical thought is especially stressed in the work of Brian Tierney; see his *Religion, Law, and the Growth of Constitutional Thought, 1150-1650* (Cambridge: Cambridge University Press, 1982).
15   Hugo Grotius, *The Law of War and Peace* (*De Jure belli ac Pacis Libri Tres*), 2 vols, trans. Francis W. Kelsey (New York: Oxford University Press, 1925; reprinted Indianapolis, IN: Bobbs-Merrill, 1962), vol. 2.
16   For the roots of the concept of sovereignty, see Kenneth Pennington, *The Prince and the Law* (Berkeley: University of California Press, 1993).
17   Hedley Bull, 'The Importance of Grotius in the Study of International Relations', Hedley Bull, Benedict Kingsbury and Adam Roberts (eds), *Hugo Grotius and International Relations* (Oxford: Oxford University Press, 1992), 65-93, 85.
18   Concerning the circumstances of the capture, see the 'Introductory Note' to Hugo Grotius, *The Freedom of the Seas*, ed. James Brown Scott, trans. Ralph van Deman Magoffin (New York: Oxford University Press, 1916), vi-vii.
19   On the beginnings of the Dutch presence in Asia, see C.R. Boxer, *The Dutch Seaborne Empire: 1600-1800* (New York: Knopf, 1965), 22-4.
20   John Lynch, *Spain under the Habsburgs*, 2 vols (New York: New York University Press, 2nd ed. 1984), vol. 1, 322-30.
21   Pope Alexander VI issued three bulls in 1493 that, along with the Treaty of Tordesillas in 1494, drew a line from pole to pole dividing the Atlantic into Portuguese and Castilian zones. The texts of the bulls and the treaty are in *European Treaties Bearing on the History of the United States and Its Dependencies to 1648*, ed. Frances Gardiner Davenport (Washington, DC: Carnegie Institution of Washington, 1917; repr. Gloucester, MA: Peter Smith, 1967), 56-100.
22   The voyage of Ferdinand Magellan, 1519-1522, led to the extension of the Line of Demarcation to the Pacific as well, by the terms of the Treaty of Saragossa in 1529. See *European Treaties*, 146-98; see also Samuel Eliot Morison, *The European Discovery of America: The Southern Voyages A.D. 1492 - 1616* (New York: Oxford University Press, 1974), 476-7.
23   On the history of the text, see Hugo Grotius, *De Iure Praedae Commentarius*, trans. Gwladys L. Williams and Walter H. Zeydel (Oxford: Oxford University Press, 1950; repr. New York: Oceana; London: Wildy & Sons, 1964), xiii-xvii.
24   On these claims see Paul Christianson, *Discourse on History, Law, and Governance in the Public Career of John Selden, 1610-1635* (Toronto: University of Toronto Press, 1996), 258-9; Grotius, *De Jure Praedae*, 246-7, 250-52; Grotius, *Mare Liberum*, 48, 53-4, 56; Frei Serafim de Freitas, *Do Justo Império Asiático dos Portugueses*, 2 vols (Lisbon: Instituto Nacional de Investigação Científica, 1983), vol. 2, 162 (XIII:13).
25   Specifically, the Danish kings 'controlled the entrance to the Baltic' by controlling the Sound that was the main route in and out of the Baltic. See Palle Lauring, *A History of the Kingdom of Denmark*, trans. David Hohnen (Copenhagen: Høst & Søn, 1960), 110-11.
26   Christianson, *Discourse on History, Law, and Governance*, 271.
27   Grotius, *Mare Liberum*, 4.
28   *Ibid.*, 1-2.
29   *Ibid.*, 2.
30   James Muldoon, *Popes, Lawyers and Infidels: The Church and the Non-Christian World 1250-1550* (Philadelphia: University of Pennsylvania Press, 1979), 11.

31   Grotius, *Mare Liberum*, 15.
32   *Ibid.*, 2.
33   *Ibid.*, 5.
34   *Ibid.*, 7.
35   *Ibid.*, 10.
36   Muldoon, *Popes, Lawyers, and Infidels*, 11, 14.
37   *Ibid.*, 148.
38   Grotius, *Mare Liberum*, 2.
39   *Ibid.*, 15.
40   *Ibid.*, 16-17.
41   *Ibid.*, 45.
42   *Ibid.*, 46.
43   Muldoon, *Popes, Lawyers, and Infidels*, 9-11.
44   *Ibid.*, 34.
45   C.G. Roelofsen, 'Grotius and the International Politics of the Seventeenth Century', Bull, Kingsbury and Roberts (eds), *Hugo Grotius and International Relations*, 95-131, 112. Grotius' different positions in these two situations has been noted by a number of authors. See Hedley Bull, 'The Importance of Grotius', 66; and C.R. Boxer, *The Dutch Seaborne Empire*, 102.
46   On Welwood and Selden see Paul Christianson, *Discourse on History, Law, and Governance*, 246-81.
47   For a brief survey of this literature see W.E. Butler, 'Grotius and the Law of the Sea', Bull, Kingsbury and Roberts (eds), *Hugo Grotius and International Relations*, 209-20, 209-12.
48   David Armitage, *The Ideological Origins of the British Empire* (Cambridge: Cambridge University Press, 2000), 110.
49   *Ibid.*, 112.
50   Christianson, *Discourse on History, Law, and Governance*, 270.
51   Armitage, *Ideological Origins*, 278.
52   On Freitas see Frei Serafim de Freitas, *Do Justo Império Asiático*, vol. 1, 34-9.
53   The importance of defending the Portuguese overseas empire within a legal order is discussed in Lauren Benton, 'The Legal Regime of the South Atlantic World, 1400-1750: Jurisdictional Complexity as Institutional Order', *Journal of World History* 11 (2000), 27-56, esp. 39; see also Patricia Seed, *Ceremonies of Possession in Europe's Conquest of the New World, 1492-1640* (New York: Cambridge University Press, 1995).
54   Freitas, vol. 2, 9 (I:25).
55   *Ibid.*, vol. 2, 44-6 (VI:1-5).
56   *Ibid.*, vol. 2, 50 (VI:18).
57   *Ibid.*, vol. 2, 90-93 (VII:1-6).
58   *Ibid.*, vol. 2, 3 (I:3).
59   There is a useful selection of relevant bulls in *European Treaties*, vol. 1, 9-100. The most complete list of relevant bulls is Charles Martial de Witte, 'Les bulles pontificales et l'expansion portugaise au XVe siècle', *Revue d'Histoire Ecclésiastique* 48 (1953), 683-718; 49 (1954), 438-61; 51 (1956), 413-53, 809-36; 53 (1958), 5-46, 443-71.
60   See Manlio Bellomo, *The Common Legal Past of Europe: 1000-1800*, trans. Lydia G. Cochrane (Washington, DC: Catholic University of America Press, 2nd ed. 1995).
61   Adam Watson, *The Evolution of International Society: A Comparative Historical Analysis* (London: Routledge, 1992), 150.

2 Orientation as a Paradigm of Maritime Modernity

ULRICH KINZEL

The aim of my paper is to reconstruct - in the abridged form of a textual diagram - a historical constellation of practices which contributed to the constitution of what may be called the oceanic turn of occidental culture in the 16th century. This turn obviously manifested itself in the voyages of discovery and circumnavigation. At the same time these events heralded a complex cultural change, the impact of which reaches far into our own modernity. The 'energetic maritime upsurge of the period', as Carl Schmitt put it in his narrative essay *Land and Sea*,[1] implies two fundamental shifts: oceanic transgression and the rule of contingency. In a culture still steeped in both the Christian demonization of the sea and the antique notion of keeping within limits, the ocean signified a marginal reality beyond an horizon that encircled the known, the secure, the civilized and the governable. 'As if it were merely an annex of the inland sea', says Braudel, the ocean in the 16th century 'did not yet have a fully independent existence.'[2] Sailing out onto the open sea thus signified a fundamental change. The same applies to the new role contingency was to play by suspending and challenging moral values which had been revived in order to base moral practices on essential principles such as constancy. Transgression and contingency signify modes of experience which dominate our present discourses as well.[3] Yet, the maritime genealogy of this part of our actual experience does not simply become evident by establishing an historical analogy; it can only be revealed by looking at the interrelation between the event of the oceanic turn and the practices which it helped to generate.

In this context it is important to consider that transgression and contingency pose the problem of orientation. A passage from James Hamilton-Paterson's *Seven Tenths* may help to see its maritime dimension and its systematic implications:

The business of orientation on the blank and shifting waters of the open sea, of establishing a fixed *point de repère* which is not a landmark, is central not merely to navigation but to various sciences coming under the general heading of oceanography. (The very word suggests a difficulty, the writing down of an ocean.) Until a certain moment in history there must have been a conceptual impossibility in the idea of a sea chart without a coastline on it, implying as it logically would the drawing of lines and boundaries - albeit notional ones - on a fluid surface. Being boatless and lost in mid-ocean at noon in the tropics at least makes vivid certain problems which have faced all navigators and carto-graphers, with the sun directly overhead and the seabed far out of sight a mile below. The panic of a careless swimmer keen to avoid joining his ancestors thus makes a good starting point as he twirls despairingly round and round like a demented compass needle in search of any bearing, any point of reference, any direction other than down.[4]

This passage articulates both the difficulty of orientation and that of representation. The swimmer is, literally speaking, in the absolute situation of being alone on the open sea (even torn away from his boat), a point on the fragile line that separates sea and sky, water and air, life and death,[5] a point which is compared to the needle of a compass trying to find either or both: position and direction. The situation of the maritime, modern subject is combined with the scientific problem of mapping something - the ocean - which does not - in the form of landmarks, coastlines, etc. - yield to any visible shape or trace. It seems as if writing the ocean can only claim a virtual reality.

Hamilton-Paterson outlines the basic problem of orientation and its con-nection with maritime experience. And in doing so, he points out two of the three fundamental concepts which should be considered when classifying practices of orientation. Orientation either implies that a *position* is fixed (on a map) or a *direction* is defined (in a route). These two modes have to be distinguished from a mode which is orientation-free and might be called *situation*, or, in terms of spatial extension, passage or way.[6] Route, which is not only characterized by direction but by recurrent passage as well, repre-sents a dynamic or procedural principle which may interfere with the other two modes. Thus the combination of position with route defines *navigation* as one type of orientation; the other being *experience*, the interference of situation and route. It is through experience that a situation is given direction, and it is through navigation that a recurrent passage is directed by fixing positions. Whereas the latter entails the use of cartographical maps, the former is encoded in cognitive or imaginary maps.

By trying to reconstruct the basic outline of three discursive practices - the art of navigation, the allegory of fortune and the practice of systematic travel observations - I would now like to historicize the question of orientation.

Navigation

Navigation in General

'We commonly call the art of navigation the science of well and safely steering and directing a ship by certain rules, from one port of call to another.'[7] This definition, to be found in John Seller's *Practical Navigation* (1669), translates a definition given a hundred years earlier by Michiel Coignet in his manual of navigation *Instructions nouvelles des poincts ... touchant l'art de naviger* (1581). Navigation here consists of governing or directing a ship, and it is both an art and a science, which is to say, it is a practice that involves knowledge or, vice versa, a science that serves the practical ends of a *techne*. Although science, as we shall see shortly, will play an important role in setting up rules of governing or conducting a ship, navigation cannot be regarded as an *episteme*, knowledge aiming at un-changeable objects or the representational mode of being, it rather has to be seen as *techne*, knowledge that relates to changing objects or the operative mode of formation.

Ten years before Coignet, John Dee provided this definition in his preface to the first English edition of Euclid's *Elements of Geometry*:

> The Arte of Navigation, demonstrateth how, by the shortest good way, by the aptest Direction, & in the shortest time, a sufficient Ship, betwene any two places (in passage Nauigable,) assigned: may be conducted: and in all stormes, & naturall disturbances chauncyng, how, to vse the best possible meanes, whereby to recouer the place first assigned.[8]

This definition, firstly, emphasizes the principle of connection. The passage of a ship is conceived of as overcoming distance, in order to connect two places in the most direct way and in the shortest time. The object of navi-gation is not passage or way but route - recurrent passage which is directed to a place assigned; furthermore, route is transformed into a geometrical line. As oceanic shipping increases and takes on the regular form of traffic, the geometrical line becomes the line of ships or shipping companies. Finding the aptest direction is, secondly, related to the sufficiency of a ship. This term refers to seamanship,[9] which comprises the design of a ship, the distribution of services and the functional differentiation and ranking of the crew, provisions for clothing, nourishment and hygiene, the handling of sails and steering, discipline and the government of a ship. One can see that navigation in the narrow sense of orientation is related to a number of practical and technical issues concerning the sufficiency of a ship. And all this together - and this is the final point - serves the purpose of safety, or, as William Bourne puts it in his *Regiment for the Sea* (1574), 'to preserue the shippe and goodes in al common disturbances'.[10]

Pilotage

So far, Coignet's and Dee's general definitions do not account for the fact that the art of navigation signified a specific and altogether new practice. Coignet continues his definition by saying that the art of navigation consists of two parts, 'la navigation commune' and 'la navigation grande', the first meaning (in Seller's words) 'Coasting or Sailing along the Shore', the second being a guide for 'the Ship in her Course through the Immense Ocean'.[11]

Shipping in the 16th century was still largely sailing along the coastline, *costeggiare*, as the Italians called it, 'hugging the shore'.[12] Braudel quotes an account according to which 'it was a matter of buying one's butter at Villefranche, vinegar at Nice, oil and bacon at Toulon', or 'of travelling from one seaside inn to another, dining in one and supping in the next'.[13] Similarly, English seamen in early Tudor times still kept to the vicinity of coasts, when sailing to the Low Countries, to Bordeaux, the Biscay ports and to Portugal and Spain in order to exchange wool and cloth for wines, fruit or iron. Thus Chaucer's shipman 'knew alle the havenes, as they were / Fro Gootlond to the Cape of Fynystere'.[14]

The ability needed for coasting was that of common navigation or the art of pilotage. It depended on the observation and knowledge of visible landmarks - 'hylles, vales, cliftes, and Castles, with steples and Churches, are the beste and most surest markes', says Bourne - or, in Coignet's words, on

> knowing perfectly by sight all the capes, ports and rivers met with, how they rise up and how they appear from the sea, and what distance lies between them, and what route or course, or rather bearing, they have one from another ...[15]

Thus pilotage rests primarily on experience and on empirical observation for which a limited number of instruments are used:[16]

- A compass (including a loadstone to magnetize it) to take the bearings of landmarks or harbours. In Atlantic shipping it was also used to fix the moon's position at high tide; thus not only the time of tides could be calculated, but also the position of a place or landmark could be fixed.
- The lead and line served to sound the depth and nature of the sea-bottom, and allowed to estimate the vicinity of a coast, cape or rock, particularly in the case of fog, or simply enabled a safe passage into a river or port.
- The log and line were a recently invented means of judging the speed of a ship.
- Time-keeping was managed with the help of a half-hour running-glass, the ship's bell and a schedule of watches. The traverse-board helped to check on the course and the distance covered each watch.
- Although the ship-master usually knew landmarks, coastlines, etc., well, they at times would use pilot-books - 'rutters' in the Atlantic or 'portolani' in the Mediterranean tradition[17] - which contained detailed information on bearings, distances between places, descriptions of landmarks, instructions for entering harbours. Northern rutters were not very precise on these points; due to the different conditions of fog, shallow waters and tides they gave detailed accounts of soundings and tides instead, supplemented by almanacs containing calenders with the phases of the moon. Another difference is that the Northern seamen did not use sea-charts until the middle of the 16th century, whereas the Mediterranean seamen did: the portolan charts were 'little outline maps with the names of ports and a compass rose and radiating lines',[18] by means of which the pilot could set his course.

Navigation

All this was the equipment of those who first set out on oceanic voyages, but very soon the need for skills that had to go beyond the art of pilotage became evident. The obvious reason is that oceanic shipping could not find its bearings in visible landmarks. Thus navigation, as Bourne put it, had to face the necessity of 'how to direct ones course vpon or thorow the sea, where he findeth no path to any place assigned'.[19] If the ocean embodies the absence of visible terrestrial objects, the only fixed marks that remain are the heavenly bodies. And while the art of pilotage cared for compass bearings, the principal care of the navigator was to determine, according to Seller, 'in what place the Ship is at all times both in respect of *Latitude* and *Longitude*',[20] and for this, knowledge of geometry, arithmetic, trigonometry and astronomy was required. Thus, in contrast to the empiricism of pilotage, 'oceanic navigation, was fundamentally scientific and depended primarily upon calculation and the observation of celestial bodies.'[21] The following means were used:

- Quadrant, astrolabe or cross-staff were developed or adjusted to observe the altitude of the Pole Star and the sun in order to find latitude.
- It was necessary to tabulate these observations methodically. For this purpose the log-book was designed, which contained the day of the month (constituting chronology), nautical data (constituting position) and remarks or discourse (constituting narrative).
- Maps were now going to play an important role in navigation. At the end of the 16th century, after a rapid development in chart-making, the navigator was equipped with a plane chart that provided a fairly proportionate representation of the continents which accounted for sphericity and an adequate projection of longitude and latitude. Other than the portolan network of compass bearings, the map was now divided up into a grid of latitudes and longitudes which enabled the navigator to mark his current position or that of newly discovered land.

The development of the art of navigation was accompanied and supported by developments and innovations in other fields. One, as already mentioned, was seamanship, another the institutionalization of navigational education and the transfer of skills and knowledge. In the second edition of his *Principal Navigations* (1600), Richard Hakluyt presents 'Certaine briefe extracts of the orders of the Contractation house of *Siuil* in *Spaine*, touching their gouernment in sea-matters; together with The streight and seuere examination of Pilots and Masters before they be admitted to take charge of ships'.[22] Earlier, in the 1560s, Stephen Borrough had brought back Martin Cortez' *Arte de navegar* from a visit to Seville - it was translated into English within a year - and written a petition to the Queen for the creation of the office of Chief Pilot: 'to make perfect mariners',[23] to examine them and to certify their skills according to their rank and function. Twenty years later Hakluyt demanded that a lectureship in the art of navigation - 'the chief ornament of an island kingdom'[24] - be established in London. All these supporting activities display the great care invested in achieving a high level of institutionalization. The immediate aim was safety: 'the advoyding of dyvers great perills and dawngers, as well the Losses of shipps and goodes, as mens lyves',[25] as Borrough said. And safety was needed to serve the prime purpose of navigation: bringing into the country 'habundaunce of Riches and cummoditie',[26] thus serving 'the common good' and giving 'a great strength and stay to the kindom [*sic*]'.[27]

Technology of Orientation

The art of navigation may be regarded as a comprehensive technology of orientation and as such it was a means to tackle oceanic transgression and to react to contingency in the form of either shipwreck or commercial chance. But in how far is it possible to say that the art of navigation marks the beginning of a new form of orientation or even the beginnings of a specifically modern need for orientation?

- Navigation answers the event or rather the advent of landlessness. It is a form of orientation under the condition of complete deterritorialization.
- In the art of pilotage, orientation was primarily linked to visible land-marks and to route. The sailing directions therefore contained informa-tion on concrete objects. In navigation, orientation is a matter of finding and fixing positions in a system of longitudes and latitudes. This implies that the route is transformed into the more abstract notion of line and connection. The more regular oceanic shipping became, the more the empty space of the ocean, into which the ships transgressed, was filled with circumnavigational lines; by and by, transgression turned into a global network of connections - it became traffic and communication.
- The abstract mode of line (as well as the older bearings on portolan charts) reflects the simple fact that the ocean does not keep the trace of a ship, there is - according to Bourne - 'no path ... assigned'.[28] Connections in navigation materialize in graphic form only, be it in the log-book or on the map. In deterritorialized orientation the mode of representation is substituted by diagrammatic virtuality.

If the awakening of maritime energies - as Schmitt put it - was one important and long-ranging event of the 16th century, the development of an art of navigation was another. And if the one is associated with merchant adventurers, discoverers and pirates, the other must clearly be seen as a practice designed to control risk, adventure and contingency. Channelling the new energies and making voyages safe served the purpose of fulfilling the promises of commercial enterprise: abundance of riches and com-modities.

Travel Observations

Among the instruments used for navigation, the log-book deserves some closer attention. In his *Ordinances, instructions, and aduertisements of and for the direction of the intended voyage for Cathaye* (1553) Sebastian Cabot advises

> that the marchants, and other skilful persons in writing, shal dayly write, describe, and put in memorie the Nauigation of euery day and night with the points, and obseruation of the lands, tides, elements, altitude of the sunne, course of the moone and starres ...[29]

The nautical data Cabot asks the merchants to note down form one part of the log-book; the other, called discourse, contains observations of the sort that Hakluyt expects the merchants of the Muscovy Company to collect:

> To note the Islands, whether they be hie land or low land, mountaine, or flat, grauelly, clay, chalkie, or of what soile, woody or not woody, with springs and riuers or not, and what wilde beasts they haue in the same. ... If you finde any Island or maine land populous, and that the same people hath neede of cloth, then are you to deuise what commodities they haue to purchase the same withall. If they be poore, then are you to consider of the soile, and how by any possibilitie the same may be made to inrich them, that heerafter they may haue something to purchase the cloth withall.[30]

These instructions are a first step on the way towards systematic travel observations which were later prepared and structured by a catalogue of questions.[31] The aim was to gain systematic knowledge of a country, its geographical outline, its natural resources, its population, its culture and society. It is in this so-called 'statistics' that orientation gains a wider perspective in so far as the descriptions of other countries and places constituted a whole discourse which shaped the perception of the other and initiated the production of knowledge.

Two interesting examples will show in a nutshell how the log-book's two registers contain the systematics of both nautical and geographical discourse. In the introduction to his *Voyage Round the World*, Georg Forster explains that he does not write about nautical observations, as Cook did, but concentrates on his domain, the description of the fauna and flora, of geographical phenomena and of the population.[32] Thus we have two different types of description of one and the same voyage. Later, Forster compensates his readers for his earlier abstention from nautical themes; in an essay dedicated solely to Cook as a person, he deals extensively with everything concerning navigation and seamanship, praising Cook in particular for having taught his officers the importance of astronomy for navigation.[33] In his final characterization, the voyage as a whole appears as a perfect fusion of competent navigation and a comprehensive description of the Pacific Islands and their inhabitants.

The second example, Kant's lectures on physical geography, allows us to consider the historical significance of Forster's fusion of discourses. The systematics of these lectures define anthropology (knowledge of the inner truth of man) and physical geography (knowledge of the outer truth of nature) as the two fundamental components of what Kant calls *Welterkenntnis*[34] (knowledge of the world). It implies and demands a globalization of the human and natural sciences at a time when Cook's travels cover the world. As the navigator holds the world in his hands like an orb,[35] the philosopher maintains that the world is the scene and substance of man's actions and skills.[36] What is remarkable now is the fact that Kant inserts a chapter on the art of conducting a ship into his lectures on physical geography.[37] This insertion marks (at least for a decisive historical moment) the entrance of nautical discourse into the empirical sciences of man and nature. It correlates with Kant's demand that physical geography should assist the subject in structuring its perception of the world so that, when new data is coming in (via newspapers), it knows where to locate and how to use them. Thus *Welterkenntnis* is not simply an extension and further systematization of travel observation, it becomes a mode of orientation in itself. Kant widened the maritime art of orientation to a cultural practice, relating it to science, globality and the subject, by demanding that this practice should allow everybody to locate everybody else's position.

Fortune

The Self and the Sea

> In sooth, I know not why I am so sad.
> It wearies me, you say it wearies you,
> ...
> And such a want-wit sadness makes of me
> That I have much ado to know myself.

says Antonio at the beginning of Shakespeare's *Merchant of Venice*, and his friend Salerio replies:

> Your mind is tossing on the ocean ...[38]

An explanation for Antonio's melancholy may be found in contemporary notions, as it is (among a legion of other reasons) the 'losse of friends, and losse of goods'[39] which produce sadness. The loss of his friend Bassanio is a theme to be treated later in the scene, the loss of temporary goods is referred to by Salerio and Solanio in their immediate response to Antonio's complaint. This loss implies the question of the self in the context of maritime experience.

In Salerio's statement, the sea serves as an image of the restless and undirected movement of the self, in the sense that, according to Robert Burton, the melancholics' 'restlesse mindes are tossed and varie'.[40] Salerio goes on to say:

> There where your argosies with portly sail,
> Like signors and rich burghers on the flood -
> ...
> Do overpeer the petty traffickers
> That curtsy to them, do them reverence,
> As they fly by them with their woven wings. (1.1.9-14)

It is interesting to note that Salerio does not follow the metaphor of the ship as self, that is to say, he does not compare Antonio's ships with his mind; they both rather exclude each other: the self is dislocated, instead of being like the stately ships, it is where they are, somewhere else. Thus Solanio links Antonio's ventures, his floating capital, to his lost sense of self:[41]

> Believe me, sir, had I such venture forth
> The better part of my affections would
> Be with my hopes abroad. (1.1.15-17)

This explanation of melancholy as oceanic dislocation of the self also controls Salerio's and Solanio's perspective on the following discourse on orientation. Solanio says:

> ... I should be still
> Plucking the grass to know where sits the wind,
> Peering in maps for ports and piers and roads ... (1.1.17-19)

And Salerio goes on to say that the wind cooling his soup would make him fear harmful winds, that the sight of a sandy hour-glass would make him think 'of shallows and of flats' (1.1.26), and that seeing the stones of a church building would make him think of 'dangerous rocks' (1.1.31). One can clearly recognize some of the dangers that pilotage was meant to overcome.[42] Yet, here the imagination of these dangers is roused by observations of land and betrays an anti-maritime attitude. To say that Antonio 'Is sad to think upon his merchandise' (1.1.40) is to say that he does not concentrate on the care of his self, but on the goods that float on the ocean, a sphere governed by the inconstancy and contingency of Fortune whose presence is felt in Salerio's words on the spices scattered around the wrecked ship:

> And, in a word, but even now worth this,
> And now worth nothing? (1.1.35-6)

And like the goods the self is tossing on the ocean, it has lost the capability of orientation.

But there is another model of experience, which Antonio claims for himself in his reply to his friends' moral critique:

> My ventures are not in one bottom trusted,
> Nor to one place; nor is my whole estate
> Upon the fortune of this present year.
> Therefore my merchandise makes me not sad. (1.1.42-5)

What Antonio conjures up here are the practical principles of the prudent merchant who sees overseas trade as a chance and calculates its risks. When he tells his friend, 'that all my fortunes are at sea' (1.1.177), he seems to be sure about the profitable chances the uncertainties of shipping offer.

Prudence

In both models of behaviour - care of the self and prudence - the opening scene of *The Merchant of Venice* relates maritime experience to the allegory of Fortune. This link indicates a fundamental change in the attitude towards contingency. In the tradition of classical moral philosophy, particularly Stoicism, Fortune represented indifferent things, things which were contingent and followed the rule of time. In order to find and practise the essential values of the good (like self-restraint or constancy), the subject had to fight and resist the inconstancy and violent attacks of fortune. To illustrate this moral combat, Seneca compares the self with a helmsman who has to steer his course 'contra fortunam'[43] - against the storm (*turbae*) of inner and outer passions - and who brings home the ship of his self to the safety of an unassailable harbour. In the political *turbae* of the 16th century, the Stoic canon is revived as a means to console and relocate a threatened self, a self that feels haunted by (as Wyatt puts it) the 'dread of mutability'.[44] The question that Lipsius poses is: how can one flee and resist the tumult of civil war which rages like the rough and stormy seas,[45] how can one flee the deceptive winds of Fortune and chance?[46] Langius, Lipsius' philosophical consoler, answers:

> As some riuers are said to runne through the sea [*per media maria*] and yet keepe their streame fresh: So shalt thou passe thorough the confused tumultes [*tumultus*] of this world ... onely take vnto thee a good courage, steere thy ship into this porte, where is securitie and quietnesse, a refuge and sanctuarie against all turmoyles and troubles [*a turbis*] ...[47]

'Fortunae resistere' worked as an exercise which was part of an ethics of the self, and the essence of the moral subject is position (the safe harbour) beyond the changing and overwhelming modes of time and the sea.

The revived battles of constancy indicate a historical change concerning the role of contingency. During the Middle Ages, Fortune - now mostly visualized as turning a crowded wheel symbolizing the uncontrollable rise and fall of worldly existence - remained a power to be excluded and suspended.[48] The 15th and 16th centuries witness a remarkable rise of the allegory of Fortune; this coincides with an iconographical change which signifies a reorganization of self-practice. Instead of turning a wheel, we now see Fortune taking the place of a ship's mast and catching the wind in her sail.[49] Here, the wind no longer foreshadows a destructive whirl,[50] it promises the energy and dynamics of a ship sailing out to bring home the riches of far-off countries. Goblets and horns of plenty are what she now holds in her hands as a reward for the successful merchant adventurer. Barabas' concern for the winds - 'But now how stands the wind?'[51] - differs completely from the Stoicists', since it is the wind which brings home 'abundance of riches':

> Thus trowls our fortune in by land and sea,
> And thus are we on every side enrich'd.
> ...
> What more may heaven do for earthly man
> Than thus to pour out plenty in their laps,
> ...
> Making the sea their servant, and the winds
> To drive their substance with successful blasts?[52]

The development towards a *fortuna di mare* shows that contingency is no longer excluded by an attitude centred around ethos; it is integrated into a new attitude centred around prudence, whose aim is to make use of Fortune's energies. Contingency becomes chance, in the equivocal sense of the word. De Bry's emblem (Figure 2.1) shows Fortune balancing on a globe in the sea; her fickle, yet upright posture divides two scenes from one another: storm and shipwreck on the one hand, calm weather and a boat returning to an island on the other. The lesson of this scene is not only that of Fortune's

FIGURE 2.1

Allegory of Fortune. Theodor de Bry, *Emblemata nobilitati et vulgo scitu digna* (1592)

arbitrary rule, of her incalculable (and often unjust) distribution of goods. Her position in between two scenes (and on the sea) also marks the route of prudence between the two possibilities of failure and success. By trying to make use of the winds, prudence, in contrast to the timeless position of the moral subject, manifests itself as timely direction. In this sense, prudence can be seen as a technique of personal orientation. As the subject here cannot refer to theory or a set of general rules, but has to deal with situations of contingency, this type of orientation is constituted by experience. It is interesting to note that because prudence, unlike science, has to cope with chance, it was compared to the open and unsteady sea.[53]

Apart from commerce, it is the court which offers itself as another 'field' of prudent behaviour. With its intrigues and the unpredictable rise and fall of favourites it is seen as a dangerous sea, and prudence as the ability to navigate in these perilous waters. Thus Boccalini in his *Ragguagli di Parnasso* (1613) recommends astrolabe, quadrant and compass to those, who want to embark on the wild seas of the court,[54] in the same way as Critilo and Andrenio, heroes of Gracián's *El Criticon*, ask for a conduct book that may direct their course through the sea of court life like a compass.[55] *El Criticon* no longer depicts the battle between land-based *constantia* and sea-borne *Fortuna*, but a journey on which the prudent subject has to wind its way through the deceptions and opportunities of contingency. For Gracián there is no timeless resort, there is only continuous change in everything. Therefore everybody needs time[56] (rather than the exclusion of it) and experience (as a spacious process[57]) to achieve their point of perfection. This revaluation of prudence, change and time is linked with maritime experience: considering the 'inconstancia de mi fortuna' Critilo believes what he was told: that he was born on the sea.[58]

Another significant point about prudence is that it entails the art of looking into the other's soul. The prudent courtier will successfully come off his voyage, if he knows how to decipher the other.[59] The aim of the voyage is no longer the return to the self, but an anatomy of the affective structure of the other which serves as an instrument in the fight against sudden attacks and veiled intentions. This shift from an ethics of the self (a passage directed to the safety of a harbour) to a hermeneutics of the other (a passage directed to the open sea) is significant, because later on, in the 18th century, knowing the other will take the form of empirical human sciences, which (in Kant's systematics) supplement the natural sciences.

There is, however, a third model of personal orientation to be thought of, which one can find in Montaigne. On the one hand, Montaigne clearly presents his reflections as attempts at a return of the self to the self. Like Lipsius, he refers to both antique tradition and the actual political turmoil: up to now you have lived swimming and drifting, Montaigne paraphrases Seneca and Epicurus, it is time now to turn back home to the harbour;[60] and this return to one's own self is a reaction to the tempests of civil war, which forces everyone to guard their own houses.[61] On the other hand, Montaigne puts the security and essence of the self in doubt.[62] The world, he says with regard to Fortune, is a permanent up and down, everything totters and swings, so that even constancy is nothing but slowed-down rocking. Thus he is unable to fix the object of his representation, the image of himself:

> I cannot settle my obiect; it goeth so vnquietly and staggering, with a naturall drunkennesse. I take it in this plight, as it is at th'instant I ammuse my selfe about it. I describe not the *essence*, but the *passage* ... My historie must be fitted to the present. I may soone change, not onelie fortune, but intention.[63]

Montaigne's mobile, time-stricken reflections on the self (rocking and travelling like a ship) stand in between the ascetic (Lipsius) and the prudent subject (Gracián);[64] they combine ethical orientation (being) with the notion of passage (being-on-the-way), essence with contingency, position with situation.

Contingency and the Novel

In the second part of his adventures Don Quixote, when approaching the Ebro, becomes aware of 'a small bark, without oars, or any sort of tackle'.[65] Visualizing another opportunity to rescue some helpless noble person - this time across a distance of 'two or three thousand leagues'[66] - he immediately embarks with his companion Sancho. The irony of this adventure lies in the diverging conceptions of space and distance. Don Quixote explains to San-cho (who despairs at the prospect of landlessness) that they must already be out on the sea and must have covered at least seven or eight hundred leagues:

> If I had here an astrolabe, to take the elevation of the pole, I would tell you how many [leagues] we have gone; though either I know little, or we are already past, or shall presently pass, the equinoctial line, which divides and cuts the opposite poles at equal distances.[67]

This reference to astronavigation is supported by Don Quixote's conception of global space as a grid of lines, parallels, points or straight lines,[68] and it is this conception which stands in ironic contrast to the less than five yards that the bark has actually moved away from the river's bank, and to the ensuing uncontrolled drift of the boat ending in shipwreck. Don Quixote's deception, which transforms the calculations of Ptolemaic geography into an imaginary map, opens up a gap between the poles of position and situa-tion, a gap signifying the absence of experience. For the land-based knight the maritime adventure becomes a chorographic failure - he fails to map the same of his country by transgressing into the oceanic other - it ends in the complete loss of orientation and announces the modern rule of 'fortune',[69] which replaces providence and the chivalrous test of virtue.[70]

Thus *Don Quixote* can be regarded as one of the first examples of what Bakhtin said about the fundamental role that the road plays in novels.[71] The road or way, as one of the major chronotopes of the novel, is defined as a space of chance encounter. It is there that the ways of the most varied individuals - 'representatives of all social classes, estates, religions, nationalities, ages'[72] - meet, and it is the road, says Bakhtin, which serves particularly well to depict events 'governed by chance'.[73] The formative function of chronotopes in general consists in providing the basis for scenes. In contrast to communication, which informs about an event, placing it in a network of temporal and spatial connections, scene concentrates and condenses events.[74] Thus the road first of all assembles events and encounters as they happen according to the mode of Fortune or 'in the flow of time'.[75] The road, in short, allows and represents situation, being without direction and position. But in the same way as Fortune allegorizes prudence and with it a practice, which gives chance a direction, narrative directs chance encounters and events by condensing them into the experience of characters (as well as readers[76]) and by establishing the logic of plot. Consequently, the mode of undirected contingency is transformed into the directed mode of route, which eventually becomes 'the route of a life'[77] or the journey of life. Orientation here implies experience, because on their way characters are time and again confronted with situations of chance, through which they have to work their way in order to set the course of their life. The meandering route of experience is thus opposed to the straight line of navigation.

Our own actuality even seems to witness a reopening of Cervantes' gap - in the postmodern vision of a text without plot and character, a text which gives up the narrative grip on chance, encounter and event, a text without direction like Rimbaud's drunken, unmanned ship drifting away and dislocating itself like Don Quixote's bark and thus producing incessant departures.[78]

If one were to describe - in terms of orientation - the essence of a moral tradition that had its origins in antiquity and was revived in early modern times, one would have to say that it consisted in a permanent resistance to time, change and contingency. This moral tradition was (other than its metaphors suggest) anti-maritime inasmuch as its orientation was directed towards the harbour, symbolizing the security and autonomy of the self. Up to the 15th and 16th centuries, this tradition coincided with a deep respect for limits, for not transgressing the pillars of Hercules which marked off the vast space of the ocean. Shipping, consequently, was coasting, avoiding the perils of the wide and uncontrollable waters.

Oceanic transgression - which must also be seen as a shift from the Mediterranean culture of self-restraint to the Atlantic civilization of transgressive individualism - introduced a new dynamics into occidental culture, whose concrete source was the winds. Their contingency promised a dynamics that the moral subject would never have taken trust in. Seen as chance and risk, double-faced contingency[79] challenges new systems of orientation: one based on a precise calculation of positions - the art of navigation - and one based on experience - the operative models of Fortune and prudence. If navigation had to make voyages safe and stabilize contingency, not by muting, but by using it (for commercial purposes), prudence, understood as a technique of personal orientation, had to govern contingency by actually facing it and giving it direction. And it seems that the more navigation turned out to be the starting point for the development of technologies of global orientation, involving an allocation of positions, a system of communication and globalized empirical sciences, the more literature insisted on and reintroduced the stifled dimension of experience, even to the point of giving up the narrative grip on contingency. However, both commercial, communicative and scientific culture which is driven by the controlled dynamics of permanent transgression, and literary culture which tries to give chance a shape, prove that in part our modern existence stems from maritime energies, from the time when the former threat of the winds began to be hailed as a promise. As our actual experience of contingency turns out to be linked with the oceanic turn, and maritime experience discloses itself as a line on the multifaced physiognomy of modernity, it also becomes clear that ours is a culture of, and in need of, orientation.

Notes

1   Carl Schmitt, *Land und Meer. Eine weltgeschichtliche Betrachtung* [1942] (Stuttgart: Reclam, 2nd ed. 1954), 22; quoted here from the English edition *Land and Sea*, trans. Simona Draghici (Washington, DC: Plutarch Press, 1997), 19.
2   Fernand Braudel, *The Mediterranean and the Mediterranean World in the Age of Philipp II*, trans. Siân Reynolds, 2 vols (London: Fontana, 1975), vol. 1, 224.
3   Cf. Michael Makropoulos, 'Modernität als Kontingenzkultur', Gerhart von Graevenitz *et al.* (eds), *Kontingenz*, Poetik und Hermeneutik 17 (München: Fink, 1998), 55-79.
4   James Hamilton-Paterson, *Seven Tenths. The Sea and Its Thresholds* (London: Hutchinson, 1992), 5-6.
5   For the image of the narrow path that separates life from death cf. Seneca, *Medea*, lines 307-8.

6   These concepts and the following enlargements modify the opposition of *carte* versus *parcours*, or, respectively, of *survey* versus *route*. Cf. Michel de Certeau, *Kunst des Handelns* [1974], trans. Ronald Voullié (Berlin: Merve, 1988), ch. 9 [English edition: *The Practice of Everyday Life*, trans. Steven Rendall (Berkeley: University of California Press, 1984)]; and Robert Lloyd, *Spatial Cognition. Geographic Environments* (Dordrecht and London: Kluwer Academic, 1997), 50.

7   John Seller, *Practical Navigation* [1669], quoted in David W. Waters, *The Art of Navigation in England in Elizabethan and Early Stuart Times*, 3 vols (Greenwich: National Maritime Museum, 2nd ed. 1978), vol. 1, 3-4.

8   John Dee, 'The Mathematicall Praeface to the Elements of Geometrie of Euclid of Megara' [1570], quoted in Waters, *The Art of Navigation*, vol. 3, 521.

9   Cf. the entry on 'seamanship', *Encyclopedia Britannica* [ed. 1911]; J.H. Parry, *The Age of Reconnaissance. Discovery, Exploration and Settlement 1450 to 1650* [1963] (New York: Praeger Publishers, 1969), ch. 4.

10 William Bourne, *A Regiment for the Sea* [1574], *A Regiment for the Sea and Other Writings on Navigation*, ed. E.G.R. Taylor (Cambridge: Hakluyt Society, 1963), 139.

11 Quoted in Waters, *The Art of Navigation*, vol. 1, 4.

12 Braudel, *The Mediterranean*, vol. 1, 103.

13 *Ibid.*, 104.

14 Geoffrey Chaucer, *The Canterbury Tales*, 'General Prologue', lines 407-8, *The Works of Geoffrey Chaucer*, ed. F.N. Robinson (Oxford: Oxford University Press, 2nd ed. 1978).

15 William Bourne, *An Almanacke and Prognostication for three yeares* [1571], *A Regiment for the Sea*, ed. Taylor, 57; Coignet quoted in Waters, *The Art of Navigation*, vol. 1, 4 (translation by Seller, see note 7).

16 For the following see Waters, *The Art of Navigation*, vol. 1, ch. 1; David W. Waters, 'The Art of Navigation in the Age of Drake', Kenneth R. Andrews (ed.), *The Last Voyage of Drake and Hawkins* (Cambridge: Hakluyt Society, 1972), 259-65; Parry, *The Age of Reconnaissance*, ch. 5; Albrecht Sauer, *Das 'Seebuch'. Das älteste erhaltene Seehandbuch und die spätmittelalterliche Navigation in Nordwesteuropa* (Hamburg: Ernst Kabel, 1997), 108-77.

17 Cf. David W. Waters, *The Rutters of the Sea* (New Haven, CT, and London: Yale University Press, 1967); Monique de la Roncière and Michel Mollat du Jourdin, *Portulane. Seekarten vom 13. bis zum 17. Jahrhundert* (München: Hirmer, 1984).

18 Parry, *The Age of Reconnaissance*, 89.

19 Bourne, *A Regiment for the Sea*, 139.

20 Quoted in Waters, *The Art of Navigation*, vol. 1, 5.

21 *Ibid.*

22 Richard Hakluyt, *The Principal Navigations, Voiages and Discoveries of the English Nation* [1600], quoted in Waters, *The Art of Navigation*, vol. 3, 555.

23 From Stephen Borrough's petition for the creation of the office of 'Pilott Maior', BL Landsdowne MS 116 [1562], quoted in Waters, *The Art of Navigation*, vol. 3, 513.

24 Richard Hakluyt, 'Epistle Dedicatory to Sir Walter Raleigh', Peter Martyr, *De orbe novo* (Paris: G. Auuray, 1587), quoted in Waters, *The Art of Navigation*, vol. 3, 546 (translation by F.C. Francis).

25 Draft of Stephen Borrough's appointment as 'Cheyffe Pylott of this our realme of Englande', BL Landsdowne MS 116 [1563/4], quoted in Waters, *The Art of Navigation*, vol. 3, 515.

26   From Borrough's petition [see note 23], quoted in Waters, *The Art of Navigation*, vol. 3, 513.

27   William Monson, 'The Convenience of a Lecture of Navigation' [c. 1624], quoted in Waters, *The Art of Navigation*, vol. 3, 568.

28   Bourne, *A Regiment for the Sea*, 139.

29   Richard Hakluyt, *The Principall Navigations, Voiages and Discoveries of the English Nation*, 2 vols (London: George Bishop and Ralph Newberrie, 1589; repr. Cambridge: Hakluyt Society, 1965), vol. 1, 259.

30   *Ibid.*, 461.

31   See Justin Stagl, 'Der wohl unterwiesene Passagier. Reisekunst und Gesellschafts-beschreibung vom 16. bis zum 18. Jahrhundert', B.I. Krasnobaev *et al.* (eds), *Reisen und Reisebeschreibungen aus dem 18. und 19. Jahrhundert als Quellen der Kultur-beziehungsforschung* (Berlin: Camen, 1980; repr. Essen: Hobbing, 1987), 353-84; Stagl (372) names as one of the first instructions for overseas travels a text called *General Heads for a Natural History of a Country, great or small*, published in the *Philosophical Transactions* of 1665; with regard to Forster see Michael Neumann, 'Philosophische Nachrichten aus der Südsee. Georg Forsters *Reise um die Welt*', Hans-Jürgen Schings (ed.), *Der ganze Mensch. Anthropologie und Literatur im 18. Jahrhundert* (Stuttgart: Metzler, 1994), 517-44, 517-33.

32   Cf. Georg Forster, *A Voyage Round the World*, ed. Robert L. Kahn, *Georg Forsters Werke*, 18 vols (Berlin: Akademie-Verlag, 1958-), vol. 1 (1968), 12. This is not to say, of course, that Cook's *A Voyage Towards the South Pole and Round the World* only contains nautical data. Yet his report is modelled more closely on the form of the log-book.

33   Georg Forster, 'Cook, der Entdecker', ed. Horst Fiedler *et al.*, *Georg Forsters Werke*, vol. 5 (1985), 191-302, 283-5.

34   Immanuel Kant, *Physische Geographie* [1802], ed. Paul Gedan (Leipzig: Dürr, 1905), 8.

35   This is the image that Forster uses in his 'Cook, der Entdecker', 208.

36   Kant, *Physische Geographie*, 9.

37   Cf. *ibid.*, 188-91.

38   William Shakespeare, *The Merchant of Venice*, 1.1.1-8. *The Norton Shakespeare*, ed. Stephen Greenblatt *et al.* (New York and London: Norton, 1997). All *Merchant of Venice* quotations are taken from this edition.

39   Robert Burton, *The Anatomy of Melancholy*, vol. 1, ed. Thomas C. Faulkner *et al.* (Oxford: Clarendon, 1989), 360 (Burton is quoting Guianerius).

40   *Ibid.*, 391.

41   Cf. Christiane Damlos-Kinzel, 'The Tension between Oeconomics and Chrematistics in William Shakespeare's *The Merchant of Venice*', Christoph Bode and Wolfgang Klooss (eds), *Historicizing / Contemporizing Shakespeare. Essays in Honour of Rudolf Böhm* (Trier: Wissenschaftlicher Verlag, 2000), 115-32, 116-18.

42   The scope of maritime experience is not limited to coasting though. Cf. what Bassanio says about Antonio's fleet: 'From Tripolis, from Mexico, and England, / From Lisbon, Barbary, and India, / And not one vessel scape the dreadful touch / Of merchant-marring rocks?' (3.2.267-70).

43   Seneca, *De providentia*, V, 9.

44   Quoted in Stephen Greenblatt, *Renaissance Self-Fashioning. From More to Shakespeare* (Chicago: Chicago University Press, 1980), 123.

45 Justus Lipsius, *De constantia / Von der Standhaftigkeit*, trans. Florian Neumann (Mainz: Dieterich, 1998), book 1, ch. 1, 10-11.
46 *Ibid.*, book 1, ch. 20: 'Ita enim Fortunae & Casus fallacem ventum fugimus' (148).
47 Justus Lipsius, *Two Bookes of Constancie*, trans. John Stradling (London: R. Johnes, 1595), book 1, ch. 6, 14.
48 Alfred Doren, 'Fortuna im Mittelalter und in der Renaissance', *Vorträge der Bibliothek Warburg* 2, no. 1 (1922/3; repr. 1965), 71-143; Howard R. Patch, *The Goddess Fortuna in Mediaeval Literature* (Cambridge, MA: Harvard University Press, 1927; repr. London: Frank Cass & Co., 1967).
49 Doren, 'Fortuna', 134-7; Samuel C. Chew, 'Time and Fortune', *ELH* 6, no. 2 (1939), 83-113, 103; Klaus Reichert, *Fortuna oder die Beständigkeit des Wechsels* (Frankfurt a.M.: Suhrkamp, 1985), 24-8. For the new association of Fortune with maritime experience cf. also William Shakespeare, *Julius Caesar*, 4.2.269-76: 'BRUTUS: We at the height are ready to decline. / There is a tide in the affairs of men / Which, taken at the flood, leads on to fortune; / Omitted, all the voyage of their life / Is bound in shallows and in miseries. / On such a full sea are we now afloat, / And we must take the current when it serves, / Or lose our ventures.' *The Norton Shakespeare*, ed. Stephen Greenblatt *et al.* (New York and London: Norton, 1997).
50 Seneca, *Naturales Questiones*, V, 16.
51 Christopher Marlowe, *The Jew of Malta*, 1.1.38. *The Complete Plays*, ed. J.B. Steane (Harmondsworth: Penguin, 1969).
52 *Ibid.*, 1.1.105-13.
53 Cf. Merio Scattola, '"Prudentia se ipsum et statum suum conservandi": Die Klugheit in der praktischen Philosophie der frühen Neuzeit', Friedrich Vollhardt (ed.), *Christian Thomasius (1655-1728). Neue Forschungen im Kontext der Frühaufklärung* (Tübingen: Niemeyer, 1997), 333-63, 336.
54 Traiano Boccalini, *Ragguagli di Parnasso*, 3 vols (Bari: n.p., 1910-48), vol. 2 (1912), 23.
55 Baltasar Gracián, *El Criticon* [1651-3], edición de Santos Alonso (Madrid: Catedra, 2000), 236.
56 Baltasar Gracián, *El Discreto* [1646], *Obra completas*, ed. Arturo del Hoyo (Madrid: Aguilar, 1967), 124-5.
57 Hans Blumenberg, *Die Lesbarkeit der Welt* (Frankfurt a.M.: Suhrkamp, 1986), 108. Blumenberg emphasizes that with Gracián experience turns into an 'extensive process' [*weitläufiger Prozeß*] which does not suffer abridgement.
58 Gracián, *El Criticon*, 99.
59 Cf. Baltasar Gracián, *El Discreto*, 129-30. Gracián makes frequent use of the sea-metaphor, cf. *ibid.*, 95, 96, 109.
60 Michel de Montaigne, *Les Essais*, ed. Fortunat Strowski *et al.*, 5 vols (Bordeaux: n.p., 1906-1933; repr. Hildesheim and New York: Olms, 1981), vol. 1, 321. For the return of the self cf. the whole essay *De la Solitude* and Jean Starobinski, *Montaigne en mouvement* [1982] (Paris: Gallimard, 1993), 38-9.
61 Montaigne, *Les Essais*, ed. Fortunat Strowski *et al.*, vol. 2, 238.
62 See *ibid.*, vol. 2, 234-5. Also, Montaigne favours travel and disregards the duties of household government (see *ibid.*, vol. 2, 207).
63 Quoted from the contemporary translation by John Florio (1603): Michel de Montaigne, *The Essays 1603*, facs. ed. (Menston: Scolar Press, 1969), 'Of Repenting',

483-92, 483 (my emphasis). For the French original, see Montaigne, *Les Essais*, ed. Fortunat Strowski *et al.*, vol. 2, 20.

64   For this reason I disagree with Blumenberg who claims Montaigne completely for the Neo-stoicist position of the harbour; cf. Hans Blumenberg, *Schiffbruch mit Zuschauer. Paradigma einer Daseinsmetapher* (Frankfurt a.M.: Suhrkamp, 1979), 18-22, 34, 39; English edition: *Shipwreck with Spectator. Paradigm of a Metaphor for Existence*, trans. Steven Rendall (Cambridge, MA, and London: MIT Press, 1996).

65   Miguel de Cervantes, *Don Quixote de La Mancha*, trans. Charles Jarvis, ed. E.C. Riley (Oxford: Oxford University Press, 1992), book 2, ch. 29, 729.

66   *Ibid.*

67   *Ibid.*, 731.

68   Cf. *ibid.*, 732.

69   *Ibid.*, ch. 30, 735.

70   Cf. Erich Köhler, *Der literarische Zufall, das Mögliche und die Notwendigkeit* (Munich: Fink, 1973), 28-31.

71   Michail M. Bakhtin, *The Dialogic Imagination*, ed. Michael Holquist, trans. Caryl Emerson and Michael Holquist (Austin: University of Texas Press, 1982), 98, 243-5. With respect to Cervantes see also Werner Krauss, *Miguel de Cervantes* (Neuwied and Berlin: Luchterhand, 1966), 148.

72   Bakhtin, *The Dialogic Imagination*, 243.

73   *Ibid.*, 244.

74   *Ibid.*, 250.

75   *Ibid.*, 244.

76   Cf. for example Henry Fielding, *The History of Tom Jones*, ed. R.P.C. Mutter (Harmondsworth: Penguin, 1966; repr. 1975), 813: 'We are now, reader, arrived at the last stage of our long journey. As we have therefore travelled together through so many pages, let us behave to one another like fellow-travellers.'

77   Bakhtin, *The Dialogic Imagination*, 244.

78   Cf. Roland Barthes, 'Roland Barthes par Roland Barthes', *Oeuvres complètes*, 3 vols, ed. Éric Marty (Paris: Seuil, 1993), vol. 3, 94, on the idea of a haiku-book; Roland Barthes, *Mythologies*, *Oeuvres complètes*, vol. 1, 612, on the incessant departures that Rimbaud's *Bateau Ivre* produces. The beginning of Rimbaud's poem refers to Cervantes' enchanted bark.

79   '(For, Fate's, or Fortune's drifts none can soothsay, / Honour and misery have one face and way)'. John Donne, 'The Storm', *The Complete English Poems*, ed. A.J. Smith (Harmondsworth: Penguin, 1971; repr. 1996), 197, lines 11-12.

3   Satan's Ocean Voyage and 18th-Century Seafaring Trade

ANNE-JULIA ZWIERLEIN

When Milton recounts the persecution of nonconformists under Archbishop Laud in *Of Reformation* (1641), stating that 'nothing but the wide Ocean, and the savage deserts of *America* could hide and shelter [them] from the fury of the Bishops' (*YP* 1: 585), the crossing of the ocean is perceived as a last resort in extremity but otherwise as undesirable as the 'savage deserts of *America*' in general.[1] The ocean, to Milton, is a hostile force, in *Paradise Lost* ambiguously associated with the chaotic structure of original matter from which God created the world but which in itself is perceived as an almost anti-vital force: 'The secrets of the hoary deep, a dark / Illimitable ocean without bound, / Without dimension, where length, breadth, and highth, / And time and place are lost' (*PL* 2.891-4).[2] The elegy *Lycidas* (1638), a tribute to Milton's deceased friend Edward King who was drowned in a shipwreck in 1637 not far from the British coast, presents the sea as a destructive force and imagines the 'sounding seas / Wash[ing] far away ... [the] bones' of King, depicting them 'beyond the stormy Hebrides' or 'under the whelming tide ... [at] the bottom of the monstrous world' (154-8).[3] And although at the end of *Lycidas* Milton evokes 'the dear might of him that walked the waves' (173), presenting Christianity as the vanquisher even of the destructive ocean, the darker forces evoked in the poem linger, especially the piece of superstition which claims King's ship, the 'fatal and perfidious bark', to have been 'Built in the eclipse, and rigged with curses dark' (100-101). The life-sustaining power of inland waters, the 'fountain, shade, and rill' of *Lycidas* (24) or the positively connoted river Severn ('the glassy, cool, translucent wave', 860) out of which arises the nymph Sabrina in Milton's masque *Comus* to tender salvation to the human protagonists in the form of 'Drops ... from my fountain pure' (911), is in Milton continuously opposed by the open sea with its apparently limitless expanse and threatening bottom which symbolize chaos and dangerous conflict.

Satan as Seafarer

In *Paradise Lost*, it is Satan's voyage through the epic's topographies that continually links references to ocean travel and maritime metaphors with spiritual symbolism. Throughout the narrative, Satan is compared to sea monsters, islands, seafarers, merchant travellers, or even a merchant vessel. In this paper I will concentrate on three stages of Satan's epic - and nautical - voyage. The first is Satan's awakening on the lake of fire in hell after his fall from heaven and the extended comparison between Satan and the sea-monster Leviathan. The second is the depiction of Satan on his throne in hell, resplendent in the treasures of 'Ormus and of Ind' with their evocations of early modern colonialism and seafaring trade. The third stage in Satan's narrative is his voyage from hell through the 'ocean' of chaos to the 'shores' of paradise in order to conquer and enslave mankind. This voyage is depicted by Milton in analogy to early modern voyages of discovery and long-distance trading and just possibly might also allude to the early modern slave trade and its oceanic routes.[4] The metaphorical level of seafaring is sustained even after Satan has invaded paradise: when trying to attract Eve's attention in the temptation scene, Satan in serpent-form undulates before her eyes like 'a ship by skilful steersman wrought / Nigh river's mouth or foreland, where the wind / Veers oft, as oft so steers, and shifts her sail' (*PL* 9.513-15).

The resonances in Milton's epic of early modern colonialism and the rise of a new seafaring merchant class have been a major focus in Milton criticism for some time, along with the vexed question about Milton's status as a poet 'for' or 'against' empire.[5] Whereas the last two books of *Paradise Lost* display a negative outlook on human empire-building, and whereas David Quint sees Satan's 'merchant voyage' as parodically inflected, the extended nautical allegory does convey the appeal of classical heroism. This is due, not least, to Milton's use of early modern travel accounts collected by Hakluyt and Purchas. Moreover, the narrative of Satan's voyage mixes classical examples of *aristeia* like Ulysses' brave encounter with the sea monsters Scylla and Charybdis and the exploits of the Vasco da Gama of Camões' *Lusiads*. But Milton's use of the tradition of classical heroism intersects with his Christian symbolic universe which, even if informed by recent findings of travellers or astronomers, is still close to the allegorical world picture preserved in Jodocus Hondius' so-called 'Christian Knight Map' (c. 1597). This map, even though using Mercator's projection, presents the world primarily as a stage for the contest between Christianity and the archaic forces of Satan, Sin, and Death (Figure 3.1). These three figures, in fact, are the 'Satanic Trinity' in *Paradise Lost*; all three voyage across the watery expanses of Milton's cosmos to bring destruction to mankind. The most salient features of Milton's oceanic symbolism, therefore, are his insistence on the physical and spiritual dangers of ocean travel and his warnings about the spiritual dangers of luxuries imported through long-distance trade. In short, the ocean in *Paradise Lost* becomes a metaphor for the uncertainty of human knowledge and the contingencies of fallen human existence.

I will follow these issues up with a brief look at worldly, patriotic 18th-century transformations of these Milton passages in commentaries and poetic adaptations.[6] Each subsection will start by discussing one of the relevant Milton passages, i.e. Satan on the lake of fire, on the throne in hell, or on his way to paradise, and subsequently I will analyse some selected 18th-century rewritings of these passages. What interests me are the ways in which Satan's trajectory was rewritten to be inserted in 18th-century discourses about the glories of the evolving British Empire, the debate between mercantilist and free trade visions of commerce, the debate about the luxuries imported via long-distance trade, and the debate about the slave trade. At the beginning of the 18th century, British trading posts had been established in India, at Surat, Madras, Bombay and Calcutta, and European ships were sailing regularly off the coasts of China and Japan.[7] The new 'global players' were not the heroes and noble soldiers of Sidney's and Raleigh's days but the newly risen merchant class.[8] Commentators like Bentley (1732), Paterson (1744), or Marchant (1751) transformed Satan's route into a eulogy of flourishing East India Company trading posts; their annotations familiarized the mythological dangers Milton's Satan encounters by proffering recent knowledge about winds or tides out of the fast-growing 'imperial archive'. As Marcus Rediker has observed, 'English trade routes constituted the arteries of the imperial body between 1650 and 1750.'[9] The cartographical revolution of these times of expansion was accompanied by profound changes in the European imagination of spaces and distances. Still, the ominous instability of the transnational space of long-distance trade, conveyed in Milton's metaphors and syntax, persisted in these adaptations.

On the whole, I will be concerned with nationalistic or even imperialistic Milton readings in the century after his own. The literary-historical *grand récit* constructed in this paper, possibly to the exclusion of other 18th-century perspectives on Milton such as that of religious nonconform-

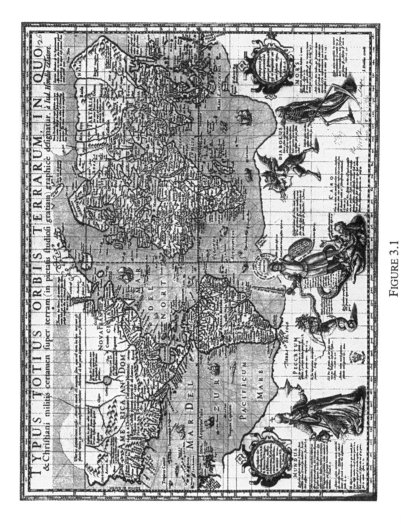

FIGURE 3.1

Jodocus Hondius, *Typus totius Orbis terrarum, in quo & Christiani militis certamen super terram (in pietatis studiosi gratiam) graphicè designatur* ('Christian Knight Map') (c. 1597)

ists, is the replacement of Milton's 17th-century spiritual and symbolic concept of space by the classified and cartographically charted space of the 18th century.[10] In a last twist, my coda will present Peter Ackroyd's 'postcolonial' mode of rewriting Satan's ocean voyage in his recent novel *Milton in America*.

Satan as Leviathan

In Milton's *Paradise Lost*, we first encounter Satan after his fall floating in chains on the burning lake in hell: 'Prone on the flood, extended long and large / [He] Lay floating many a rood' (*PL* 1.195-6). His huge bulk is compared to that of the 'sea-beast / Leviathan, which God of all his works / Created hugest that swim the ocean stream' (*PL* 1.200-202). The symbolic connotations of the ocean imagery follow immediately: Satan's 'metamorphosis' into Leviathan, the archetypal monster of *Job* 41, is connected in an extended simile with the famous travellers' tale of the ship's pilot taking Leviathan for an island and anchoring his ship in the monster's 'scaly rind':

> Him haply slumbering on the Norway foam
> The pilot of some small night-foundered skiff,
> Deeming some island, oft, as seamen tell,
> With fixed anchor in his scaly rind
> Moors by his side under the lea, while night
> Invests the sea, and wished morn delays:
> So stretched out huge in length the arch-fiend lay
> Chained on the burning lake ... (*PL* 1.203-10)

This is an allegory about Satan's powers of deception and man's defective powers of perception, and it was a traditional item in medieval bestiaries and Renaissance emblem books,[11] most prominently perhaps in a 1511 *Bestiarium* preserved in the Bodleian Library which recounts the spiritual meaning of this travellers' anecdote[12] (Figure 3.2). The anonymous writer of this Bestiary recounts that the beast he calls 'Balena' resembles the one that swallowed Jonah ('except ionam') and was associated with hell even in the Old Testament: 'tantae magnitudinis fuit ut putaret infernum dicente ipso iona. Exaudivit me de ventre inferi.' ('It was so huge that he believed it to be hell, so that Jonah himself exclaimed: God heard me even from the very maw of hell.') Our travellers' tale is recounted immediately after this:

> Et in medio pelagi elevat dorsum suum super undas maris tumque stat in uno loco quo adusque de sabulo maris vento aquato planities fiat virgultasque

quiaquil mari uuuunt. ut wce. cocodrlui ypota
ru. b. eft equi fluccualef.   Ðᴇ ʙᴀʟᴇɴᴀ.

Eft belua inmari q grece afpido delone dr. latine u
afpido teftudo. lete i dicta. ob immanitatem cor
poral. e. enim fic ille qui excepit ionam. cuiuf aluif

FIGURE 3.2
Anon., *Bestiarium* (12th century)

crescant ibi. Qua re navigantes insulam esse putantes amplicant naves. Deinde faciunt suos focos. Et illa sentiens ardorem ignis subito se in aquam immergit et navem secum in profundum trahit; Sic illi patiuntur qui in credulo animo sunt. Ignorant diaboli astucias spem suam in eum ponentes. Atque suis opibus se obligantes simul iunguntur cum illo in gehennam ignis.

['And in the middle of the ocean the monster elevates its body above the waves and remains in the same spot without moving for so long that the wind carries sand onto its back where it forms a soil for bushes to grow on. The navigators therefore believe it to be an island and anchor their ships there; then they start making fire. But as soon as the monster feels the burning of the flames, it plunges abruptly into the ocean and trails the ship along with it into the deep. This is what befalls those who are too easily deceived; they ignore the tricks of Satan and put their faith in him. Thus as they have linked themselves to Satan's earthly works, they are similarly linked to him in the fires of hell.']¹³

But this plain religious and moral tale which foregrounds, via the oceanic imagery, Satan's deceitfulness and the sinful state of mankind is rewritten in the 18th century. Satan's metamorphosis into the sinister Leviathan is rewritten from a symbolic narrative into a worldly narrative of travelling, of discovering and exploiting material resources: the time of the Restoration, to set the scene for these 18th-century transformations, coincided with the foundation of the Royal Society which institutionalized the Baconian 'zealous yet skeptical inquiring spirit' that assumed 'a knowable, unmysterious world ready to yield up its secrets to the patiently inquiring mind'.¹⁴ In his *Annus Mirabilis*, written in 1667, the same year as Milton's *Paradise Lost* and Thomas Sprat's *History of the Royal Society*, Dryden celebrated the increase of human knowledge with Baconian enthusiasm; in an 'Apostrophe to the Royal Society' he proclaimed that all the yet unsolved mysteries of the earth 'Shall in this Age to *Britain* first be shewn, / And hence be to admiring Nations taught'. Ship-building becomes a metaphor for the progress of empire and commerce in Dryden's *Digression concerning Shipping and Navigation*.¹⁵

The Baconian spirit of inquiry into the newly accessible world to fill in the last white spaces on the maps became pervasive in the 18th century, and Pope in *Windsor-Forest* (1713) echoes Dryden when his happy vision of Windsor's trees converted into ships deliberately rewrites the negative image in Ovid where ship-building initiates the hardships of the iron age - Pope represents Britain's imperial glory through the exploits of her navy.¹⁶ The new 18th-century 'planetary consciousness among Europeans' expressed itself in an impulse for the 'systematizing of nature'.¹⁷ Among the objects analysed and listed by natural historians, Georges-Louis Buffon in 1749 enumerates a 'prodigious multitude of Quadrupeds, Birds, Fish, Insects, Plants, Minerals, etc.' which 'offers a vast spectacle to the curiosity of the human spirit'.[18] The allegories and icons used to fill in the blank spaces on nautical maps (of a religious nature, as in Hondius' 'Christian Knight Map', or of a near-mythological nature as dragons, Amazons or Leviathans) gradually gave way to more exact descriptions and classifications of flora and fauna; this was always connected with the epoch's expanding search for commercially exploitable resources or markets.

Milton's sea-beast Leviathan accordingly lost its spiritual terror during the 18th century and became an item of foreign fauna to be catalogued and possibly exploited; very often whales were addressed poetically as 'leviathans' in the literature of the time but left devoid of their biblical connotations. Already Andrew Marvell had no scruples about transforming the traditionally Satanic Leviathan into an emblem of the British navy, 'a hideous shoal of wood-leviathans' which instil horror into Britain's enemies.[19] Moreover, in 'Bermudas' Marvell contemplated the eponymous islands, discovered in 1515, as the place 'where he the huge sea-monsters wracks, / That lift the deep upon their backs' and where the whales leave the treasure of their 'ambergris on shore'. This divested the beasts of their religious connotations and transformed them into commercial commodities, although Philip Brockbank rightly remarks that, in comparison with contemporary poems like Waller's 'Battle of the Sommer Islands' (1645), 'Marvell keeps his distance from direct allusion to the economic resources of the islands, and to their exploitation and spoliation. Marvell's island in comparison is a symbolic, not an actual, destination.'[20] James Paterson in his 1765 Milton commentary on the Leviathan passage pondered more bluntly the materiality of the beasts which he defined as 'Whales': 'The Whales live in these cold Northern Seas, and also in the cold Coast of *Pataegonia*, near the Straits of *Magellan*, in great Abundance; but rarely in the warm, because of their excessive Fatness; for they would melt and be parboiled in hot Waters.'[21] Instead of reading Leviathan as the traditional allegory about good and evil forces battling for man's soul, the secularized 18th century produced these new materialistic readings.

Finally, the spiritual allegory in *Job* which takes Leviathan as an emblem of man's comparative smallness and feebleness compared with other works of God's creation, was also domesticated in the 18th century. God had asked Job, implying an *adynaton*: 'Canst thou draw out leviathan with an hook?'; 'Canst thou fill his skin with barbed irons?' But 18th-century rewritings of the biblical and Miltonic Leviathan depicted man as indeed capable of overcoming the monster and even 'part[ing] him among the merchants' (*Job* 41:1, 7, 6). A case in point is Elizabeth Tollet's 1756 poem 'The Microcosm, asserting the Dignity of Man',[22] which praises God not for the overwhelming creation depicted in *Job* but for creating mankind, endowed with reason: 'To rule the Brutes [God] made thee more wise than they'. Again, the felling of 'the lofty Pine' and the building of ships take on the positive connotations of Pope's *Windsor-Forest*. Mankind is exhorted to 'steer thy Course, where, by the frozen Poles, / *Leviathan* upon the Ocean rolls'. Tollet proceeds, in direct opposition to the biblical tale, to relate man's triumph over the beast:

> When from thy Hand the piercing Barb is thrown
> The Monster trembles, tho' his Heart be stone:
> Wounded he roars, and drags the length'ning Line,
> And mingled with his Blood he spouts the Brine,
> Lash'd by his ample Tail the frothy Surges shine:
> Then to the shallow Shores for Safety flies;
> While on his Back whole Groves of Lances rise.[23]

The 18th-century transformations of the Leviathan episode were on the whole straightforwardly affirmative of the idea of progress. Milton's allegory of the deficiencies of human perception and the biblical insistence on man's humbleness in *Job* were turned into affirmations of man's imperial dignity, rationality, and superiority over the rest of God's creation. The political implications of this transformation with respect to the British are nowhere more obvious than in Edward Young's 1729 poem *Imperium Pelagi: A Naval Lyric*, where Britain's dominion over the seas is epitomized in this proud line: 'O Britain! The leviathan is thine.'[24]

Satan and the Wealth of Ormus

The next oceanic location that is connected with Milton's Satan in *Paradise Lost* is the island of Ormus, an important part of the British imperial stage. The 'wealth of Ormus and of Ind' decorates Satan's throne in hell at the opening of book 2:

> High on a throne of royal state, which far
> Outshone the wealth of Ormus and of Ind,
> Or where the gorgeous East with richest hand
> Showers on her kings barbaric pearl and gold,
> Satan exalted sat ... (*PL* 2.1-5)[25]

Located in an important strategic position at the mouth of the Persian Gulf, the island of Ormus guaranteed to its possessor control of the seaway between Persia and India: '[the Portuguese] fortifications at Ormus dominated the narrow strait that forms the only entrance to the Persian Gulf, and their galleons swept the Arabian Sea so that no ship might sail between Persia and India without their special licence'[26] (Figure 3.3). Held by the Portuguese since 1508, it developed into a trading centre of legendary wealth. Marvell in 'Bermudas' mentions 'jewels more rich than Ormus shows', and Purchas described 'Hormuz [as] among the richest Countries of the India one of the richest, for the many and great merchandize that come to it from all places ... And so the Inhabiters of Hormuz doe say, that all the world is a ring, and Hormuz is the stone of it.'[27] The island was the goal of the disastrous expedition of the *Tyger* in 1583, mentioned in *Macbeth*. In 1622, the British East India Company, whose ships were repeatedly denied thoroughfare by the Portuguese, joined forces with the Persian Shah Abbas to recapture Ormus, paying huge bribes afterwards to Buckingham and James I, who was, to Milton, another hellish monarch.[28] After their victory the island's wealth was transferred to Bandar Abbas. Four years after the sack, Ormus was described as 'the most disconsolate Place in the World, which was latterly the Glory of the East'.[29] Thus Ormus, to Milton, is a symbolic place-name synonymous both with excessive luxury and worldly fallenness. This beginning already metaphorically comprises Satan's entire journey: 'the wealth of Ormus and of Ind' decorating his throne in hell symbolizes his own paradoxical fallen glory.

In the 18th century, however, Milton's Ormus was discussed in different terms; it offered an opportunity to discuss various concepts of trade and exchange. Long-distance trade had opened up entirely new vistas onto immense foreign resources. While 18th-century anxieties about the depraving dangers of luxury will be discussed below, the new economic possibilities also triggered debates about the intrinsic versus extrinsic value of goods; and, of course, the later 18th century witnessed the contest between mercantilist concepts of commerce and the free-trade ideas of Adam Smith. Richard Bentley's 1732 edition of *Paradise Lost* offers an example of the influence of mercantilist thought on literary criticism. Bentley, in fact, takes exception to Milton's use of 'Ormus' on the grounds of the island's factual poverty by the time of Milton's writing:

> *Ormus*, a small Island in the *Persian* Gulph, unnam'd by antient Poets, a mere Rock of Salt, infamous for Heat and bad Air; has no native *Wealth*, but what is brought thither as a Center of Commerce by Ships at Sea, and Caravans at Land; not to be lodged there, but transfer'd to other Countries.[30]

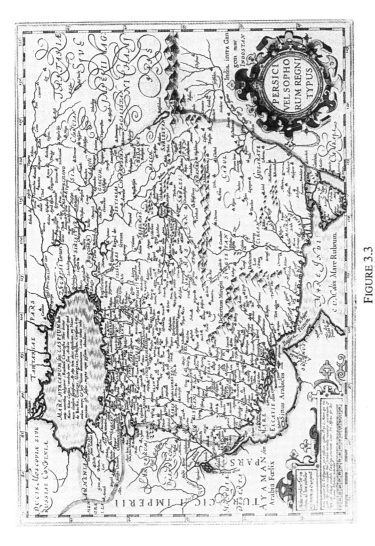

FIGURE 3.3

Gerard Mercator, Jodocus Hondius and Joannes Janssonius, *Atlas or a geographicke description of the world* (1636), 'Persici vel Sophorum regni typus' (The island of Ormus, 'Ormus emporium', is located in the Persian Gulf.)

English merchants, in Bentley's account, bestow wealth upon the island temporarily before transferring it elsewhere; mercantilist theory, in fact, prescribed the importation of spices 'in order [for them] to be recirculated, at a greater profit, in an act which the economic writer Thomas Mun described in 1621 as *Transitio*'.[31] A curious feature of Bentley's Milton censure is the intertextual presence of Milton's fallen paradise in his own text: Milton's archangel Michael tells Adam that during the Deluge paradise shall be dislocated and 'take root' in the Persian Gulf as 'an island salt and bare' (*PL* 11.858-9).[32] Bentley's association of a lack of riches with the Miltonic passage about lack of grace is thus nearly indistinguishable from mercantilist homologies between money and grace.[33] As paradise is degraded through the fall, so is Ormus, for its lack of natural resources, excluded from Bentley's version of Milton's text. What Bentley offers instead are 'Hermus' and 'Tage', 'Rivers with Golden Sands, ... celebrated by all Poets for original and inexhaustible Wealth'.[34] Bentley's insistence on 'original', intrinsic value is in conflict with mercantilist economy where colonies are seen as 'regions capable of producing whichever of the world's consumer items suited the demand of the empire ... The image of colonies as transmutable regions of exchange value ... prevailed during the heyday of mercantilism, the 1720s and 1730s',[35] and thus precisely at the time when Bentley was drafting his commentary on *Paradise Lost*.[36] The taintedness of Satan's hellish riches seems less important to Bentley than his own ambivalent stance towards mercantilist theory and his desire for historical accuracy based not on the findings of navigatory exploration but on the classical tradition.[37]

But at the end of the 'Long Eighteenth Century', the overwhelming emphasis in rewritings of Milton's Ormus imagery is on the commodities the island bestows on Britain through maritime exchange. In Miss Christian Cann's *Scriptural and Allegorical Glossary to Milton's Paradise Lost* (1828), Ormus is described in vague terms as part of 'Asia', 'the richest and most fruitful part of the world', a colonial site which 'supplies us with the richest spices, drugs, diamonds and other precious stones; with silks, muslins, coffee, tea, &c'. The 'West Indies' feature in her commentary as the islands 'from whence come our spices'.[38] Exotic luxuries have been naturalized to such an extent that even before reaching Britain they have become 'our spices', fully integrated into the framework of domestic necessities. The attributes of Milton's hell have turned into the celebrated features of a British consumers' paradise. Finally, the spiritual dangers of Milton's symbolic universe are explicitly redressed in Henry Jones' 1767 poem *Kew Garden*, which integrates Ormus into a positive and even paradisal vision of Britain's peaceful commerce. The royal gardens, symbolizing Britain, are by George III himself reconstituted as a paradise regained: he imports foreign flowers, appropriating the wealth of the earth's regions 'from pole to pole'. Space simultaneously expands and contracts as he assembles 'all that Ormus, India, or that Pontus lend' in the 'narrow room' of his royal hothouses that imitate the unfallen state of Milton's paradise (*PL* 4.207).[39] Milton's dangerous and delusive ocean has turned into the British passage to paradise, and the tainted riches of Milton's Ormus have turned into the well-deserved tribute owed to Britain by her colonies. In these patriotic transformations of Milton's epic, his spiritual allegory has become the worldly success story of Britain's rise to maritime supremacy. The ideologies of the *pax Britannica* and the 'circular flow of trade' are effortlessly combined with the idea of British soldiers invading foreign trading posts. As already Dryden's *Annus Mirabilis* (1666) would have it: 'Thus to the Eastern wealth through storms we go' (1213), on a 'British Ocean'.

Satan's Ocean Voyage

The third part of Satan's trajectory through the Miltonic narrative is his voyage across the ocean of chaos from hell to paradise. As all early modern travellers, Satan has many misgivings before setting out into the unknown seas: at the outset of his voyage, Satan is lingering on the brink of the 'illimitable ocean' (*PL* 2.892): 'Into this wild abyss the wary fiend / Stood on the brink of hell and looked a while, / Pondering his voyage; for no narrow frith / He had to cross' (*PL* 2.917-20). Satan's knowledge of the 'new world', earth, consists entirely of rumours,[40] similar to the vague conjectures about undiscovered islands or immense golden riches that initiated many early modern voyages. Milton's own examples of Hudson's 'imagined way' to Cathay and of Raleigh's elusive El Dorado are directly pertinent. Satan's erroneous trajectory, the tainted origin of all subsequent human endeavours, strikingly contrasts with the archangel Raphael's comfortable voyage and correct knowledge. These two figures, Raphael, heavenly messenger, and Satan, infernal imperialist, enact the most prominent and sustained 'travel narratives' in *Paradise Lost*; both are travelling to paradise, the one from heaven and the other from hell. Raphael's immediate departure to earth, 'Nor delayed the winged saint / ... up springing light, / Flew through the midst of heaven' (*PL* 5.247; 250-51), obviously contrasts Satan's above-quoted static verb 'Stood' (*PL* 2.918) with Raphael's line-opener 'Flew' (*PL* 5.251). The rest of both voyages is similarly contrasted: whereas everything 'gave way' to Raphael (*PL* 5.252), the gate of heaven 'self-opened wide' to let him pass (*PL* 5.254) and the winds support his flight, Satan battles with hostile elements throughout:

> ... all unawares
> Fluttering his pennons vain plumb down he drops
> Ten thousand fathom deep, and to this hour
> Down had been falling, had not by ill chance
> The strong rebuff of some tumultuous cloud
> Instinct with fire and nitre hurried him
> As many miles aloft ... (*PL* 2.932-8)

Satan's movements, too, are very different from Raphael's purposeful 'steady wing' and 'quick fan': as if incorporating, already at this point, a whole swarm of different creatures, the fiend 'with head, hands, wings, or feet pursues his way, / And swims or sinks, or wades, or creeps, or flies' (*PL* 2.949-50). In his depiction of Satan's voyage Milton deploys his knowledge of the dangers of ocean travel. Fernand Braudel has commented on the hardships of early modern long-distance sea travel; he especially emphasizes the dangers of having to sail against or cut across the trade winds on return journeys from the South Seas or Africa, and the hazards of sailing on the open ocean (as opposed to the much preferred alternative of keeping close to the coast line).[41] Satan, however, 'sometimes / ... scours the right hand coast, sometimes the left; / Now shaves with level wing the deep', resembling a fleet 'by equinoctial winds / Close sailing from Bengala' (*PL* 2.633-4; 2.637-8), thus incurring virtually the entire range of dangers that early modern ocean travel, based on fragile navigational calculations and theories, had to offer. Tellingly, Satan's 'travelled steps' (*PL* 3.501) when arriving at the globe of the earth imply experience in travel as well as tiredness. Here he is upon arriving, finally, at his destination, when he discovers to his relief that 'his sea should find a shore' (2.1011):

> ... Satan with less toil, and now with ease,
> Wafts on the calmer wave by dubious light,
> And, like a weather-beaten vessel, holds
> Gladly the port, though shrouds and tackle torn ... (*PL* 2.1041-4)

What Milton never fails to foreground are the frustrations and setbacks of maritime exploration. In 1608 Henry Hudson had endeavoured to find a north-eastern sea-way to Cathay, and failed, as his route was barred by ice. Milton provides a spiritual etiology for Hudson's failure: after Satan has successfully invaded paradise, his hellish offspring, Sin and Death, create a 'passage broad / ... down to hell' to facilitate mankind's expected mass exodus through the ocean of chaos into hell. In so doing, Sin and Death paradoxically obstruct the sea-way to Cathay to any future human discoverers: they 'together drive / Mountains of ice, that stop the imagined way / Beyond Petsora eastward, to the rich / Cathaian coast' (*PL* 10.304-5; 10.290-93).[42] Rich Cathay, in Milton's time often seen as a symbol of paradisal wealth,[43] is thus forever removed from human reach through the fall and the workings of Sin and Death. Bruce McLeod claims that in Milton 'the truly heroic adventures of England's finest are associated with elements and forces as treacherous as Satanic achievement',[44] and according to Stevie Davies Milton here emphasizes that '[t]he world we think we know is a patchwork of apparently verifiable data joined at the seams by conjecture, desire (gold) and corporate illusion.'[45] For all the meticulous geographic detail, Milton's concept of space is not empirical, but hermeneutical: space is constructed through perception, and the uncharted ocean becomes a symbol of the instability of human knowledge. Satan is almost always situated in an uncertain space *between* land and sea, or between heaven and the sea, as when he is described as a ship 'hanging in the clouds'; sailing past regions that are 'neither sea, / Nor good dry land', regions where he needs 'both oar and sail' (2.939-40, 942). Moreover, Hudson's way is obstructed by the same 'polar winds' that actually help Raphael on his way. Reaching back to the themes of man's credulity and Satan's deceitfulness in the Leviathan episode, Milton presents the archangel's intuitive knowledge and instinctive gift of orientation as opposed to the fragmentary and conjectural perception of Satan and fallen mankind.[46]

Critics have variously remarked on Milton's anti-commercial stance; David Quint, for instance, sees Satan's voyage as accomplishing 'merely temporal (hence Satanic) ends and accordingly belong[ing] exclusively to the world of time and chance'. For him, Milton deflates Satan 'into a representative of the East India Company'.[47] Keith Stavely surmises that the negative depiction of Satan's merchant voyage is a veiled allusion to Cromwell's foreign policy, whose Navigation Acts of 1650 and 1651 were an attempt to establish 'a monopoly area of privilege for British merchants ... Satan may embody both the sweep and grandeur of the emergent capitalist revolution and also the license it would for generations and centuries give to diverse forms of self-interest, jealousy, and ambition.'[48] This is the passage from Satan's voyage most frequently discussed in this context:

> As when far off at sea a fleet descried
> Hangs in the clouds, by equinoctial winds
> Close sailing from Bengala, or the isles

> Of Ternate and Tidore, whence merchants bring
> Their spicy drugs; they on the trading flood,
> Through the wide Ethiopian to the Cape,
> Ply stemming nightly toward the pole: so seemed
> Far off the flying Fiend (*PL* 2.636-43).

The two islands of the Moluccas in the East Indies here mentioned, Ternate and Tidore,[49] were described by Purchas as 'Ilands of the Spicerie, ... because all the Pepper, Cloves, Sinamon, Ginger, Nutmegs, and Masticke that is spent in Europe is brought from them'. Some of the Spice Islands, as Gilbert in his *Geographical Dictionary* states, were also mentioned by Milton 'in his papers setting forth the claims of the English for satisfaction for injuries inflicted by the Dutch'.[50] (In the early 1650s Milton had to draft reparations claims for the Dutch seizure of Amboyna in 1623 in his official capacity as Latin Secretary.[51]) If the ship in the simile were a Dutch merchant vessel, as Timothy Morton claims, the negativity of the image, *pace* Quint and Stavely, would be part of a patriotic agenda rather than criticism of commerce. Robert Markley, too, sees Satan as a 'thinly veiled indictment of a European archrival - the Dutch', and connects the voyage to paradise with 'English anxieties about the Dutch monopoly in the East Indies'.[52] Indeed, the continuing trade hostilities with the Dutch are the subtext in Miss Christian Cann's annotations in her Milton *Glossary*; about 'Ternate and Tidore' she states that 'their chief produce consists of cloves, mace and nutmegs, in vast quantities, which are monopolized by the Dutch.'[53] But in fact, it is impossible to determine which, if any, nationality Satan is meant to represent. His movements are variously described as erratic and erroneous; he keeps metamorphosing into different shapes (*PL* 2.632-5, 2.927-50, 3.741). This 'syntactical instability of Satan's journey', according to Morton, points towards the 'radical, or structural, instability of the space of trade, capital and colonialism'.[54]

In terms of Milton's spiritual symbolism, however, Satan's representation as a merchant vessel evokes the debate about 'luxury' that was to continue well into the 18th century. Milton emphasizes the potential enslavement of the self through luxury; Balachandra Rajan has analysed the function of the term 'spice' in Milton's poems as 'a synecdoche for the entire range of conspicuous consumption'. Adam and Eve's fall, in fact, 'joins original sin to all subsequent excesses in consumption ("Greedily she engorged without restraint", *PL* 9.791)'.[55] Excess is censured in terms reminiscent of Satan's merchant voyage in *Samson Agonistes* where the seductress Dalila appears

bedecked, ornate, and gay,
... this way sailing
Like a stately ship
Of Tarsus, bound for th' isles
Of Javan or Gadire
With all her bravery on, and tackle trim,
Sails filled, and streamers waving,
Courted by all the winds that hold them play,
An amber scent of odorous perfume
Her harbinger, a damsel train behind (*SA* 712-21).

Samson, in thrall to his wife, is compared to a 'vessel ... gloriously rigged' (*SA* 199-200), 'softened with pleasure and voluptuous life' (*SA* 534). Milton's fascination with exotic riches is always coupled with a marked insistence on their potential to deprave, as in his famous invective in *A Brief History of Moscovia* (1682) against the 'excessive love of Gain and Traffick' displayed by the discoverers of the seaway to Moscovia (*YP* 8:524). Milton represents the shifting value of transported goods in Satanic metaphors: the 'trade winds' topos, part of the contested figuration of trans-national trade, is prominent in his description of Satan's voyage. But his emphasis is on the very instability of this topos about spicy breezes floating across the ocean. Spice and the trade winds, metaphors for commercial exchange, can mark the 'blessed space of Paradise' as well as stake out the dangerous terrain of devilish machinations.[56]

Luxury goods, imported into Europe through long-distance trade, retained their negative connotations far into the 18th century. Until Adam Smith declared luxury an important instigator in a potentially unlimited commercial process, luxury was usually denounced in moralistic tones, and 'outright hostility to emergent consumerism' was demonstrated 'in the name of traditional religious, moral and socio-political values'.[57] But although the Ovidian and Miltonic denunciations of luxury persisted throughout the century, in most 18th-century readings of *Paradise Lost* there is a marked emphasis on the fascination of long-distance trade. 18th-century Milton annotators testified to the more assertive ideas about human exploratory potential that were developing along with British maritime supremacy. Like the island of Ormus, the islands of Ternate and Tidore were appropriated to the British Empire. Already in Hume's 1695 annotations, Milton's '*Ternate* and *Tydore*' are described as those islands 'whence our Merchants bring the *East-India* Spices'.[58] Here there is no doubt about the nationality of the merchant travellers. At the same time, the pleasures of conspicuous consumption are acknowledged; Paterson's commentary expands Milton's 'Sabean odours' transported by the trade winds into an enticing mixture of 'cinnamon, cassia, frankincense, myrrh, and other sweet spices'.[59] Milton's intimations of transcendent truth give way before 18th-century emphases on the here-and-now of the evolving empire.

In the nautical passages of Dyer's 1757 poem *The Fleece*, finally, Satan's death-bringing voyage is poetically transformed into the glorious enterprise of British mariners. The British poet patronizingly asks the 'soft sons of Ganges': 'Can ye the weather-beaten vessel steer, / Climb the tall mast, direct the stubborn helm, / Mid wild discordant waves, with steady course?' Satan's erratic way through chaos and his struggling like a 'weather-beaten vessel' (*PL* 2.1043) have turned into the glorious British conquest of the seas and a 'steady course' to victory. Raleigh's and especially George Lord Anson's ocean voyages are praised as entirely positive versions of Satan's:[60]

> Though that wide sea, which spreads o'er half the world,
> Deny'd all hospitable land or port;
> Where, seasons voyaging, no road he [= Anson] found
> To moor, no bottom in th' abyss, whereon
> To drop the fastening anchor; ...
> Still ...
> ... his wave-worn bark
> Met, fought, the proud Iberian, and o'ercame.
> So fare it ever with our country's foes![61]

Anson here triumphs over the existential uncertainties of Milton's ocean; finding no place to anchor one's ship is here not emblematic of spiritual destitution as in the Leviathan episode but a merely practical problem which cannot bar Britain's way to imperial glory.

And in 1875, James Russell Lowell in an essay on Wordsworth compares the 'sublimity' of *Paradise Lost* to the sublimity of American seafaring trade and the American 'Manifest Destiny'. Here Milton's ocean turns into the supreme location of national glory. In Lowell's metaphorical language, the texture of Milton's epic itself parallels the grandeur of maritime commerce and nautical warfare:

Paradise Lost ... like the trade-wind, gathered to itself thoughts and images like stately fleets from every quarter; some deep with silks and spicery, some brooding over the silent thunders of their battailous armaments, but all swept forward in their destined track, over the long billows of his verse, every inch of canvas strained by the unifying breath of their common epic impulse.[62]

In this last stage in the evolution of post-Miltonic nationalistic rhetoric in Miltonic language, the epic itself becomes an ocean swept by ships proceeding on their nation's 'destined track'. Here the ocean, Milton's metaphor for the contingencies of fallen human existence, turns into the sublime image of mankind's greatest achievements.

Satanic Middle Passages

Up to here, this paper has traced the development of Milton's symbolic and transcendence-orientated universe into the 18th-century worldly and empire-affirmative world picture. I have recounted three stages of Satan's voyage, from the fiery lake in hell and Leviathan, to the Satanic throne with its evocations of Ormus, to the voyage to paradise. But this last item in the narrative, the ocean voyage, was exploited in yet another, very different way in the 18th century: British abolitionists translated the episode into an illustration of the fatal Middle Passage of the slave trade and employed the Satanic connotations of the Milton text to spell out their own humanitarian protest against slavery. While both the anti-luxury debate and the anti-slavery debate were not anti-imperial discourses but merely set out to redress specific negative extremes or abuses perceived in the imperial system, at least they demonstrated in what ways the Miltonic passage lent itself to writers whose purpose was not to glorify but to criticize aspects of the British Empire.

While the British slave trade was already in full gear by Milton's time, Charles II having continued Cromwell's slave-trade policy by granting a 1000-year monopoly to the 'Company of Royal Adventurers Trading into Africa',[63] there are no explicit references to black slaves or the slave trade in *Paradise Lost*. The only recent attempt to link Milton with the slave trade was made by Maureen Quilligan,[64] but her interpretation of Satan as an allegory of a slave merchant can only suggest potential meanings; they become actual in 18th-century Milton readings and adaptations. In *Paradise Lost* itself, the idea of slavery, following the Church Fathers, serves as a spiritual or political metaphor and is always coupled to ideas of military conquest or a nation's voluntary self-enslavement.[65] Moreover, in interpreting Satan as an affirmative or at least neutrally descriptive allegory of a slave merchant, Quilligan neglects the fact that Milton's ambiguous heroization of the merchant voyager also partly satanizes him.

My first example of 18th-century Miltonic abolitionist writing is James Montgomery's *West Indies*, written as part of the collection *Poems on the Abolition of the Slave Trade* (1809) celebrating the achievement of abolition in 1807; it concludes with an acknowledgement that Britain 'shared the gain, the glory, and the guilt' of the slave trade. Montgomery transfers the narrative frame of Milton's epic to his own poetic retracing of the trajectory of slaves: the sugar cane, main crop of the West Indian slave plantations, was imported 'among the bowers of paradise' like the baneful 'tree of knowledge with forbidden fruit'. The Edenic fall repeated itself on Caribbean ground, due to the curses of long-distance travelling and trade: 'While with vain wealth it gorged the master's hoard, / And spread with manna his luxurious board, / Its culture was perdition to the slave, - / It sapp'd his life, and flourish'd on his grave.' Montgomery aligns the degradation of the slave with the fall of Adam; indeed, the importation of black slaves from West Africa is described in terms of Satan's voyage through chaos to enslave Adam and Eve. The Spanish slave vessels alarm the ocean by this assembly of 'fiends' crossing his surface: 'Old Ocean shrunk, as o'er his surface flew / The felon-cargo, and the daemon crew'.[66] This is a version of Milton's chaos, 'anarch old' (*PL* 2.988), confused when the rebel angels are falling through him into hell: 'Confounded chaos roared, / And felt tenfold confusion in their fall' (*PL* 6.874-5).

In my second example, Jamieson's poem *The Sorrows of Slavery. Containing a faithful Statement of Facts respecting the African Slave Trade* (1789),[67] the Middle Passage is also described in terms of chaos and a Miltonic personification of death. Jamieson depicts the interior of a slave vessel: 'The half-chew'd fragments of a thousand meals / Devouring Death has made, his many mouths / Of melancholy, madness, famine, sword, / Scourge, halter, musket, manifold disease / Wide-opening, as his changeful taste requir'd; / The mangled morsels left to fill his maw, / his appetite when keener!' (469). In *Paradise Lost*, on hearing of Satan's plan to invade paradise and enslave mankind, Death had 'blessed his maw' (*PL* 2.847); part of his rich repast here consists in the cargo of the slave vessels. Very similarly, in James Grahame's *Africa Delivered; or, The Slave Trade Abolished*, my last example, the miseries on the slave ships are evoked by an epigraph from *Paradise Lost* which originally described the diseases in the 'Lazar House' (*PL* 11.501-2): 'DIRE WAS THE TOSSING, DEEP THE GROANS: DESPAIR / BUSIEST FROM COUCH TO COUCH TENDED THE SICK (*PARADISE LOST*)'.[68] In all three examples, the slave ship is described as a Miltonic Pandemonium, complete with Milton's vision of diseases.

In the high-strung rhetoric of British abolitionism, the baneful connotations of Satan's and his offspring Sin and Death's voyages across the ocean of chaos were employed to present as a sin of biblical dimensions what Britain had by then more or less successfully legitimized as a subsection of her trade. But although such writing was subversive to some extent, its revolutionary energies were always contained within the larger framework of the evolving British Empire. Even though abolitionists were attacking one of the most violent manifestations of empire, they did not directly question its existence. Like the debates about luxury and depravation or the contest between different economic systems, the anti-slavery discourse set out to redress, with some rhetorical help from Milton, 'blemishes' on the otherwise spotless imperial surface (such metaphors were used with frequency).[69] It now remains to observe, in a brief 'coda' to this paper, how Milton's Satanic ocean voyage with all its implications is rewritten in the late 20th century from a postcolonial and perhaps postimperial perspective.

Coda: Ackroyd's *Milton in America*

From a late 20th-century, postcolonially inflected perspective, Satan's ocean voyage is read very differently again; the 18th-century glories of discovery and discussions about foreign trade are erased and replaced by a general scepticism far surpassing the specific criticism of the 18th-century British anti-slavery movement. In Peter Ackroyd's recent novel *Milton in America* (1996), 'Milton', the protagonist, is himself associated with British imperialism and consequently identified with the Satan of *Paradise Lost* and sent on a very similar journey across the ocean - into a Puritan colonial settlement in America. Ackroyd's narrative hypothesis derives from Milton's own dictum in *Of Reformation*, with which this paper started, that 'nothing but the wide Ocean, and the savage deserts of *America* could hide and shelter [the Puritans] from the fury of the Bishops' (*YP* 1: 585); here, Milton himself is included among the Puritan exiles. But the frenetic empire-building in which Ackroyd engages his Milton figure makes 'Milton' a version of his own Satan, whose concept of meliorism was subjected to continual criticism in *Paradise Lost*. Just as Satan had erected Pandemonium and subsequently conquered the 'new world' of paradise, Ackroyd's 'Milton' addresses the New England colonists in a Satanic speech:

> 'I share with you hopes of a glorious rising commonwealth. I see the prospect of another world, the happy seat of some new race, a bright isle and clime, where one day, by policy and long process of time, will rise a mighty empire. Long has been the way, and hard, that from the hell of impiety and sacrilege has led you toward this dawn.'[70]

Ackroyd's 'Milton' is a caricature Puritan, castigating 'vice' wherever he finds it, unsuccessfully fighting the wilderness and battling against American natives.[71] Divided, rather obviously, into two sections entitled 'Eden' and 'Fall', the narrative has 'Milton' re-enact the loss of innocence through his own personal transgression; the end of the novel shows 'Milton' blind and lost among the woods. Yet Ackroyd's narrative premise entirely distorts Milton's transcendental message and equates Milton with his own creature Satan.

From the very beginning of the novel, it is the image of the ocean which casts 'Milton' in the role of Satan. Shipwrecked on the New England coast, 'Milton's' ship (tellingly named *Gabriel*) 'was being lifted by the waves between two great rocks; it seemed to hang there suspended above the waters for a moment', and for 'Milton', washed out into the ocean and holding on to a piece of wood, 'there was now no time and no motion. He was suspended between two worlds, and a general quietness gathered about him'. These are faint echos of the Holy Ghost hovering upon the waters before the creation but also of Satan on the burning lake in hell. The symbolic situation 'between two worlds' reflects the novel's postcolonial perspective on the European exile alienated in an America incomprehensible to him. The novel's first sentence, 'Come on board, friend Menippus, and float in the Tartarean air' initiates an interior-monologue dream vision that rewrites the opening scene of book 1 of *Paradise Lost*. Addresser and addressee recall Satan and Beelzebub, 'weltering' (*PL* 1.78) on the burning lake, 'a fiery deluge, fed / With ever-burning sulphur unconsumed' (*PL* 1.68-9). In the Ackroydian 'Milton's' imagination, '[t]he sparkling waves do smoke again and there is sorrow on the sea' - the ship on the ocean here becomes an intimation of Milton's epic hell. 'Milton's' cry from the abyss, '[f]rom the face of the deep, I call to thee', is a reminiscence of Jonah and the whale; in fact, 'Milton's' voyage to America is beset by dangers of the imagination such as 'Sirens. Leviathan', bequeathed to Ackroyd by Homer's and Milton's epics respectively.

The closing sentences of the exposition juxtapose the external calm after the storm with 'Milton's' still troubled mind: 'Fair blow the winds, now strike your happy sails. Port after stormy seas is best. Spice, and ivory, and apes. The unmeasured ocean of my mind is forever beating.' Similarly but less internally harrowed, Milton's Satan had emerged after the hazardous voyage through chaos, as we have seen above: 'Satan with less toil, and now with ease, / Wafts on the calmer wave by dubious light, / And, like a weather-beaten vessel, holds / Gladly the port, though shrouds and tackle torn' (*PL* 2.1041-4). Like Joseph Conrad's *Heart of Darkness*, Ackroyd's novel uses the exotic setting to reveal the abyss in the protagonist's soul.

On the other hand, what 'Milton' summarizes as 'Spice, and ivory, and apes' is a western, utilitarian perspective on the exploitable resources of the newly discovered regions. Again, this connects Ackroyd's 'Milton' with Milton's Satan who had voyaged as a merchant vessel from Ternate and Tidore, carrying 'spicy drugs'. Ackroyd's introductory paragraph thus evokes in a nutshell Satan's awakening on the 'burning lake' (*PL* 1.210), his voyage through chaos to earth, and even his recognition that 'within him hell / He brings, and round about him, nor from hell / One step, no more than from himself, can fly / By change of place' (*PL* 4.20-23). In fact, Ackroyd's 'Milton' hastes to assure his amanuensis that '[t]he mind has its oceans, too ... It has its gulfs and currents. You have often told me that the sea is mild and temperate, but I have my own inward sight that reaches the highest altitudes and the furthest depths ... to bring angels or devils back into the thoughts of men'.[72]

Ackroyd, as an 'honorary' postcolonial writer, in this novel deconstructs western imperial mythologies which posit the moment of discovery by western explorers as the 'origin' of the overseas regions. But, in fact, Milton himself ironizes assumptions of imperial destiny in his epics, emphasizing his transcendental vision in their stead; these ironies are lost in 18th-century remodellings of Milton as a national poet. They are also lost in rewritings which equate Milton with his creature Satan. After the 18th century had rewritten Milton's texts as hailing the expansive spirit of their own imperial age, in the late 20th century empire-building is, again, identified as Satanic. The question, however, remains precisely who is imagined as the seafarer across the Miltonic oceans to conquer foreign shores, be it paradise or America. Is Satan imagined as a merchant and slave trader, or does Milton himself become the adventurous long-distance traveller setting out to conquer and colonize? Postcolonial strategies of rewriting Milton hinge upon this question,[73] depending on whether late 20th-century authors believe or disbelieve in the epic's denunciatory strategy which consists, as has been argued in this paper, in presenting Satan as the prototype of all subsequent human ocean voyagers, be they Hudson, Raleigh, Anson, Dutch or British East India Company officials, slave traders, colonizers, or perhaps tourists.

Notes

1   Milton's prose is quoted from *The Yale Complete Prose Works of John Milton*, ed. Don M. Wolfe *et al.*, 8 vols (New Haven: Yale University Press, 1953-82), here cited as *YP*. Milton's poetry is quoted from *Paradise Lost*, ed. Alastair Fowler (London: Longman,

2nd ed. 1998), and *Complete Shorter Poems*, ed. John Carey (London: Longman, 2nd ed. 1997).

2   Milton's God creates the world from this 'Outrageous ... sea, dark, wasteful, wild' (*PL* 7.212); Milton follows, with Augustine's *De Genesi* and Philo's *De opificio mundi*, Plato's *Timaios* and even Ovid's *Metamorphoses* where a certain 'matter unformed' is assumed before the creation (*PL* 7.23). In *De Doctrina* 1.7 (if it is his) Milton rejects the doctrine of *creatio ex nihilo*.

3   If the manuscript of *Lycidas* is taken into account, Milton's relationship with the watery element seems unassured to an even greater extent: an initial comparison between Edward King and the Greek shepherd Narcissus was later erased by Milton, probably because with reference to a drowned man this mythological image would imply that King brought on his fatal disaster himself.

4   See below the subsection 'Satanic Middle Passages'.

5   See J. Martin Evans, *Milton's Imperial Epic:* Paradise Lost *and the Discourse of Colonialism* (Ithaca: Cornell University Press, 1996); David Quint, *Epic and Empire: Politics and Generic Form from Virgil to Milton* (Princeton: Princeton University Press, 1993), chs 6 and 7; Bruce McLeod, *The Geography of Empire in English Literature, 1580-1745* (Cambridge: Cambridge University Press, 1999), ch. 4; Balachandra Rajan and Elizabeth Sauer (eds), *Milton and the Imperial Vision* (Pittsburgh: Duquesne University Press, 1999). For article-length statements on Milton's imperialism or anti-imperialism see Paul Stevens, '*Paradise Lost* and the Colonial Imperative', *Milton Studies* 34 (1996), 3-21; and David Armitage, 'John Milton: Poet Against Empire', Armitage *et al.* (eds), *Milton and Republicanism* (Cambridge: Cambridge University Press, 1995), 206-25.

6   Some aspects of 18th-century Miltonic writing discussed in this paper are treated in more detail in my *Majestick Milton: British Imperial Expansion and Transformations of* Paradise Lost, *1667-1837* (Münster: LIT, 2001); see also notes 65 and 73.

7   Douglas Chambers, *The Reinvention of the World: English Writing 1650-1750* (London: Arnold, 1996), 23.

8   See the accounts by J.G.A. Pocock in his *The Machiavellian Moment: Florentine Political Thought and the Atlantic Republican Tradition* (Princeton: Princeton University Press, 1975), and *Virtue, Commerce, and History: Essays on Political Thought and History, Chiefly in the Eighteenth Century* (Cambridge: Cambridge University Press, 1985).

9   Marcus Rediker, *Between the Devil and the Deep Blue Sea: Merchant Seamen, Pirates, and the Anglo-American Maritime World, 1700-1750* (Cambridge: Cambridge University Press, 1987), 21.

10 Of course there were other, not directly nationalistic constructions of the ocean in the 18th century, for instance the discourse of sublimity which Marjorie Hope Nicolson has traced in her *Mountain Gloom and Mountain Glory: The Development of the Aesthetics of the Infinite* (New York: W.W. Norton, 1959): 'During the eighteenth century the ocean came to share with mountains the "sublime"' (xii); an example is the Addison essay in *Spectator* 489 where the 'floating mountains' of the 'troubled ocean' are said to raise 'in [one's] thoughts the idea of an Almighty Being' (306-7). These developments are not my concern here.

11 See *Paradise Lost*, ed. Fowler.

12 *Bestiarium. Facsimilé du manuscrit du bestiaire Ashmole 1511, conservé à la Bodleian Library d'Oxford, accompagné des commentaires de Xénia Muratova et Daniel Poirion et de la traduction en français de Marie-France Dupuis et Sylvain Louis* (Paris: Club du Livre, 1984), n.p.

13   The translations are mine.

14   John McVeagh (ed.), *All Before Them: 1660-1780. English Literature and the Wider World* (London: Ashfield Press, 1990), 9.

15   John Dryden, *Annus Mirabilis* [1667], *The Works of John Dryden*, 20 vols, gen. ed. Alan Roper *et al.* (Berkeley: University of California Press, 1956-96), vol. 1 (1956): *Poems 1649-1680*, ed. Edward Niles Hooker and H.T. Swedenberg, Jr., 47-105; stanzas 155-64, 161, lines 3-4. Dryden correlates the progress of ship-building, from the primitive logs of the Irish and Indians (157) to the British navy, with the progress of commerce (158).

16   Alexander Pope, *Windsor-Forest* [1713], *Pope: Poetical Works*, ed. Herbert Davis (London: Oxford University Press, 1966), 37-50, lines 385-6. See Ovid: 'vela dabat ventis (nec adhuc bene noverat illos) / navita; quaeque diu steterant in montibus altis, / fluctibus ignotis insultavere carinae' (*Met.* 1.132-4). In Horace's *Ode* 1.3 this blasphemy has already taken place; 'inpiae ... rates' are ploughing the waves (1.3.23-4).

17   Preceding quotations: Mary Louise Pratt, *Imperial Eyes: Travel Writing and Transculturation* (London: Routledge, 1992), 29-30.

18   Georges-Louis Buffon, *Histoire naturelle, générale et particulière*, 36 vols (1749-88), quoted in English translation by Pratt, *Imperial Eyes*, 30.

19   Andrew Marvell, 'The First Anniversary of the Government under His Highness the Lord Protector', *The Major Works*, ed. Frank Kermode and Keith Walker (Oxford: Oxford University Press, 1990), 92-102, 101, line 361.

20   Andrew Marvell, 'Bermudas', *The Major Works*, 16-17, lines 9-10, 28; Philip Brockbank, 'The Politics of Paradise: "Bermudas"', C.A. Patrides (ed.), *Approaches to Marvell: The York Tercentenary Lectures* (London: Routledge, 1978), 174-93, 185. See also Margarita Stocker, '"English All the World": Marvell in Europe and Beyond', McVeagh (ed.), *All Before Them*, 65-80, 76, on English whale-hunting expeditions in northern Norway.

21   James Paterson (ed.), *Paradise Lost ... A New Edition*, 2 vols (Edinburgh: John Wood, 1765), vol. 1, 11-12, *ad* 1.203.

22   The poem is introduced by the Ovidian epigraph '*Sanctius his Animal, mentisque capacius altæ*' which contests the biblical humility of *Job* (Ovid, *Met.* 1.76).

23   Elizabeth Tollet, 'The Microcosm, asserting the Dignity of Man', *Poems on Several Occasions: With Anne Boleyn to King Henry VIII, an Epistle* [*in verse*] (London: John Clarke, 1755), n.p., lines 126, 113-14, 128-34.

24   Edward Young, *Imperium Pelagi: A Naval Lyric* [1729], *Edward Young: The Complete Works, Poetry and Prose*, ed. John Doran, 2 vols (London: William Tegg and Co., 1854), vol. 2, 1-31, 16 (3.13.6).

25   On Satan as an oriental monarch see Patricia Springborg, *Western Republicanism and the Oriental Prince* (Cambridge: Polity Press, 1992).

26   John W. Draper, 'Milton's Ormus', *Modern Language Review* 20 (1925), 323-7, 325.

27   Samuel Purchas, 'Relation of Ormuz, and of the late taking thereof by the English and Persians' [1625], *Hakluytus Posthumus or Purchas His Pilgrimes*, 20 vols (Glasgow: James MacLehose and Sons, 1905), vol. 10, 318-74, 324.

28   On the Anglo-Persian attack on Ormus see P.J. Marshall, 'The English in Asia to 1700', *The Oxford History of the British Empire*, gen. ed. W. Roger Louis, 5 vols (Oxford: Oxford University Press, 1998), vol. 1: *The Origins of Empire*, ed. Nicholas Canny, 264-85, 272-3; and John C. Appleby, 'War, Politics, and Colonization, 1558-1625', *Oxford History of the British Empire*, vol. 1, 55-78, 76-7.

29   See Draper, 'Milton's Ormus', 326.

30   Richard Bentley (ed.), *Milton's* Paradise Lost. *A New Edition* (London: Jacob Tonson, 1732), *ad* 2.2.

31   See Timothy Morton, 'Trade Winds', Kate Flint (ed., for the English Association), *Poetry and Politics*, Essays and Studies 1996 (Cambridge: Brewer, 1996), 19-41, 22. Thomas Mun famously stated that '[o]ur stock may be much increased by Trade from Port to Port in the *Indies*' and that investing in foreign trade means only 'transmutations and no consumptions of the Kingdomes stocke'. *A Discourse of Trade, From* England *unto the* East-Indies*: Answering to diverse Obiections which are usually made against the same* (London: Nicholas Okes for John Pyper, 1621), 21, 25. Mun's most important theory was that of 'artificial wealth' created by foreign trade (see his 1664 *England's Treasure by Foreign Trade*). On his important new idea of commerce as a 'self-contained system, controlled ... by impersonal market forces, not government policies, let alone moral or religious precept', see Wilfrid Prest, *Albion Ascendant: English History, 1660-1815* (Oxford: Oxford University Press, 1998), 7-8.

32   This intertextual presence becomes even clearer when we remember the moral Michael had extracted from his account: 'God attributes to place / No sanctity, if none be thither brought / By men who there frequent, or therein dwell' (*PL* 11.860-62). Only the 'commodity' is different: God's grace with Milton, merchandise with Bentley.

33   Nigel Smith provides an analysis of the 'literalisation within the new civic religion [after the Restoration] of the metaphor of grace as money in Christian theology'. 'The English Revolution and the End of Rhetoric: John Toland's *Clito* (1700) and the Republican Daemon', Flint (ed.), *Poetry and Politics*, 1-17, 13. J.G.A. Pocock in *The Machiavellian Moment* describes in more detail the 18th-century discursive shift away from the language of grace to that of virtue and commerce (423-505).

34   Dryden in *Annus Mirabilis* also refers to 'wealthy *Tagus*' (299.1) but prophesies that its wealth will eventually be eclipsed by the commercial riches of 'silver *Thames*' (298.1).

35   David S. Shields, *Oracles of Empire: Poetry, Politics, and Commerce in British America, 1690-1750* (Chicago: University of Chicago Press, 1990), 19.

36   While preparing his own 1732 edition, Bentley annotated a 1720 Tonson edition now in the Cambridge University Library: John Milton, *The Poetical Works* (London: Jacob Tonson, 1720), CUL Adv.b.52.12.

37   On the 'Old Whig' tendencies in Bentley's annotations see also William Kolbrener, *Milton's Warring Angels: A Study of Critical Engagements* (Cambridge: Cambridge University Press, 1997), 107-28.

38   Miss Christian Cann, *A Scriptural and Allegorical Glossary to Milton's* Paradise Lost (London: C. and J. Rivington, 1828), *ad* 2.2.

39   Preceding quotations: Henry Jones, *Kew Garden* (London: J. Browne, 1767), 1.162-5, 1.355, 1.221.

40   'There is a place / (If ancient and prophetic fame in heaven / Err not) another world, the happy seat / Of some new race called man, about this time / To be created like to us' (*PL* 2.345-9).

41   Fernand Braudel, *Capitalism and Material Life 1400-1800*, trans. Miriam Kochan (London: Fontana, 1974), 136.

42   See Allan H. Gilbert, *A Geographical Dictionary of Milton* (Ithaca: Cornell University Press, 1919).

43   Robert Markley claims that at the time, '[t]o imagine the revolution of the saints was, in some measure, to dream that the "destin'd Walls" of this infinitely wealthy and fertile country were within the reach of virtuous and enterprising merchants.' But even Milton's

early millennarianism was never as narrowly materialistic as this. '"The destin'd Walls / Of *Cambalu*": Milton, China, and the Ambiguities of the East', Rajan and Sauer (eds), *Milton and the Imperial Vision*, 191-213, 209.

44   Bruce McLeod, 'The "Lordly eye": Milton and the Strategic Geography of Empire', Rajan and Sauer (eds), *Milton and the Imperial Vision*, 48-66, 65.

45   See Stevie Davies, *Milton*, Harvester New Readings (New York: Harvester Wheatsheaf, 1991), 123.

46   Satan's faulty perception is compared to that of humans: to Galileo's 'less assured' observation of 'imagined lands and regions in the moon', and to a sailor who perceives as a 'cloudy spot' in the distance either 'Delos or Samos', he cannot be sure which (*PL* 5.262-6). For Amy Boesky, the Galileo motif in *Paradise Lost* represents 'both the powers of mortal vision and its fallibility'. 'Milton, Galileo, and Sunspots: Optics and Certainty in *Paradise Lost*', *Milton Studies* 34 (1997), 23-43, 23.

47   Quint, *Epic and Empire*, 256, 266. Quint interprets Satan's merchant voyage as either 'a revision of the earlier epic tradition' to accommodate the replacement of aristocratic heroes by merchant adventurers, or as 'an indictment of European expansion and colonialism' (265).

48   Keith W.F. Stavely, *Puritan Legacies*: Paradise Lost *and the New England Tradition, 1630-1890* (Ithaca: Cornell University Press, 1987), 63.

49   Camões mentions them in the *Lusiads*: 'Look there, how the seas of the Orient, / Are scattered with islands beyond number; / See Tidore, then Ternate with its burning / Summit'. Luís Vaz de Camões, *The Lusiads*, trans. Landeg White (Oxford: Oxford University Press, 1997), 10.132.1-4.

50   *Purchas His Pilgrimes*, 3.904; Gilbert, *Geographical Dictionary*, s.v. Ternate, 290-91.

51   In *Of Reformation* (1641) Milton had still advocated a League of Protestant Nations especially between the English and the Dutch, even 'though their Merchants bicker in the East Indies' (*YP* 1:587).

52   Markley, '"The destin'd Walls"', 205. For evidence of this theme in Milton see John Milton, *A Common-Place Book of John Milton*, ed. Alfred J. Horwood (London: Camden Society, 1877; repr. New York: Johnson Reprint Corporation, 1965), last entry: '*de re nautica*'.

53   Cann, *Scriptural and Allegorical Glossary*, *ad* 2.639.

54   Morton, 'Trade Winds', 25.

55   Balachandra Rajan, 'Banyan Trees and Fig Leaves: Some Thoughts on Milton's India', *Under Western Eyes: India from Milton to Macaulay* (Durham: Duke University Press, 1999), 50-66, 55.

56   Morton, 'Trade Winds', 19.

57   John Brewer and Roy Porter, 'Introduction', Brewer and Porter (eds), *Consumption and the World of Goods* (London: Routledge, 1993), 1-15, 7. On the increasing 18th-century demands for luxury imports see also Paul Langford, *A Polite and Commercial People: England 1727-1783* (Oxford: Oxford University Press, 1989), 68-71. On the growth of middle-class consumerism and conspicuous consumption see Peter Earle, *The Making of the English Middle Class: Business, Society and Family Life in London, 1660-1730* (Berkeley: California University Press, 1989), 281-2, 336.

58   Patrick Hume, *Annotations on Milton's* Paradise Lost (London: Jacob Tonson, 1695), 78, *ad* 2.637.

59   James Paterson, *A Complete Commentary ... on Milton's* Paradise Lost (London: R. Walker, 1744), 158, *ad* 4.162.

60   George Lord Anson is connected with the nautical feat of circumnavigation, with the sea victory against the Spanish in 1740 and against the French in 1747.

61   Quotations: John Dyer, *The Fleece* [1757], *The Works of the English Poets from Chaucer to Cowper*, ed. Alexander Chalmers [1810], 21 vols; repr. Anglistica & Americana 51 (Hildesheim: Olms, 1971), vol. 13, 228-50, book 3, 242, book 4, 249.

62   James Russell Lowell, 'Wordsworth' [1875], *English Critical Essays: Nineteenth Century*, ed. Edmund D. Jones (1916; London: Humphrey Milford, 1922), 558-610, 598.

63   See David Richardson, 'The British Empire and the Atlantic Slave Trade, 1660-1807', *Oxford History of the British Empire*, vol. 2: *The Eighteenth Century*, ed. P.J. Marshall, 440-64, 444.

64   Maureen Quilligan, 'Freedom, Service, and the Trade in Slaves: the Problem of Labor in *Paradise Lost*', Margreta de Grazia *et al.* (eds), *Subject and Object in Renaissance Culture* (Cambridge: Cambridge University Press, 1996), 213-34.

65   See my chapter 'Milton and the Anti-Slavery Movement', *Majestick Milton*, 353-98.

66   Preceding quotations: James Montgomery, *The West Indies, a Poem. In four Parts*, James Montgomery, James Grahame and E.E. Benger, *Poems on the Abolition of the Slave Trade* (London: R. Bowyer, 1809), 1-53, 11-12, 16. The British 'Black Legend' about the Spanish comes to the fore in these emphases on Spain's cruel slave traders.

67   Quoted in *The Critical Review* 67 (1789), 468.

68   James Grahame, *Africa Delivered; or, The Slave Trade Abolished. A Poem*, Montgomery, Grahame and Benger, *Poems on the Abolition of the Slave Trade*, 57-100; Milton quotation: epigraph to Part II.

69   See also the debate among historians about the mixed motives for abolition; generally, 'moral values', enlightenment thought and evangelical movements are cited alongside purely economic reasons. See Eric Williams, *Capitalism and Slavery* (Chapel Hill: University of North Carolina Press, 1944); J.R. Ward, 'The British West Indies in the Age of Abolition, 1748-1815', *Oxford History of the British Empire*, vol. 2, 415-39.

70   Peter Ackroyd, *Milton in America* (London: Sinclair-Stevenson, 1996), 87-8.

71   One of the numerous intertexts, apart from Milton's own texts, seems to be Nathaniel Hawthorne's story 'The May-Pole of Merry Mount' (1837) with its colony of joy-loving High Church men opposing the rigid rules of the Puritan colony: 'Jollity and gloom were contending for an empire.' *Twice-Told Tales*, ed. William Charvat *et al.*, *The Centenary Edition of the Works of Nathaniel Hawthorne*, 14 vols (Ohio: Ohio State University Press, 1962-1980), vol. 9 (1974), 54-67, 54-5.

72   All preceding quotations: Ackroyd, *Milton in America*, 18-19, 5, 11.

73   See my chapter 'Postcolonial Epilogue', *Majestick Milton*, 341-54.

4 Class War and the Albatross: The Politics of Ships as Social Space and *The Rime of the Ancient Mariner*

SARAH MOSS

Coleridge begins both *A Moral and Political Lecture* and the 'Introductory Address' to *Conciones ad Populum* with the metaphor of the Ship of State:

> When the Wind is fair and the Planks of the Vessel sound, we may safely trust everything to the management of professional Mariners; but in a Tempest and on board a crazy Bark, all must contribute their Quota of Exertion ... Even so, in the present agitations of the public mind, everyone ought to consider his intellectual faculties as in a state of immediate requisition.[1]

This explicit connection between the ship in trouble and the state in disarray can be seen as fundamental to a reading of the importance of long-distance journeying in Coleridge's work. The image was well established in both radical and conservative writings on the state of the English body politic in the 1790s,[2] but it is also central to Coleridge's writing from *Lectures 1795* to the biography of Alexander Ball in *The Friend*. Auden writes in *The Enchafèd Flood*, '[t]he state ship that deliberately chooses the high seas is the state in disorder, the Ship of Fools',[3] and most of Coleridge's ships, choosing the high seas, are ships of state and many are ships of fools, from the slavers whose rotting planks he graphically describes in 'On the Slave Trade' to the man-of-war, captained by Alexander Ball whom Coleridge came to admire. This uneasy conflation of the Ship of State and the Ship of Fools epitomizes the ambivalence of Coleridge's view of the Establishment throughout his career, for the ship figures as both the vindication of Tory hierarchy and the site of social transgression and even anarchy.

Very few of Coleridge's references to ships and seafaring can be read straightforwardly. The details of his biography, the extent of his reading of travel writing, and his profound engagement with a politics much exercised by the Navy and various forms of colonial trading, and the sheer weight of references to these things in Coleridge's work demand a reading of his *oeuvre* that is acutely sensitive to these concerns. In this paper I will focus on *The Rime of the Ancient Mariner* as the major work most explicitly concerned with seafaring and exerting influence on almost all subsequent writing about the sea in English.

Since the 1960s, literary criticism of *The Ancient Mariner* has been exploring the context of Coleridge's interests in the slave trade and the politics of nascent colonialism. This began in 1964, when William Empson suggested that 'it would not be right to say that the Albatross was a "symbol" of the ill-treated natives, but the terrible cry, "I didn't know it was wrong when I did it" belongs somehow naturally to the whole set-up of the exploring ship.'[4] In 1972, J.R. Ebbatson expanded on Empson's intuition to announce that 'the central act of *The Ancient Mariner*, the shooting of the albatross, may be a symbolic rehearsal of the crux of colonial expansion, the enslavement of native peoples; and that the punishments visited upon the Mariner, and the deaths of his shipmates because of their complicity, may represent European racial guilt, and the need to make restitution.'[5] The critical tendency to convict the Ancient Mariner of participation in the slave trade continues in Patrick Keane's *Submerged Politics*.[6]

The problem with this is that Coleridge is meticulous in mapping the Mariner's voyage, and it is clear that the ship clears the harbour, drops 'Below the Kirk, below the Hill, / Below the Light-house top',[7] and sails with sunrise on the left (due South) until the sun is directly over the mast at noon (on the equator). Then the storm and wind drive the ship along 'like chaff' (line 49) for days and weeks until it grows 'wond'rous cold' (line 51) and ice mast-high comes floating by as green as emerald (line 52). They stay among the Antarctic ice until the Ancient Mariner has shot the albatross and then the sun comes up upon the right and goes down on the left and there is a strong south wind, so the ship is heading due North quickly. Then 'the bloody sun at noon / Right up above the mast did stand' (lines 108-9) (they are back at the equator again) and the wind fails. Like many other sailors before and since, the Mariner and his crew stay becalmed in the equatorial Pacific for weeks, running out of food and water in seas too far from anywhere else to hope for rescue. Then the polar spirit moves the ship until it is within reach of the pilot, in whose small boat the Mariner rows himself back to his 'own Countree' (line 603). No landfall is made, and this is very much the pattern of the voyages of Antarctic exploration of the late 18th century and bears no relation to the triangular slave-trading voyage. While all late 18th-century voyaging takes place against the background of the slave trade and other forms of colonial exploitation, it seems perverse to ignore Coleridge's very precise account of exactly where the Mariner goes, especially as the navigational precision is marked in an otherwise unearthly poem. The point about the Antarctic is that it has no legends, no language, no culture, no history but geology. Going to the Antarctic is fundamentally different from going anywhere else on earth; it is a place where there is literally nothing to see, where what there is to see is greater expanses of nothing than on any other continent. It seems at least unlikely that Coleridge, whose extensive reading of polar travel writing is used more in this poem than anywhere else, includes such a distinctive topos as casually as readings in terms of the slave trade and imperial guilt would suggest.

The obvious difficulty with this is that the central problem of *The Ancient Mariner*, the moral challenge of outrageous suffering out of all proportion to any mistakes made or offences committed, remains unanswered. It is possible, as Coleridge suggested when asked to explain the poem's moral, that there isn't one and that this is simple and gratuitous story-telling at its most extravagantly amoral. The problem with this reading (apart from its unsatisfactoriness to the inquiring mind) is that there is nothing in a South Sea voyage that would offer the opportunity not to think about domestic politics. Ships at this date (shortly after hugely publicized court martials following the *Bounty* mutiny, and during the mutinies of the entire Naval fleet at Spithead and the Nore), especially on long voyages, functioned both for those aboard and for those reading about them at home as microcosmic Englands where all power relations and conflicts were intensified. Coleridge not only shared in but perpetuated such perceptions of the 'crazy bark', and readings of some of his probable sources for *The Ancient Mariner* make clear just how obviously politicized these 'supernatural voyages' could be. Coleridge's sources also demonstrate what should be more horrifying than the idea that the Mariner suffers through unwarranted visitations of the supernatural: that, seen beside contemporary voyage narratives, the skeletal crew 'for charnel dungeon fitter' (line 441), the slimy things crawling with legs, the biscuit worms and the weight around the Mariner's neck are not merely natural but realistic. If so, then it seems possible that at least one of the things this poem is 'about' is the sea as social space in the English body politic.

Several historians comment that ships are what the sociologist Erving Goffman has defined as 'total institutions', places such as asylums and prisons where inmates are completely enclosed and, within that enclosure, completely public: 'A total institution may be defined as a place of residence and work where a large number of like situated individuals, cut off from the wider society for an appreciable period of time, together lead an enclosed, formally administered round of life.'[8] Although the idea of the total institution has been challenged and complicated, in the case of ships at sea where the very simple and important binary construction of on board / overboard is always valid it remains fruitful. On 18th-century ships communal isolation is compounded by a caste system in which the captain must not fraternize with his officers lest he lose authority over them and the officers must not fraternize with the 'men' for the same reason. Any attempt on the part of the officers to behave sociably towards the captain, or the crew towards the officers, may be interpreted as an attempt to violate this hierarchical order. This is mutiny, or, if only one person is involved, mutinous behaviour, and the punishment is death by hanging for the men and dismissal for the officers. If the captain chooses not to have the crew member executed, he may do instead whatever occurs to him: the man cannot complain because the captain's alternative was to kill him and the Admiralty Board, the body to which he might complain, will do so if he admits the capital offence of mutinous behaviour. The sorts of things that might occur to isolated men with absolute power to do to someone whom they perceive to have threatened this absolute power, thousands of miles from home, with witnesses over whom they have similar power, can probably safely be left to the imagination.[9]

In theory there were limits on captains' power. If they wanted to give a seaman more than 36 strokes with the cat-o'-nine-tails, they needed Admiralty permission. There are hundreds of instances of captains ordering or giving more strokes than this - including James Cook - and no records of anyone requesting permission. Other common punishments, such as hanging seamen in the rigging by their arms for hours at a time, often in extreme weather and with heavy lead weights around their necks ('Instead of the Cross, the Albatross / About my neck was hung' [lines 138-9]), or 'running the gauntlet' where the crew were forced to form a double line through which the miscreant walked at gunpoint while his fellow workers hit him with metal belaying pins or whatever else took the captain's fancy, were officially outlawed but in fact remained normal into the 19th century. In practise, the far South was a very long way from the Admiralty headquarters, there was no possibility of communication and witnesses could always be intimidated or, if necessary, forcibly silenced. The Admiralty very rarely took the side of the crew anyway, so there was almost no possibility of redress. Most of the time, at sea, there was no possibility of escape either. Desertion and attempted desertion were also capital offences, and anyone found or known to have been ashore when the ship was in port without express permission could be accused and punished accordingly. Sleeping on watch, failing to carry out an order (for whatever reason), stealing (however little and however great the need, including, for example, water in great heat), homosexuality and drunkenness were among the misdemeanours attracting the same punishment. Since most ships worked a four-watch system, which meant that two groups took turns to work alternate four-hour periods unless the weather was bad or the captain for some other reason felt that circumstances required more than half the available labour, when everyone had to remain on watch for as long as it took, it was never possible to sleep for more than four hours at a time. Failure to carry out an order covered everything from reluctance to do an unpleasant job, through refusal to do something deemed by an experienced sailor to be unnecessary and dangerous, to ignoring a nonsensical order given by a drunk, seasick or inexperienced officer. All this is to say, a captain who was trying could find a reason to flog most of the crew on most days, resulting in an extremely stressed as well as exhausted, malnourished and alcoholic crew. Coleridge read many journals of such voyages, including that of Shelvocke who is conventionally cited as the source for the killing of the albatross and Bligh, in the context of whose loss of control the *Rime* has occasionally been read. There is also another, less widely acknowledged influence, suggested by Bruce Chatwin in *In Patagonia*.[10]

In 1593 John Davis set off as second-in-command to Thomas Cavendish on a South Sea voyage that reached Antarctica but went horribly wrong. Coleridge had access to Davis' *Last Voyage of the Worshipfull M. Thomas Cavendish* in Hakluyt's *Principal Navigations* of 1600, and Chatwin's thesis is compelling. This voyage bears comparison with Shelvocke's in being jeopardized by power struggles between the captain, the crew and the officers from the beginning and Davis, like Shelvocke, ended up by requiring his crew to sign 'a testimonial acquitting him of having purposely and designedly abandoned his general'.[11] The expedition had left England in two ships, with Cavendish as captain of the *Galeon* and Davis, subordinate to him, in charge of the *Desire*. Like most later expeditions, the two ships were running out of food by the time they reached South America, and after several fights and disasters and many deaths, they reach the Antarctic underprovisioned and with a reduced crew. Davis writes, 'all the sicke men in the Galeon were most uncharitably put a shore into the woods in the snowe, raine and cold, when men of good health could skarcely indure it, where they ended their lives in the highest degree of misery, master Candish all this while being aboard The Desire' (97). The accusation of negligence is veiled but it is clearly implicit, and as conditions worsen and more of the crew die of exposure and hunger, the crew and Davis give Cavendish a petition begging him to turn back rather than keep heading South into the ice with 'no more sailes than mastes, no victuals, no ground-tackling, no cordage more than is overhead ... and but foureteene saylers' (98). It is at a similar moment that Shelvocke and Bligh lose even the nominal and sym-bolic control they had previously managed to exert and Cavendish is simi-larly inflexible, similarly unable to understand that his power does not exist when his crew ceases to believe in it. Cavendish reacts by giving orders to continue South. Shortly afterwards the ships are mysteriously separated (hence Davis' need of the testimonial) and, Davis claims, the *Desire* is damaged, so he plans to set off alone to report to Cavendish while the others repair the *Desire*, but is regrettably prevented by a mutinous crew. As Davis clearly knew, it seems at best to show an unnatural devotion to the letter of the law if a crew who have expressed their urgent desire to turn round subsequently lose the general who refuses their demands at sea and then try their best to return to him but are sadly prevented by an unruly majority, who subsequently conspire

> [i]n a night to murther our Captaine and Master, with my selfe, and all those that they thought were their friendes. There were markes taken in his caben how to kill him with muskets through the shippes side, and bullets made of sil-ver for the execution, if their other purposes should fail ... The Captaine being thus hardly beset, in perill of famine, and in danger of murthering, was con-strained to use lenitie, and by courteous meanes to pacifie this furie ... the Cap-taine desired then to shewe themselves Christians, and not so blasphemously to behave themselves, without regard or thanksgiving to God ... alleaging many examples of Gods sharpe punishment for such ingratitude. (102)

This sermon, Davis claims, is effective and indeed prophetic, for the matter 'after came to a most sharpe revenge even by the punishment of the Almightie'. It is clearly unlikely that mutiny was deflected by a sermon, especially by a sermon containing no threats because the captain has realized that he is 'hardly beset' and 'in danger of murthering' and must resort to 'lenitie' and 'courteous meanes' and to this extent, Davis' account offers its own contradiction. The point, always, is that there is no way of knowing what happens at sea. Nevertheless, in this testimony the Lord's vengeance is swift and disproportionately terrible. Storms batter the ship whose 'shroudes are all rotten' (the shrouds are in this context the ropes that hold up the masts but the effect is no less alarming for that) and 'not having a running rope whereto we may trust ... neither have we any pitch, tarre or nailes, nor any store for the supplying of these wants' (105). The extremity of the state of the ship's fabric is evident from Davis' listing these problems before he comes onto the absence of food: without a ship, they will die in minutes while they could live for days without food. Some mussels are found, and eventually the storm abates and the crew find that 'after wee had rested a little our men were not able to move; their sinewes were stiffe, and their flesh dead, and many of them (which is most lamentable to bee reported) were so eaten with lice, as that in their flesh did lie clusters of lice as big as peason, yea, and some as big as beanes' (117). ('They raised their limbs like lifeless tools / We were a ghastly crew' [lines 334-5].) But the worst is yet to come. The ship comes upon an Antarctic island covered in penguins and seemingly without inhabitants, so they spend days killing, drying and salting twenty thousand of the flightless birds which are so unused to predators that they allow themselves to be picked up and killed ('And every day for food or play / Came to the Marineres hollo' [lines 73-4]). Some of the men disappear and are presumed killed by 'savages' (125), and then one night,

> [m]any of our men in the ship dreamed of murther and slaughter: In the morning they reported their dreames, one saying to another; this night I dreamt thou wert slaine; another answered, and I dreamed that thou wert slaine: and this was general throughout the ship. (124)

Again, this proves prophetic, for by the end of the day the shore party has been massacred by 'savages' and Portuguese sailors, presumably also stocking up on penguins, leaving twenty-seven of the original seventy-six crew. Most of these are also fated:

> But after we came neere unto the sun, our dried Penguins began to corrupt, and there bred in them a most lothsome and ugly worme of an inch long. This worme did so mightily increase and devoure our victuals, that there was in reason no hope how we should avoid famine, but be devoured of these wicked creatures: there was nothing that they did not devoure, only yron excepted: our clothes, boots, shooes, hats, shirts, stockings: and, for the ship, they did so eat the timbers as that we greatly feared they would undo us by gnawing through the ships side ... the more we laboured to kill them the more they increased; so that at the last we could not sleepe for them, for they would eate our flesh and bite like Mosquitos ... after we had passed the Equinoctiall toward the North, our men began to fall sick of such monstrous disease, as I thinke the like was never heard of. (126)

The disease is indeed monstrous; in the course of three days, the victims' 'cods and yardes' swell up so much that they 'can neither stand, lie, nor goe' (126) and then they slowly go mad and die, leaving sixteen survivors of whom five are still able to move across the worm-infested ship.[12] Utterly helpless, 'without victuals, sails, men or any furniture, God onely guided us into Ireland' (130) from where Davis, the only one who can still walk, goes alone to Padstow to announce the return of the *Desire*.

Apart from the obvious connection, pointed out by Chatwin, between these worms and the 'slimy things', the *Rime* is infested with decomposition in the same way as Davis' account, for both have dead and dying human flesh lying around the ship and both narrators see

> The many men so beautiful
> And they all dead did lie!
> And a million million slimy things
> Liv'd on - and so did I. (lines 231-4)[13]

Both ships are sailed by crews whom the narrators have called 'dead', both crews endure terrible thirst and hunger, both see the Antarctic ice and the albatrosses that wheel around it. The suggestion that Davis' *Last Voyage* is an important influence on the *Rime* is strengthened by the similarity of the routes taken; both leave England and make a quick passage to the far South, encounter storms and bad weather in the Antarctic ice and are disastrously becalmed just south of the equator before being miraculously taken home in seriously disabled ships without enough surviving crew to get them back. There are, of course, many other probable and possible influences on Coleridge at this period, but the claim here is that a few texts to which he is known to have had access, that exemplify the literature of Antarctic voyaging, offer a previously unconsidered context for the central problems of the *Rime*.

Several critics have pointed out possible connections between Coleridge's stance on the political regimes of England and France at this time and the imagery of the *Rime*. Robert Maniquis in particular suggests that the gratuitous suffering at the centre of the poem can be related to the terror of the French Revolution:

> When the Ancient Mariner recounts how he let the arrow of his cross-bow fly and murdered the albatross, we are thrust into violence as yet untransformed and unsymbolized. The poem is the imagination of a pure act of violence before interpretation, not yet fitted into the discourses of symbolic exchange.[14]

This is acute and extremely interesting in the context of the Romantic apprehension of political violence, but it can be argued that there is a context in which 'pure' or gratuitous violence aboard a ship is already and intrinsically politicized. The voyage narratives of Bligh, Shelvocke, Cook,

William Wales and John Davis are among the more obvious influences on
The Rime of the Ancient Mariner, and each text is defined and fundamentally shaped by the captain's need to maintain a power that is in fact merely
symbolic so far from home, and by the crew's need to resist being con-
sumed as labour, to define themselves outside the economy of the voyage.
Starving and sleepless, living below decks where if the sun 'peers through
the dungeon grate' (line 179) it is all the natural light that can be hoped for,
they labour on because there is no alternative but intolerable physical abuse
and an earlier death. In this context the ceaseless labour which almost
makes a refrain in the *Rime*, the bodies that continue to work after the
sailors are dead and the ship has stopped, can be read as satirical:

> The helmsman steerd, the ship mov'd on;
> Yet never a breeze up-blew;
> The Marineres all gan work the ropes,
> Where they were wont to do:
> They rais'd their limbs like lifeless tools -
> We were a ghastly crew. (lines 330-35)

The crew's working of ropes and the helmsman's steering are constantly
reiterated until the Mariner's trance is abated and the two voices have left
him to his renewed life, from when 'The Ice did Split with a Thunder-fit; /
The Helmsman steered us through' (lines 68-9) until

> The body of my brother's son
> Stood by me knee to knee:
> The body and I pull'd at one rope,
> But he said nought to me. (lines 335-9)

The Wedding Guest tries to make a move, but the Mariner holds him,

> Never sadder tale was heard
> By man of woman born:
> The Marineres all return'd to work
> As silent as beforne.
>
> The Marineres all 'gan pull the ropes,
> But look at me they n'old. (lines 366-71)

The alienation of the sailors' labour in these stanzas is so clearly enunciated
as to verge on the parodic and make all comment clumsy by comparison.
The Mariner's life, his continuing subjectivity, is very obviously marked

where he refers to himself as 'I' and 'me' but to his colleague as 'the body' that labours and the 'he' that is now silenced. It seems possible that the careful precision of 'The body of my brother's son' can be related to the naval and seafaring tradition whereby young boys are enlisted on their uncles' ships as midshipmen but also as unofficial apprentices, in hopes that the family connection will protect the child from the worst excesses of nautical 'discipline' and offering the possibility that the Mariner, among other unexplained and inexplicable causes of guilt, fails in a duty of care assigned in his 'own Countree' (line 603). It is not possible to tell whether the sailors refuse to look at and speak to the Mariner and give him 'The curse in a dead man's eye' (line 253) simply because they are dead and he is alive or because his killing of the albatross gives these undead reason to hate and resent him. This crew of hostile spectres, skeletal and even decomposing, who would not be blurring the boundary between the living and the dead except that they continue to labour even as the worm is on their cheeks, can be no more finally diagnosed than the victims of any other instance of evil, be it the sugar plantations of 18th-century West Indies or the guillotine wielded by the mob. The sailors on the Mariner's ship are recognizably in the same physical state as abused subaltern populations in industrialized and capitalist societies from 18th-century West Africa through 19th-century England to 20th-century Poland, and it is this state that critics finding references to the slave trade and the starving mobs of 1790s England and France have identified.[15] I would like to speculate - and this can only be a speculation although I hope it is a fruitful one - that the combination of the Mariner's undefined role aboard the ship and Coleridge's gratitude for sadistic treatment at school and subsequent approval of some of the more extreme forms of naval discipline suggest that the Mariner's guilt may be in some sense that of the collaborator, of the Shelvocke or Davis who, understandably and in peril of his life, tries simultaneously to please Authority and appease the mob.[16] In the history of long-distance or perilous travel where resources are limited, the lone survivor has traditionally been treated with suspicion and often assumed to be a cannibal. A contemporary example would be John Adams, the only survivor of the group which accompanied Fletcher Christian to Pitcairn, whose account of his companions' fate was regarded with deep suspicion from his first telling of it, and there is also the Native American tradition of the Windigo, a humanoid cannibal who may begin as a traveller forced to resort to the survival cannibalism of his companions. The problem with all of these situations is exactly the same as that of sea-stories; there is no way of telling, anything could have happened out there and often it probably had. Edward Bostetter's comment is potentially illuminating:

Like the figures in a dream, they [the sailors] have no identity apart from the dreamer. We have no awareness of them as living human beings; we watch their deaths without surprise and without feeling, except insofar as they affect the Mariner. When, dying, the men fix their eyes upon the Mariner, the effect is not only to intensify his sense of guilt but to emphasise his importance.[17]

As the narrator and sole survivor, it could be said that the Mariner's importance needs little emphasis; it is his story and his story alone. But there is certainly at least a tacit hierarchy on the Mariner's ship, since someone, presumably the resentful crew, hangs the albatross around his neck (the seven-foot wingspan, objected to by some critics, would have been no barrier to men who required boys to climb the rigging with hundred pound weights around their necks) and the Mariner, as the only survivor, is somehow on top of the hierarchy by the end. The suggestion here, and it can and should be no more than a suggestion, is that the Mariner may fruitfully be considered as, if not captain, then intimately involved in the violent power struggle of life at sea.

Notes

1   Samuel Taylor Coleridge, *Lectures 1795 on Politics and Religion*, ed. Lewis Patton and Peter Mann (Princeton: Princeton University Press, 1971), 33.
2   For a more detailed discussion of the ship of state in the literature of this period, see Tim Fulford, 'Romanticizing the Empire: The Naval Heroes of Southey, Coleridge, Austen and Marryat', *Modern Language Quarterly* 60, no. 2 (1999), 161-96; and Tim Fulford, 'Britannia's Heart of Oak: Thomson, Garrick and the Language of Eighteenth-Century Patriotism', Richard Terry (ed.), *James Thomson: Tercentenary Essays* (Liverpool: Liverpool University Press, forthcoming).
3   W.H. Auden, *The Enchafèd Flood, or The Romantic Iconography of the Sea* (London: Faber and Faber, 1951).
4   William Empson, 'The Ancient Mariner', *Critical Quarterly* 6 (1964), 298-319, 305.
5   J.R. Ebbatson, 'Coleridge's Mariner and the Rights of Man', *Studies in Romanticism* 11 (1972), 171-206, 198.
6   See Patrick J. Keane, *Coleridge's Submerged Politics. The Ancient Mariner and Robinson Crusoe* (Columbia and London: University of Missouri Press, 1994).
7   Samuel Taylor Coleridge, 'The Rime of the Ancient Mariner', *Poems*, ed. John Beer (London: Everyman, 1993), 214-55, lines 27-8. All further references are to the 1798 version in this edition. Line numbers are quoted in brackets.
8   Erving Goffman, *Asylums: Essays on the Social Situation of Mental Patients and Other Inmates* (London: Penguin, 1968).
9   Should imagination fail, see B.R. Burg, *Sodomy and the Pirate Tradition* (New York: New York University Press, 1995) on sadism at sea; and Marcus Rediker, *Between the Devil and the Deep Blue Sea. Merchant Seamen, Pirates, and the Anglo-American Maritime World, 1700-1750* (Cambridge: Cambridge University Press, 1987), ch. 5.

10   Bruce Chatwin, *In Patagonia* (London: Pan, 1979), 87.

11   John Davis, *Voyages and Works of John Davis, the Navigator*, ed. Albert Hastings
      Markham (London: Hakluyt Society, 1880), xlix. All further references are to this
      edition. Page numbers are quoted in brackets.

12   Deborah Lee suggests in 'Yellow Fever and the Slave Trade: Coleridge's "The Rhyme
      of the Ancient Mariner"', *English Literary History* 65, no. 3 (1998), 675-701, that this
      disease can be read as yellow fever which killed thousands of sailors in the slave trade,
      which both complicates and complements my reading.

13   That Coleridge was concerned by the political context of such images is clear from the
      zeal with which he collects naval reports and associated news in *The Watchman*. For
      example, 'About 70 men of the 20th regiment landed at Plymouth on Tuesday last
      from on board a transport lately arrived from the West-Indies. Many of them are in an
      unhealthy state. They are the remains of 700 fine fellows, who have been thus reduced
      by the ravages of the yellow fever.' Samuel Taylor Coleridge, *The Watchman*, ed.
      Lewis Patton (Princeton: Princeton University Press, 1970), 332.

14   Robert M. Maniquis, 'Holy Savagery and Wild Justice: English Romanticism and the
      Terror', *Studies in Romanticism* 28, no. 3 (1989), 365-97, 390.

15   Coleridge's awareness of the economic motivation in such situations is clear in the
      essay 'On the Slave Trade': 'And indeed the evils arising from the formation of the
      imaginary Wants, have in no instance been so dreadfully exemplified, as in this
      inhuman Traffic. We receive from the West India Islands Sugars, Rum, Cotton,
      Logwood, Cocoa, Coffee, Pimento, Ginger, Indigo, Mahogany and Conserves. Not
      one of them is at present attainable by the poor and labouring part of Society. In return
      we export vast quantities of necessary Tools, Raiment, and defensive Weapons, with
      great stores of Provision. So that in this Trade as in most others the Poor are employed
      with unceasing toil first to raise, and then to send away the Comforts, which they
      themselves absolutely want, in order to procure idle superfluities for their Masters.'
      The Watchman, 133.

16   For a closer analysis of these late essays, see Tim Fulford, 'Romanticizing the
      Empire'.

17   Edward E. Bostetter, *The Romantic Ventriloquists: Wordsworth, Coleridge, Keats,
      Shelley, Byron* (Seattle: University of Washington Press, 1963), 111.

5 Walter Scott's *The Pirate*: Imperialism, Nationalism and Bourgeois Values

ARNOLD SCHMIDT

In Walter Scott's journal entry for 16 June 1829, pirates figure as images of chaos and existential angst. Scott had been at work on his contribution to Thomas Moore's 1830 *Letters and Journals of Lord Byron*, when he wrote:

> I did not get on with [my work on] Byron so far as I expected ... Met Captain Hamilton who tells me a shocking thing. Two Messrs. Stirling of Drumpellar came here and dined one day and seemed spirited young men. The younger is murdered by pirates. An Indian vessel in which he sailed was boarded by these miscreants who behaved most brutally and he offering resistance I suppose was shockingly mangled and flung in the sea. He was afterwards taken up alive but died soon after. Such horrid accidents lie in wait for those whom we see all joyous and unthinking sweeping along the course of life, and what end may be waiting ourselves - Who can tell?[1]

Byron had died five years earlier in Greece. Scott infuses the scene with recollections of Byron, whom he liked and with whom he agreed on 'everything except politics and religion'.[2] The pirates here serve as markers for fundamental questions about the meaning of life: how can such unexpected evil come to those who, like the sailor or Byron, are 'joyous and unthinking', in some sense, innocents. The final question, 'Who can tell?', however, concerns Scott himself, as it must anyone confronted with the arbitrary nature of death and the ephemerality of existence.

In some ways, the title character in Scott's 1821 novel *The Pirate* resembles the actual pirates described in his diary above. Both narratives of piracy, violent and disruptive, evoke existential questions for which there seem no satisfactory answers, though the novel ties up the loose ends that history leaves dangling. In *The Pirate*, Scott's principal maritime novel, the

sea carries a variety of significations.³ Aesthetically, it offers an arena for
the expiation of sin, for the development of selfhood, and for escape. It
provides both the site of exotic and erotic adventure, and a psychological
frontier. While Scott's works became very popular with general readers,
critics responded to his novels in different ways. Contemporary reviews
clearly treat his fiction as an intervention into the political discourse. So
while *The Pirate* raises philosophical issues, it can also be read as a commentary on the ethics of Regency society and on England's relations with
Scotland in the United Kingdom of Great Britain.

In *The Pirate*, Scott uses representations of maritime practices to
explore these social and political issues. In its images of wrecking, smuggling, impressment, and piracy, the novel reveals how closely crime and
commerce are intertwined. By the 1820s, according to Graham McMaster,
Scott had broken with the Scottish Enlightenment's generally teleological
and progressive views of history, and had begun to doubt 'the value of
material progress.'⁴ Britain's agricultural and industrial revolutions, which
depended on and produced a wage-based, credit-driven colonial economy,
brought great prosperity to some. Others, however, paid the price of rural
and urban poverty which undermined the traditional lifestyles that Scott
valued so highly. His doubts about the relationship between prosperity and
social responsibility become central to *The Pirate*'s critique of Regency
ethics and the slippage between piratical and bourgeois values.

The novel fictionalizes the history of pirate John Smith (alias Gow). Set
around 1700⁵ during the heyday of West Indian piracy, the novel's action
takes place on the Orkney and Shetland Islands, where many inhabitants
engage in smuggling and salvaging shipwrecks.

The narrative begins when Basil Mertoun arrives in Shetland from the
mainland; he seduces and abandons Norna, Magnus Troil's cousin.
Magnus' bloodline links him with the island's hereditary Norse monarchs,
who ruled until disempowered by Scotland in 1477. Mertoun leaves, taking
his illegitimate son, Cleveland, to the West Indies. There Mertoun marries a
Spaniard, and has a second son, Mordaunt. Discovering his wife guilty of
infidelity, Mertoun murders her.⁶ He leaves Mordaunt in school and takes
Cleveland to Tortuga, where, in desperation, they become buccaneers.
After a stint as a pirate, and believing Cleveland dead, Mertoun reclaims
Mordaunt and returns to Shetland, to live as a recluse in Jarlshof.

In time, Mordaunt has a flirtatious relationship with Magnus' daughters
Minna and Brenda. After a storm, Mordaunt saves the life of a shipwrecked
sailor, who is, unknown to him, his half-brother Cleveland. Scott incorporates the Norse superstition that rescuing a drowning man brings bad luck,
which becomes a metaphor for the link between social responsibility and

economic prosperity.[7] The superstition seems to be true, as Cleveland's arrival precipitates a rift between Mordaunt and the Troils. Scott, however, undermines belief in superstitions, and Mordaunt's falling out has a rational explanation, stemming from exaggerated rumours spread by the travelling salesman Bryce. This gossip exacerbates the rivalry between Mordaunt and Cleveland for the affections of Magnus' daughters. Cleveland falls in love with Minna and resolves to give up pirating. After saving Mordaunt's life during a whaling expedition, the pirate states that he has repaid Mordaunt for saving his life earlier. Cleveland then declares his hostility toward Mordaunt. These two outsiders have defied local custom - both rescued a drowning man - and suffer the consequences; bound together by transgression, their mutual antagonism separates them.

For Edgar Johnson, *The Pirate* reveals tension between 'long-established tradition and a disruptive iconoclasm. ... The central theme of the novel is the threat to ... [the islanders'] society created by the intrusion of strangers with alien and unsympathetic ways of thinking and feeling.'[8] This may be true, but it is also true that the strangers' intrusion reveals similarities between the islanders' values and those of the pirates whose criminality they condemn. In broader terms, the hypocrisy evident in the novel mirrors contradictions in 19th-century British society, where the civic virtues of a seemingly ethical society conflict with the imperial economy that makes that society possible. Enlightenment deism collided with evangelicalism to bring religious debate to the fore, but without resolving the tensions between imperial social practices and Christianity. Although Parliament outlawed the slave trade in 1807, slavery continued under the guise of slave apprenticeship until 1838, and Regency society prospered from the proceeds of slavery-driven colonialism.

Influential sectors of British society profited from the Napoleonic Wars, not least gentry grain growers, arms manufacturers, and speculators in land, commodities and bonds. The war itself, whose rhetoric announced as its goal the preservation and expansion of English liberty, resulted instead in Europe-wide post-Napoleonic reaction. Tens of thousands of sailors and soldiers returned home to find high inflation and unemployment, as well as continued resistance to political reform. The abolition debate challenged Britain's vision of itself as a Christian nation; profits from colonial endeavours and speculation undermined belief in the work ethic, and a war fought to preserve liberty ended with the Bourbon restoration. In all these ways, Britain's public virtue was undermined by the imperial economy that supported it. So too the ethics of many in *The Pirate* seem hypocritical in the face of their economic practices.

According to Leith Davis, the Waverley novels transform the physical boundary between Scotland's Highlands and Lowlands into a symbolic border that underscores Britain's 'heterogeneous history' geographically embodying the clash among Celtic, Roman, Saxon and Norman cultures.[9] I believe that Scott, while frequently using land as a border, in *The Pirate* considers the sea a symbolic physical boundary, because any border, whether land or sea, connects as well as separates peoples and cultures. These contested areas become what Mary Louise Pratt terms 'contact zones ... social spaces where disparate cultures meet, clash, and grapple with each other, often in highly asymmetrical relations of domination and subordination'.[10] This accurately characterizes the conflicts in *The Pirate*, which take place on or adjacent to the ocean which connects and separates Shetland's bourgeois and Udaller cultures, the colonial West Indies from whence the pirates come, and the colonizing mainland of Scotland itself. But Scott's focus goes beyond geographical borders to the borderline between past and present, mourning the passage of an earlier epoch of social order and responsibility. In that sense, Scott seems to be looking forward and backward simultaneously. On the one hand, as Miranda Burgess observes, Scott advocates 'retrogression, an ideology of return brought about by an eruption of energies linked with ancient magic, pre-commercial domesticity, and organic feudal tradition'.[11] On the other hand, though, Scott shares the Whigs' goal of offering 'a model for the United Kingdom in which lasting peace and social cohesion lock in the best of all possible improvements.'[12] Scott's fiction, then, tries not to valorize the past, but to write a genealogy of the present, to ascertain how the present came to be. Fascinated with the temporal, he inquires into the ways social systems function over time, hence his faith in the rule of law.

The Pirate illustrates Scott's anxiety about order and about the boundary as the maintainer of that order. The pirate, a border figure, serves as the locus of that anxiety, revealing the criminality latent in the bourgeoisie. Cleveland resembles the legitimate island merchants who occupy an ethical grey area and sell illegally gained goods. He commits crimes, but Britain's middle class, profiting from a slave-based imperial economy, remains complicit in the seemingly more respectable crimes of empire. As a pirate, Cleveland resists excessive violence and restrains the cruelty of those around him. As a wooer of Minna, he aspires to hearth and home, until events make their union impossible. Consequently, throughout the novel, he straddles the margins of pirate and bourgeoisie, never entirely in- or outside either community. The law condemns Cleveland's piracy, though his actions seem no more pernicious than the worst of the islanders' offences, wrecking. To the island residents, though, Cleveland's wealth makes him socially acceptable. He also succeeds in changing occupations, illustrating the ease with which one can move from piracy to respectability. At the novel's end, Cleveland joins the British Navy, hoping to use his pirate skills 'for the service of our country'.[13] Only a short distance separates the pirate from the patriot. But are not pirates' values radically different from those of the public at large? Not if the public consists of an island community which survives by smuggling and salvaging, and allows men to drown in order to steal their wares.

Wrecking, by far the most insidious of the islanders' traditional occupations, can be defined as anything from the 'pocketing of articles cast up by the sea to the deliberate luring of vessels ashore'.[14] During an 1839 inquiry into wrecking in Cheshire, one witness said that '"[t]he greatest portion [of the] ... men call[ed] themselves fishermen ..."', while another added that though he was a long-time resident, he had 'neither seen nor tasted fish'.[15] The folklore of wrecking includes the story of a clergyman who, 'on hearing of a wreck, admonished his congregation who were rushing out of church to slow down and given [*sic*] him an equal chance'.[16] In Scott's novel, both pirates and islanders steal and sell their plunder for profit. As Francis Hart points out, the 'islanders' code concerning their right to whatever the sea brings them ... ironically makes them as piratical as the Pirate ... [They] persist in the ruthlessly mercenary belief that it is dangerous to save a drowning man. If there are no survivors, the ship is lawful plunder.'[17] More accurately, ownership of salvage reverts to the sovereign, usually in the person of the preeminent magistrate,[18] in this case, Magnus Troil.

In addition to wrecking, many of the islanders participate in the profits of smuggling. As Mordaunt struggles to revive the rescued Cleveland, he asks for assistance from Bryce, a travelling salesman of merchandise legal and illegal, who refuses to help for fear he will lose a chest of valuables on the beach nearby. Mordaunt exclaims: 'You cold-blooded, inhuman rascal! either get up instantly and lend me your assistance to recover this man ... or I will beat you to a mummy ... [and] inform Magnus Troil of your thievery, that he may have you flogged till your bones are bare.'[19] During a later scene in Magnus' residence, we realize the irony of suggesting that he will enforce laws against wrecking and smuggling. Magnus personifies conspicuous consumption, and his hall overflows with contraband, for the crime of smuggling involves not the poor alone, but all social classes. During a party, Magnus asks his servant '"has the good ship the Jolly Mariner of Canton, got her cargo on board?" "Chuckfull loaded ... with ... Jamaican sugar, Portugal lemons, not to mention nutmeg"', comes his butler's reply. They then drink a toast from 'a punch-bowl of enormous size, the gift of the captain of one of the Honourable East India Company's vessels, which ... had there contrived to get rid of part of the cargo, without very scrupulously reckoning for the King's duties.'[20]

Just as islanders of all classes ultimately participated in the profits of smuggling and wrecking, so in Britain, during the Napoleonic Wars, some of the most respectable segments of society profited from the conflict. Throughout the war, trade continued between Britain and France, with French traders getting around embargoes by opening offices in London. Though most people wanted a short war and a good harvest to reduce food prices, some farmers and traders toasted to a long war and short harvest to keep prices inflated.[21] International trade, even between and among belligerents, proved too lucrative to be terminated. While the pirates' crimes remain blatantly offensive, the mercenary transgressions of respectable society become invisible. Privateers must reform, but war profiteers need not.

The practice of naval impressment provides another example of Britain's piratical values. Contemporaries recognized the hypocrisy when their society, built upon respect for property rights, neglected the poor's right to the property of their own bodies. People of all political stripes, from David Hume to Samuel Taylor Coleridge to John Thelwall, railed against impressment. In *Common Sense*, Thomas Paine argued that 'impressment [was] a reason for rejecting monarchy', and Benjamin Franklin believed that 'impressment was a symptom of injustice built into the British Constitution.' He wrote that if '"impressing seamen is of right by common law in Britain ... slavery is then of right by common law there; there being no slavery worse than that sailors are subjected to.'" Thomas Jefferson 'likened the practice [of impressment] to the capture of Africans for slavery. Both "reduced [the victim] to ... bondage by force, in flagrant violation of his own consent, and of his natural right to his own person."'[22]

Scott himself feared impressment during the 1814 lighthouse inspection tour on which he first learned Captain Gow's history. Britain had been at war with America since 1812, war precipitated in part by Britain's impressment of American sailors. Scott realized that he had no immunity from impressment, for despite his age and bad leg, he was a passable seaman. He contemplated 'what a pretty figure we should have made had the voyage ended with our being carried captive to the United States.'[23] The image of forced inclusion, which reproduces the dynamics of impressment, runs throughout *The Pirate*. The English pressed Triton into the army as a young man; the pirates hinder Cleveland's attempts at reform by forcing him to re-join their crew, and pirates kidnap the Troils.[24] Most explicitly, the impressment of a group of islanders into naval service reveals the popular abhorrence of the practice. When Mordaunt asks Bryce if any vessels have been seen, the peddler responds, 'None ... since the Kite

Tender sailed with the impress men. If it was His will, and our men were out of her, I wish the deep sea had her!'²⁵

The novel's dramatization of forced inclusion makes an important comment on contemporary society, for the functioning of impressment microcosmically reproduced the workings of Britain's imperial economy. The agricultural and industrial revolutions drove rural workers from farming into wage labour. Many of those farmers turned to the navy and merchant shipping as declining wages and hunger drove the poor to become sailors. Thus, if impressment forces reluctant inclusion in the navy, then Britain's economic policies reproduce impressment, driving unwilling labourers into maritime service. Consider the relationship among impressment, piracy and colonialism, three mutually dependent economic activities. Impressing seamen does to individuals what piracy does to ships; in each case, brute power enables possession of an unwilling individual or vessel. Colonialism operates the same way, removing the rights to self-determination and property from indigenous inhabitants and transferring them to the colonizing power. Impressment reproduces piracy as piracy reproduces colonialism.

In some ways, *The Pirate* revisits themes already encountered in Scott's earlier novels, which he generally sets during contentious historical periods and among divided peoples, telling tales that begin with division and end in integration. As Davis points out, 'Scott's novels present a complicated view of ... Scottish and English identity, showing the existence of difference within the ostensible picture of national unity.'²⁶ *Waverley* takes place during the 1745 Jacobite rebellion, in which Scottish Highlanders supported by the French fought to replace Britain's Protestant Hanoverian kings with the ousted Catholic Stuart monarchy. The rebellion ended with the defeat of the Highlanders and the decimation of clan power. Similar themes recur in *Ivanhoe*, which tells of the strife between indigenous Saxons and invading Normans after the Conquest. The romances that conclude these novels offer a way to interpret the one that closes *The Pirate*'s narrative, uniting Mordaunt, the outsider son of a pirate, with Brenda, the indigenous heiress to Magnus' Norse bloodline. In all three novels, the pattern of inclusion and exclusion reflects the tenuous state of Scotland's Union with England. In *The Pirate*, however, Scott's introduction of particular elements of pre-feudal property law gives that allegory greater specificity.

Attention to when *The Pirate* is set and when it was written clarifies the political issues at stake. Scott set the novel around 1700, and its characters lived during the 1707 Act of Union, which bound Scotland with England and Wales to form Great Britain. At the time, expectations that the Act would meld English and Scottish identities into a British nation initially evoked scepticism. As Linda Colley writes, the 'idea that Scots and English were "all one" would have been virtually unthinkable back in 1707, and not much more congenial ... even sixty years later.'[27] Though the Act of Union eliminated customs duties on trade across the border, a power differential existed between the two nations. England's larger economy translated into greater political clout. As the contemporary phrase the 'British Empire in Europe' makes clear, England did not limit its colonialism to the Indies and Africa.[28]

Scott composed *The Pirate* during the uncertain decade of the 1820s, when activists called for parliamentary reform and broader voter eligibility. Their demands at times verged on insurrection. E.P. Thompson describes the four years between Waterloo and Peterloo as 'the heroic age of popular Radicalism.'[29] Burgess emphasizes that 'internal divisions' remained in British society, and little unified the divergent groups of 'Whigs, anti-Jacobite Tories, and disillusioned former Jacobites' who supported the Hanoverian succession.[30] Radical action horrified Scott, who opposed greatly increasing voter eligibility, but who also realized that something must be done to address the era's social injustices.

To discover the ways Regency society understood the politics of Scott's novels, one need only read contemporary reviews. For instance, consider the anonymous review of *The Pirate*, published 30 December 1821 in Leigh Hunt's radical *Examiner*,[31] in which the reviewer's vocabulary strikingly calls to mind the polemical confrontation thirty years earlier between Edmund Burke and Thomas Paine. While discussing *The Pirate*, the reviewer evokes Burke's ideas about tradition, habit, prejudice and government as expressed in his 1790 *Reflections on the Revolution in France* and echoes the response Paine made in his 1791 *Rights of Man*. For instance, commenting on *The Pirate*'s satire of agricultural improvement, the reviewer writes that 'ridicule of mere theory as opposed to practice is fair enough; but is a bad plough, like a vicious mode of government, to be retained simply because it is ancient.'[32] But Burke, not Scott, advocates retaining a government because of its antiquity. For Burke, the best government has evolved over time, a product of change and continuity, war and peace, famine and surplus. He likens the English government as organized in the settlement of 1688 to a forest of sturdy oaks or to 'the foundations of a noble and venerable castle',[33] popular 18th-century symbols of common law as described by Blackstone, among others.

When analysing Scott's portrayal of the conflict between traditional and modern society, the reviewer claims that readers of *The Pirate* 'might be led to regard all improvement as useless innovation; and to sanctify ignorance and prejudice as estimable per se. Notions and habits are too often

exalted by Sir Walter Scott into principles.'[34] While reformers might consider the word 'prejudice' pejorative, readers of Burke would find it laud-
able. In his *Reflections*, Burke writes: 'We fear God; we look up with awe
to kings; with affection to parliaments; with duty to magistrates; with rev-
erence to priests; and with respect to nobility. Why? Because ... it is natural
to be affected ... we cherish [these feelings] because they are prejudices.'[35]

Paine takes Burke to task on exactly these points. Paine condemns
Burke's prejudice in favour of monarchy, believing a traditional government authorized by the past to be inferior to one ratified by voters in the
here and now. Paine declares: 'Every age and generation must be as free to
act for itself, in all cases, as the ages and generations which preceded it ...
The parliament of 1688 might as well have passed an act to have authorized
themselves to live for ever, as to make their authority live for ever.'[36] Burke
claims to be moved to awe by nobility, and his description of Marie
Antoinette during the storming of the palace at Versailles leads him to
exclaim that 'the age of chivalry is gone.'[37] In the years to come, however,
the age of chivalry will live on in Scott's novels, particularly *Ivanhoe* and
The Talisman. This pinpoints the real issue for the *Examiner* reviewer,
which brings together Scott, Burke and Paine in such an intriguing constellation.

It may be true, as McMaster states, that Scott's 'politics were designed
for implementation of a social order that was to remain the same, if more
justly the same',[38] but the ways Scott sought that justice had a Whiggish
strain to them. For instance, as a solution to reforming the Poor Laws, Scott
suggested public works projects and an income tax, not conservative Tory
positions. He 'advocated an income tax upon manufacturers, regulated in
proportion to the number of hands normally employed, with the funds obtained being devoted to relief, education, and public works.'[39]

The *Examiner*, in its review of *The Pirate*, condemns Scott for
nostalgically longing for feudal values. While Scott realizes that those
values provided community and prosperity, he also realizes that they were
imperfect and have been superseded, for better or worse, by employer-
employee wage relationships. For Scott most deplored the new generation
of capitalist factory operators, who hired and fired workers depending on
the economic cycles, who 'herded workmen into city slums and then left
them stranded and helpless there when business fell off and ... [who] could
discharge them and have no further obligation toward them.'[40] Scott
recognizes the conflict between two lifestyles, one agrarian and traditional,
the other industrial and reformist. He condemns the abuses of industrial
capitalism, and laments the passing of the feudal order, not because it was
perfect, but because of its social cohesion.

The Pirate, whose narrative acknowledges that the ethical basis of social relations has changed, presents two alternative political models that address inequities of power and property. First, Scott presents an image of piracy as republicanism. During the early 18th century, piracy flourished for many reasons, in part because the socialistic nature of pirate communities made them attractive alternatives to conventional shipboard life. In contrast to the 'near-dictatorial arrangement of command in the merchant service and the Royal Navy', the pirate ship's 'hallmark was a rough, improvised, but effective egalitarianism that placed authority in the collective hands of the crew.' Pirate crews elected their captains, allocated authority, distributed plunder, and enforced discipline. They reached major decisions collectively and democratically by vote in council,[41] a process *The Pirate* satirizes. Pirate pay eliminated the hierarchic system used in merchant and naval vessels, and reduced pay disparity by dividing sailors into three rather than the customary twelve categories. Pirates also distributed the workload differently than merchant seamen, carrying larger crews requiring less work per sailor. Finally, since pirates lacked life or disability insurance, they placed a percentage of their profits into a 'common fund' to compensate men disabled or wounded and unable to fight.[42]

Given legitimate reservations about considering a criminal venture uto-pian, the pirates' social structure reproduces elements of ideal communities generally, looking back in time to those of the Levellers and Diggers during England's Civil War, and forward to those of social reformers like Thomas Spence and Robert Owen. Significantly, piracy combined the modern technology of sailing ships with feudal labour relations to create egalitarian, democratic communities. Moreover, pirate experiments at the margins of society reflected the political thinking at its centre. Arguably, pirates enacted several of the egalitarian practices discussed by Cromwell's New Model Army in the 17th century and advocated by the London Corre-sponding Societies and the United Irishmen of the late 18th century. For while such Enlightenment social theorists as John Locke and the *Philoso-phes* revolutionized concepts of political theory, pirates and colonial communities such as those of the 'Baymen' experimented with alternative forms of social relations, non-hierarchic and non-nationalistic.

In *The Pirate*, Scott satirizes these republican tendencies in a scene in the buccaneer council. The narrator explains that voting provides an op-portunity for drunkenness, during which a few demagogues join together to make decisions, then cajole the drunk or hung over into believing that they too consented to the proposal.[43] Swagger and emotion sway simple-minded buccaneers incapable of reason. I find it tempting to read Scott's satire of the bungling pirates' democracy as a satire of the bungling participants in the 1820 Cato Street Conspiracy. Led by Arthur Thistelwood, the rebels planned to kill Cabinet members at dinner, then announce a provisional government. Before they could act, however, an agent-provocateur communicated these plans to the authorities, including the theatrical speeches the rebels had practiced to deliver during the attack. The conspirators were apprehended and executed.[44]

Whether Scott based his buccaneer council on any specific rebellious act, the scene does reveal his concern about the ongoing movement to expand manhood suffrage. The reform movement's popular resistance heightened his anxiety about what Thompson describes as 'organized forms of sustained illegal action or quasi-insurrection.' These include the rise of Luddism and machine-breaking (1811-13), the East Anglian riots and Spa Fields uprising in 1816, and the Pentrige 'Rising' of 1817.[45] Scott had personal knowledge of popular uprisings, from his own experiences as a lawyer, land-owner and militia member.

In *The Pirate*, the early 18th-century colonial relationship between Scotland and the islands parallels the early 19th-century colonial relationship between Great Britain and Scotland. If republicanism offers no means for the equitable distribution of political power, what governmental structure might? The novel offers that of an allodial arrangement,[46] territories which David Hume describes as of 'free title' and not 'subjected to ... feudal tenures'.[47] Under an allodial or Udal system, according to Knut Robberstad, 'there exists no presumption of *functio juris* saying that the king or the crown has been the owner of the entire territory.'[48] This is the system that exists in *The Pirate* among Udallers like Magnus Troil.

Between the 9th and 13th centuries, Norse settlement of Orkney and Shetland introduced this pre-feudal system of land ownership. The Shetland Islands, which had been under Norwegian jurisdiction as Hjaltland before they became Scottish in 1472, retained the Norse 'language, folklore and legal system ... for centuries'.[49] As Scott explains in a footnote to *The Pirate*, Udallers, as '*allodial* possessors of Zetland [i.e. Shetland] ... hold their possessions under the old Norwegian law, instead of the feudal tenures introduced among them from Scotland.'[50] Norse law had been codified in the lawbook of Magnus the Lawmender and practised until the early 17th century.[51] Ironically, Scott names the fictional Magnus, a character who selectively enforces and violates the law, after a foundational figure of Norse jurisprudence. Scott's antiquarian interests led him to Scandinavian culture and sagas as early as his student days in Edinburgh, when he gave papers on 'Northern' customs and mythology at the Literary Society.[52] He studied at the University when William Robertson was Principal,[53] and surely knew his immensely successful *History of the Reign of Charles V*, which traces the evolution of feudal society. Robertson defines allodial possessions as unentailed lands, inheritable by the owner's children, over which 'the possessor had ... entire right ... and dominion[;] he held of no sovereign or superior lord, to whom he was bound to do homage and perform service.'[54] Consequently, as Barbara Crawford notes, the 'Dano-Norwegian kings had no control over the odallers' possessions and were not, in feudal terms, the superiors of the odallers', though they did have to pay *skatt* or 'payments of tribute' to the crown.[55] Allodial property, then, is neither a completely independent country, nor a feudal fiefdom; as such, an Udaller like Magnus presents an unusual model of sovereignty. This system of government has much to say for it, with Udallers both independent and connected. With Udal law as with piracy, Scott looks backward in time to find an alternative social system which addresses contemporary concerns. A confederation of equals, allodial incorporation offers a model of balanced power-sharing for the English-Scottish Union.

Ultimately, Scott's principal maritime novel dramatizes the myopia produced by social insularity, and the pirate serves as a locus, if not always the source, of ethical and commercial anxiety. A figure at the margin, the pirate marks the outer boundary of social and economic behaviour, and serves as counterpoint for and measure of the social centre's validated behaviour. But the pirate as border cannot be maintained because society in general evidences and even applauds piratical values and behaviours. Cleveland as pirate, a criminal and adventurer, must be condemned. But he also accumulates capital, and a society admiring his wealth blinds itself to the ways he acquired it. The islanders' fear of outsiders raises anxieties about borderlines - national, social, economic, ethical - which the pirate violates. The islanders' parochialism leads them to colour foreigners with the symbolic capital of Otherness, itself a function of fear, but with economic implications which shield them from ethical inconsistencies. The ships which run aground on their shores belong to outsiders. Smuggling goods steals only from the government on the Scottish mainland, perhaps the ultimate outsider to this island community. The human cost of their unauthorized salvage trade shows how economic self-interest blinds the islanders to ethical responsibility. The folklore that rescuing drowning men brings bad luck justifies murder by inaction. Crime permeates the island's social fabric and indicts the entire cultural community.

Most significantly, however, the community fails to recognize these ethical contradictions. This mirrors the predicament of Regency Britain's bourgeoisie, blind to the imperial violence that supported its lifestyle. Scott's individual characters also symbolize social collectives, though, enabling his works to be read as a sort of political parable. Still, *The Pirate* begins with social division and ends with national reintegration. Scott recognizes the corruption of Regency society, but his solution leans neither toward *laissez-faire* capitalism nor radical republicanism, but advocates the enlightened monarchism of *noblesse oblige*, ideally with the independence seen in allodial relationships.

Notes

1   Walter Scott, *The Journal of Sir Walter Scott 1825-32. From the Original Manuscript at Abbotsford* (Edinburgh: Davis Douglas, 1891), 718.
2   Edgar Johnson, *Sir Walter Scott: The Great Unknown* (New York: Macmillan, 1970), 492.
3   Writers like James Fenimore Cooper have resisted defining *The Pirate* as a maritime novel because it focuses primarily on the pirate's shoreside relationships, rather than his shipboard experiences. See Thomas Philbrick, *James Fenimore Cooper and the Development of American Sea Fiction* (Cambridge, MA: Harvard University Press, 1961), 14. I disagree, as Scott's novel gives us glimpses into the lives of the Orkney Island fishermen, incorporates a dramatic whaling episode, as well as scenes of kidnapping and the pirates' council which take place on board ship.
4   Graham McMaster, *Scott and Society* (Cambridge: Cambridge University Press, 1981), 77.
5   The exact date of the novel's narrative remains elusive. In the 'Advertisement' to the 1831 edition, Scott, under his pseudonym the 'Author of Waverley' dates Gow's arrival at the Orkney Islands as 1724-25. Walter Scott, 'Advertisement', *The Pirate* (Edinburgh: William Paterson, 1886), 5-6. Johnson, however, sets the novel's action 'around 1700'. *Sir Walter Scott*, 816.
6   Mertoun does not acknowledge the murder explicitly, but when asked if he murdered her for perceived infidelity, he replies that he did what was necessary.
7   Coleman Parsons suggests that this belief may come from the physical danger involved in the rescue, 'desire for undisputed possession of flotsam, or [fear of the] vengefulness of water-monsters deprived of their prey'. *Witchcraft and Demonology in Scott's Fiction* (Edinburgh: Oliver & Boyd, 1964), 253.
8   Johnson, *Sir Walter Scott*, 816-21.
9   Leith Davis, *Acts of Union: Scotland and the Literary Negotiation of the British Nation, 1707-1830* (Stanford: Stanford University Press, 1998), 154.
10   Mary Louise Pratt, *Imperial Eyes: Travel Writing and Transculturation* (New York: Routledge, 1992), 4.
11   Miranda Burgess, *British Fiction and the Production of Social Order, 1740-1830* (Cambridge: Cambridge University Press, 2000), 203.
12   Davis, *Acts of Union*, 157.
13   Walter Scott, *The Pirate* (Edinburgh: William Paterson, 1886), 446.
14   John Rule, 'Wrecking and Coastal Plunder', Douglas Hay *et al.*, *Albion's Fatal Tree: Crime and Society in Eighteenth-Century England* (New York: Pantheon, 1975), 167-88, 169.
15   *Ibid.*, 173.
16   *Ibid.*, 184.
17   Francis Hart, *Scott's Novels: The Plotting of Historical Survival* (Charlottesville: University Press of Virginia, 1966), 300-301.

18   Rule, 'Wrecking and Coastal Plunder', 177-8.
19   Scott, *The Pirate*, 85.
20   *Ibid.*, 149.
21   See Boyd Hilton, *Corn, Cash, Commerce: The Economic Policies of the Tory Governments 1815-1830* (Oxford: Oxford University Press, 1977).
22   Jesse Lemisch, 'Jack Tar in the Streets: Merchant Seamen in the Politics of Revolutionary America', *William and Mary Quarterly* 25, no. 3 (1968), 371-407, 383, 386, 394, 389.
23   Scott, 'Introduction', *The Pirate*, 1-4, 2.
24   Scott, *The Pirate*, 102, 363-5, 380-82.
25   *Ibid.*, 164.
26   Davis, *Acts of Union*, 157.
27   Linda Colley, *Britons: Forging the Nation 1701-1837* (London: Vintage, 1996), xi.
28   C.A. Bayly, *Imperial Meridian: The British Empire and the World 1780-1830* (London: Longman Group, 1989), 6.
29   E.P. Thompson, *The Making of the English Working Class* (New York: Vintage, 1966), 603.
30   Burgess, *British Fiction and the Production of Social Order*, 18-19.
31   According to John O. Hayden, the 'review is signed "Q.", a probable indication that it was written by Albany Fonblanque, later editor of the *Examiner*'. '*Examiner*, 30 December 1821', *Scott: The Critical Heritage*, ed. John O. Hayden (New York: Barnes & Noble, 1970), 256-60, 256.
32   *Ibid.*, 258.
33   Edmund Burke, *Reflections on the Revolution in France* (Harmondsworth: Penguin, 1986), 181, 121.
34   Hayden, '*Examiner*, 30 December 1821', 258.
35   Burke, *Reflections*, 182-3.
36   Thomas Paine, *Rights of Man* (New York: Penguin, 1985), 41, 44.
37   Burke, *Reflections*, 170.
38   McMaster, *Scott and Society*, 100.
39   Edward Wagenknecht, *Sir Walter Scott* (New York: Continuum, 1991), 180.
40   *Ibid.*
41   Marcus Rediker, *Between the Devil and the Deep Blue Sea. Merchant Seamen, Pirates, and the Anglo-American Maritime World, 1700-1750* (Cambridge: Cambridge University Press, 1987), 262-3, 261.
42   *Ibid.*, 254-87.
43   Scott, *The Pirate*, 359-65.
44   Thompson, *The Making of the English Working Class*, 700-710.
45   *Ibid.*, 63, 389.
46   I am deeply indebted to Prof. James Muldoon for suggestions regarding contemporary discussion of allodial possessions. Those seeking to engage the current debate should see Susan Reynolds, *Fiefs & Vassals: The Medieval Evidence Reinterpreted* (Oxford: Clarendon Press, 1995).
47   David Hume, 'Appendix II - The Feudal and Anglo-Norman Government and Manners', *The History of England from the Invasion of Julius Caesar to the Revolution in 1688* (New York: Liberty Classics, 1983), vol. 1, 455-88, 459.
48   Knut Robberstad, 'Udal Law', Donald J. Withrington (ed.), *Shetland and the Outside World 1469-1969* (Oxford: Oxford University Press, 1983), 59.
49   James Reed, *Sir Walter Scott: Landscape and Locality* (London: Athlone Press, 1980), 139, 144.
50   Scott, *The Pirate*, 13n1.
51   See Donald J. Withrington, 'Introduction', Withrington (ed.), *Shetland and the Outside World*, 1-7.

52   Reed, *Sir Walter Scott*, 140.
53   Johnson, *Sir Walter Scott*, 57.
54   William Robertson, *The History of the Reign of the Emperor Charles V, with a View of the Progress of Society in Europe; From the Subversion of the Roman Empire, to the Beginning of the Sixteenth Century* (New York: Harper & Brothers, 1838), 507-8n8.
55   Barbara Crawford, 'The Pledging of the Islands in 1469: the Historical Picture', Withrington (ed.), *Shetland and the Outside World*, 32-48, 45.

6 Death by Water: The Theory and Practice of Shipwrecking

INA HABERMANN

I

Laurence Coupe begins his recent book on myth by identifying four mythic paradigms - the 'fertility myth', the 'creation myth', the 'myth of deliverance' (following Northrop Frye), and the 'hero myth' - which can be exemplified, respectively, in stories from ancient Egypt (the love of Isis and Osiris), Mesopotamia (the struggle between Tiamat and Marduk), Israel (Moses' parting of the Red Sea), and Greece (the deeds of Perseus).[1] The focus on narrative induces Coupe to add the fifth paradigm of 'literary myth', or 'mythic literature' (exemplified in a story from early modern England, Shakespeare's *The Tempest*), which presupposes an 'overarching framework of fertility, cosmology, deliverance and superhuman heroism'.[2] Comparing his five stories, Coupe notes that 'the obviously common factor is the symbolism of the sea, in each case associated paradoxically with both death and new life ... Such a symbol is recurrent enough to be called an "archetype" (literally, an original image, or founding figure).'[3] In this essay I will take my cue from Coupe to make this archetype central to a project of mythography. More specifically, the focus will be on shipwreck as an important aspect of the symbolism of the sea.

Shipwreck as the potential, if not inevitable, result of the sea-voyage of life is a prominent image in philosophical discourse. Rather than striving for philosophical abstraction and unwittingly succumbing to the logic of the image, however, I will focus on the image itself, trying to keep in view both its 'timeless' quality as a negative version of Coupe's third mythic paradigm, the 'myth of deliverance', and its specificity and variety as a historical practice. The latter aspect also leads to a consideration of wrecking as an *activity*. I will offer a historical reading of the myth of shipwrecking on the various but intrinsically related levels of philosophical thinking, historical practice and (mythopoeic) literary representation.[4]

The philosopher Hans Blumenberg has famously traced the changes that the metaphor of the 'shipwreck with spectator' has undergone in philosophical discourse from antiquity to modernity.[5] Sailing and shipwreck as images of 'being' have a venerable history based on the simple paradox that, while human beings live on the earth, they conceptualize life as a perilous sea-voyage and connect their existence with the element water. From classic to early modern times, philosophers emphasized the aspect of transgression involved in challenging the foreign element, a transgression implying the probability of failure or retribution, that is, the probability of shipwreck. With his dictum 'Vous êtes embarqué', Blaise Pascal gives what Blumenberg calls 'the nautic metaphor' a new turn in the early modern period: to live means already to be on board - there is no initial decision to travel since the journey has always already begun. Nietzsche later takes up this thought and carries it to an existentialist conclusion: not only is life a sea-voyage, but we are always already wrecked.

As Blumenberg shows, the metaphor of shipwreck has always been connected to the idea of a spectator. Lucretius, drawing on Epicurean philosophy, explains his concept of happiness in terms of such a spectator who becomes aware of the absence of personal pain and hurt while watching others go down. Much has been made by later philosophers of the position of this spectator. His moral standing, for instance, was a prominent subject of debate. Is the curiosity of watching, even if no help can be given, morally sound? Thinkers like Voltaire interpreted this curiosity as a passionate drive, thereby disputing the disinterestedness of any spectator and somehow implicating him in the action. While Goethe simply expresses contempt for the spectator, in idealist philosophy there is a tendency to completely exculpate the looker-on whose position allows him to see the individual loss and calamity as a means in a higher order of things - distance becomes a precondition of self-knowledge. This is a problematic twist for Blumenberg because it philosophically justifies the cruelty of indifference in the face of suffering. Herder conceives of shipwreck as a didactic spectacle directed by Providence, though chances are that the spectator himself might be cast into the water by some evil spirit. Schopenhauer finally equates shipwrecked and spectator, the faculty of reason putting men in a position to observe their own calamity. In his distance from nature and from himself, the (male?) spectator gains the experience of transcendence. These philosophical reflections conceive of the development and definition of the self as a spectacle reminiscent of the Lacanian mirror stage, although the spectator does not experience *jouissance* through the identification with an ideal self, but through the perception of distance from an afflicted self. This appears to me as a rather dire vision of an isolated creature poised between tragedy and farce.

II

The theatricality of the shipwreck observed suggests a relation with theatre, an institution which had always emphasized its mirroring function. Safely seated - or standing - the audience watches the calamities of others from a privileged vantage point. The moral or didactic dimension is obvious, but moving the spectator from the shore to the theatre also implies a shift towards the aesthetic and the fictional. By taking away the moral rigours placed on the reactions and thoughts of somebody witnessing a real catastrophe, the simulation of shipwreck with spectator on stage supplies both the spectacle and the distance necessary for self-interrogation. Although Blumenberg does not mention this particular text, I suggest that Shakespeare's *The Tempest* interrogates the philosophical metaphor of the shipwreck with observer in ways which prefigure the philosophical debate that, in Blumenberg's summary at least, postdates the play.[6] In the prologue, the audience has to face a storm and the existential fears of those threatened by drowning; the cry 'Boatswain!' (1.1.1)[7] opening the play could be taken as an appeal to God who steers the world through the universe. The play immediately establishes different layers of reality: the audience know that this is no real storm, but they think it is supposed to be one in the world of the play. In this, they are as deceived as the spectator on stage, Miranda, whose empathy for the victims is not called for - she is informed that her father Prospero ordered the storm for a higher purpose. Neither to the victims nor to the spectator is this initially transparent, but the experience is immediately put in perspective by the story of Prospero's own 'sea-sorrow' (1.2.171) when he himself, cast out of his dukedom of Milan, was helplessly adrift on the sea and eventually arrived on the island with the help of 'providence divine' (1.2.160). Thus, *The Tempest* offers a huge interrogative gesture - what is the purpose of the journey of life, where does it lead, and who directs the sail?

The island itself, strangely unlocalized as it is, soaked with and surrounded by water, is similar to a ship adrift in the ocean, and a ship of fools for that matter. The 'real', the imagined, outward and inward storms which drive all beings to madness and despair may or may not have been whipped up according to some purpose, and those who are the spectators or who are inflicting pain on others in one moment may be subject to it in the next. Thus, on a very abstract level, the play presents an allegory of the world drifting through the universe, life as a sea-voyage, suggesting to the audience by means of an endless *mise-en-abîme* that they are implicated in the action, that their status as spectators may be, and probably is, an illusion. This impression is kept alive by the frequent false suppositions that are voiced by different characters. Some think they have seen with their own eyes how the king's ship was wrecked and the king's son drowned - this same son thinks he saw how his father was wrecked, and Prospero thinks he sees and controls everything with the help of his magic. When he is just about to tell Ferdinand, and, as it were, the audience, that what they thought they saw in the *masque* was only 'thin air' (4.1.150), he remembers Caliban's plot and is unpleasantly shocked into recognition of the fact that he himself is not omniscient.[8]

At this point, Prospero admits the treacherous character of all that seems evident and important to human beings, and he connects the nautic and the theatre metaphors in a sceptical pun: the 'insubstantial pageant' - the *masque*, also suggesting the moveable stage waggon - fades and leaves 'not a rack behind' (4.1.156). 'Rack' means 'cloud', denoting 'no remainder of a vision' (or a tempest, for that matter), but the word is also homophonic with 'wreck'. Read as a pun, the passage generates a double meaning in the nautic metaphor that Blumenberg also draws attention to: the surface of the water is as undisturbed when a vessel has progressed through it on a prosperous voyage as when the ship has sunk. Time and perspective limit the possibilities of human perception which Prospero tries to extend with his magic. When he decides to relinquish this magic, his book is laid to rest in the 'oozy bed' (5.1.153) of the ocean, 'deeper than did ever plummet sound' (5.1.56). Prospero's means of, and aspirations to, supernatural power suffer shipwreck - they sink down to a remote place outside the sphere of human life. But the renunciation of his magic is the basis for Prospero's improved humanity: 'with my nobler reason 'gainst my fury / Do I take part. The rarer action is / In virtue than in vengeance' (5.1.26-8). At the same time he acknowledges a need for the recognition of others - 'Gentle breath of yours my sails / Must fill' he addresses the spectators of his renewed sea-voyage, his audience, in the epilogue (lines 11-12). At the end of *The Tempest*, Shakespeare evokes the whole scope of the nautic metaphor: the 'shipwreck' of others observed in the relative security of the theatre might induce the audience to meditate on the nature of happiness, of being, of life, or the destiny of the world. *The Tempest* does not, however, allow such abstract reflections to create emotional detachment. The play ends with a personal appeal to the audience not to be indifferent, but, even in the face of injustices and legitimate grievances, to offer prayer and help for other voyagers, not only because they themselves could in the future stand in need of it, but from an intrinsically ethical stance - as Prospero says to Caliban, 'with human care' (1.2.349). *The Tempest* offers a variation of the myth of deliverance. Pushed in the direction of philosophical abstraction, the issue is indeed 'humanity', transformed (and improved?) by the powerful experience of near-annihilation in shipwreck. But the play also invites the audience to 'historicize', to take circumstance seriously. The 'insubstantial pageant', an allegorical spectacle which draws on classical mythology, is swept away to make room for Caliban's abortive rebellion. Thus, *The Tempest* also points to the power politics of Renaissance Europe, to racism and colonial expansion, and speaks to those still waiting for deliverance.[9] Historical specificity makes myth political.

The ethical stance is a conspicuous feature of a large number of shipwreck narratives, a particular type of travel literature which emerged in the late 17th century and continued to be popular in the following two centuries.[10] Margarette Lincoln argues that

> [s]hipwreck narratives record moments of crisis in which social conventions are tested in isolation from the conditions that normally support them. They are moments in which assumptions about divine Providence, about national character, about gender roles, about civilised behaviour, are placed at risk or thrown into unusually sharp definition.[11]

These narratives cater to a reading public's wish for gripping entertainment, but they are at the same time mythopoeic: seeking meaning in disaster, they offer a means to come to terms with a harsh reality. Since early modern times and well into the 19th century, thousands of mariners were shipwrecked and drowned each year. I suggest that a lofty ethical debate, entertainment through popular fiction and socio-historical reality may be fruitfully seen as elements of one discourse. My analysis deliberately cuts across generic and disciplinary divides in order to show that the accidents and cares of the everyday interact with archetypal patterns of meaning. In order to highlight the socio-historical aspect, I will not concentrate on tales of calamity originating in the works of 'divine providence', or chance, and the moral lessons to be drawn from them, but I will focus in this essay on more earthly factors which could, and did, influence the fate of those who ventured out to sea. I propose to shift the perspective from those suffering shipwreck to 'wrecking' as an activity. What if Blumenberg's 'spectator' on the coast was delighted at the sight of a ship in distress? What if he, or she or they, neglected to help the wrecked while helping themselves to the ship's cargo? And, even worse than that, what if the ship came to grief as a result of human intervention?

III

In his book *Cornish Seafarers*, A.K. Jenkin provides some information on wrecking. The term may denote no more than collecting the 'flotsam and jetsam which the sea casts up upon the coastline', but 'very different from this was the businesslike spirit in which wrecking was conducted in the more distant past.'[12] Originally, the right to wreckage belonged to the crown, but it was increasingly in 'the hands of the lords of the coast-lying manors',[13] as Jenkin states, and the local population also tried to secure what they considered their share: 'When Sir John Killigrew erected the first lighthouse at the Lizard in 1619, he stated that most of the houses in the district were built of ruined ships, and that the inhabitants were enraged by his action, complaining that "I take away God's grace from them".'[14] When the first light tower on the Scilly Isles was built in 1680, the Scillonians

> used their light to assist, rather than hinder, their relations engaged in the family
> occupation of wrecking. For over a century the St. Agnes light was a public
> scandal. Sometimes it shone brightly; sometimes so dimly that it could not be
> seen from St. Mary's; sometimes it was put out altogether.[15]

The population in the coastal regions was extremely poor, and most made a precarious living out of working in the tin mines. Jenkin quotes George Borlase, who stated in 1753 that the tinners left their mines when a ship was wrecked and that '[t]hey'll cut a large trading vessel to pieces in one tide, and cut down everybody that offers to oppose them.'[16] The lives of those who survived the actual wreck were additionally imperiled by the fact that English law defined a ship as 'a wreck of the sea' only when nobody escaped to shore alive. In his very useful historical overview of wrecking, John Rule gives the following account:

> Wrecking had been the subject of a specific prohibitive statute as early as the
> reign of Edward I ... An act of 1713 ... was designed to reinforce existing
> legislation. It stressed that part of 3 Edward I. cap. 4. which stated that where
> any living creature escaped alive out of a ship, that ship could not be regarded
> as a wreck, even by those who claimed the right of wreck in a particular
> vicinity. This act was ordered to be read four times a year in all the churches
> and chapels on the sea coast. ... [A statute of 1753] made it a capital offence to
> 'plunder, steal or take away, cargo, tackle, provision or part of such ship',

whether any living thing remained on board or not. It also made it a capital offence to beat, wound or hinder the escape of any person trying to save his life from the wreck, or to put out 'any false light or lights with intention to bring any ship or vessel into danger'.[17]

Despite such legislation, wrecking continued unabated; it rather increased due to the considerable expansion of trade in the 18th century. Wrecks supplied the coastal population not only with food, drink and goods to be sold, but also with the much needed timber for building. Wrecking in the sense of 'rescuing' cargo was a crowd activity, and people were always on the look-out for ships in distress. Cornwall was particularly notorious, but wrecking took place all along the coastline and on the islands. Sometimes, as Rule notes, thousands of wreckers would reach the shore the moment the ship hit the cliff, equipped with crowbars, buckets and the like. So wrecking was a huge problem for merchants and insurance companies. Tom Bennett states in his *Shipwrecks Around Anglesey* that

> Liverpool opened its first large dock in 1715 and soon developed to be a lead-ing port in the British Isles. The Liverpool Corporation sought improvements around the coast, lighthouses and coal burning beacons were constructed to identify the hazards. The Skerries had a beacon built upon it by private enter-prise in 1716.[18]

Lewis Morris, Customs Officer at Holyhead, carried out pioneer work in that he produced a detailed chart of the coast of Wales. He complained in 1741 that 'false charts serve but as false lights laid by villains along ye coast to lead poor sailors to destruction.'[19] Bennett mentions an incident where '[a] sloop the "Charming Jenny" wrecked as a result of false lights, near Rhosneigr and was robbed by the local people in 1773. Three men, known as "*lladron creigiau Crigyll*", *the robbers of Crigyll rocks*, were found guilty.'[20] In the first decades of the 19th century, a system of coast-guards and patrols of revenue cutters was introduced to prevent smuggling and wrecking, and rescue became more organized. Lifeboats were estab-lished and societies founded, first on private initiative, like that, for exam-ple, of the Reverend James Williams and his wife Frances, who founded the 'Anglesey Association for the Preservation of Life from Shipwreck' in 1828.

Of course wrecking was also a painful issue with those who felt in charge of people's souls. The Reverend George Charles Smith toured the countryside near the coast, preaching and distributing his tracts. He de-scribed his experiences in letters to wealthy citizens in order to raise money to employ an itinerant preacher for the region. On his tour he also visited two new lighthouses, and his account, interspersed with descriptions of his meals and his tearful exertions when preaching, gives a very good idea of contemporary paternalism:

> A light keeper attended us to inspect one of [the lighthouses]. The lantern is a fine object, exhibiting a number of superb argand lamps and silver reflectors. I entered into a religious conversation with this man, who ingenuously confessed that he had been a great sinner, but was just on the point of turning, and wished candidly to know my opinion of the right way; this, of course, produced much profitable conversation. On leaving him I walked to the house of the other light keeper, and took the liberty of opening the door, as I saw four or five persons standing in his room. I was surprised to find the room covered with pictures and caricatures many of which were quite obscene. I addressed him in the firmest tone of reproof and admonition, and reasoned with him as a husband, a father, and a man.[21]

In 1850, the Reverend Charles Crump published a poem called *The Morte Stone*. In his preliminary note, he states that 'an allusion to the wreckers who infest the shore of Morte Bay, arose naturally from the subject. The daring outrages of these lawless people have long been a source of just complaint, and they still continue unrepressed.' To him, the sons of Morthoe are

> ... a rugged race,
> Who tread their fathers' footsteps, and disgrace
> Their better fame, (if men say sooth,) to join
> With waves and rocks, from sea-wrecks to purloin;
> Plunder the dead, nor timely help afford,
> Unholy deeds, by God and man abhorred;
> Nor heed they warning; nor the chastening voice
> Of christian pastor, but as fiends, rejoice
> Amid the tempest's gloom, some sail t'espy,
> Nearing their rocks of death, nor heed the cry
> Of drowning men, eager to seize their prey,
> As rabid wolves; the vampires of Morte Bay.[22]

A petition for a new lighthouse signed by the worthies of the region is attached to Crump's poem. Methodists in particular were exhorted by John Wesley to desist from the sin of wrecking. The efforts to make the coast more secure continued throughout the 19th century. By the second half of the century, the coastguard had become much more effective: 'Like their close confederates, the smugglers, those who continued to indulge in wrecking found that nimble wits and a ready hand were increasingly necessary in order to evade the officers of the law.'[23] It is difficult to ascertain how often it actually happened that ships were deliberately lured to destruction - wrecks occurred frequently enough as it was. Jenkin, who is thanked by Sir Arthur Quiller-Couch 'for having, without prejudice or *parti pris*, reduced the old legend of "wrecking" to history and proportion',[24] maintains that the brutal wrecker is 'dear to the heart of the novelist' and that many sins have been attributed to the people of Cornwall 'in the pages of popular fiction'.[25] In his opinion it is 'an ironical fact that for the world at large, the deeds attributed by fiction to the wreckers of long ago still excite more attention than all the life-saving by which [the Cornishmen's] sins have surely been atoned.'[26] What might be the reason for this? In his brilliant book on the 'discovery of the seaside', Alain Corbin notes that '[n]ear the strand, that indeterminate place of biological transitions, the links connecting mankind with the mineral, vegetable, and animal king-doms can be seen with exceptional clarity. ... By the sea, the animal nature hidden in man erupts with particular ferocity.'[27] The issue is one of mythic proportions, since the wrecker represents the 'animal nature' (*homo homini lupus*) while the rescuer embodies the divinely heroic human capacity for self-sacrifice. So these two images of the human coexist, one the shadow of the other, in a precarious and uncanny equilibrium.

IV

Wrecking captured the romantic imagination. It did not lose its appeal when wrecking gradually ceased to be a social reality. In a collection of stories called *The Romancist and Novelist's Library*, William Hazlitt includes a gothic tale set in Cornwall in the 16th century, entitled 'The Wrecker', which contains many typical motifs: 'Terloggan, like the vulture, ever watchful for his prey, was more than usually observant of the signs of the heavens; nor was any one more capable than himself of discovering the most distant indications of a tempest.'[28] The wrecker, goaded on by his witch-like wife, lures a ship to the coast with false lights and watches, gratified, until all the sailors have drowned: 'Unmoved by the horrid spec-tacle (for the moon had broken from the clouds by which she had before been concealed), he stood awhile gazing upon the scene of desolation around him as if at a loss where first to begin his work of rapine.'[29] While he collects his loot, he discovers that one sailor is yet living. He strikes him dead, searches his pockets and takes a ring from his finger. Nemesis follows apace: back home, Terloggan discovers that the ring had belonged to his only son, a sailor. Distracted and guilt-ridden, he hurls himself from a cliff, and his wife dies some weeks later when her hut collapses during a storm.

The rugged coast, the wild and raging sea, the stormy night, an evil villain, violence, fear and greed, guilt and poetic justice are the ingredients of the wrecking tale, merging the picturesque and the sublime, and somehow, there is always a full moon. Gender roles are conventional: the principal villains are male while female wreckers spell particular depravity. The archetypal victim is a woman with a child in her arms, her long, loose hair streaming down her back. The stories are narratives of transgression, which makes them attractive to many readers, but the element of containment is strong. Conventional social hierarchies are hardly ever questioned, authority is usually depicted as benevolent, and the stories express a belief in progress, the worst abuses always being relegated to a distant past. Some tales use the gothic setting for a romantic love story, as the novel *The Wreckers* by Rosa Mackenzie Kettle or the opera of the same title,[30] others emphasize adventure, as J. Macdonald Oxley's *The Wreckers of Sable Island*. The hero of this story is the boy Eric who is shipwrecked and has to spend a dreary winter on an island with a gang of wreckers. Here, the principal villain is Evil-Eye, a brutal and superstitious drunkard. As many of his kind, he is haunted by *Macbeth*-style visions:

[T]he whole hut was suddenly aroused by an appalling yell from Evil-Eye. Starting up, his companions saw him, by the light of a moonbeam that strayed in through one of the portholes, rise to his feet with an expression of the most frantic terror upon his hideous countenance, as he shrieked at the top of his voice, - 'I will - I swear I will - if you'll only let me alone!' Then, throwing up his arms, he fell over, foaming, in a fit. ... It seemed that the evening Evil-Eye had acted so strangely he had been awakened from his drunken sleep about midnight by a startling vision. It was the form of a tall man in a military uniform dripping with sea-water and soiled with sand. On his face was the pallor of death, and his eyes had an awful, far-away expression, as though they were looking through the startled sleeper. Fixing them steadfastly upon Evil-Eye, whose blood seemed to freeze in his veins, he held up his forefinger as if commanding attention, and pointed to the bunk where Eric lay sleeping.[31]

True to the conventions of the adventure tale, Eric is instrumental in delivering Evil-Eye and his gang up to the authorities.

Daphne du Maurier, a successful novelist occasionally accused of producing middlebrow yarns, chose the gothic theme of wrecking for one of her Cornish novels, *Jamaica Inn*, which was first published in 1936 and is set around 1810.[32] Du Maurier was an avid reader of tales of adventure, and as the daughter of a well-to-do actor-manager based in London, she was at home in the world of popular entertainment and thus ideally placed to pick themes with a certain currency and popular appeal. However, the interest of *Jamaica Inn* in the context of my argument goes beyond du Maurier's skilful weaving together of the strands of the wrecking tale. She uses the gothic mode to combine the formula of the adventure tale with elements of romance, at the same time aiming for psychological realism and exploring the philosophical implications of the wrecking myth. In the remainder of this essay, I will read *Jamaica Inn* as a 'fiction of the sea' which integrates the various levels of the cultural myth of shipwreck.

V

After the death of her mother, young Mary Yellan leaves the English south coast and travels to Cornwall to her aunt, a frightened creature terrorized by a brutal husband. He is the landlord of Jamaica Inn, a haunted house on the high road between Bodmin and Launceston. Mary soon discovers that her uncle is not only a smuggler, but that he is part of a large organization of wreckers who muffle the bell-buoys and place false lights on the cliffs in stormy nights to lure ships to destruction. Once the ship has crashed into the rocks, the wreckers kill everybody who swims to land and dispose of substantial cargoes under cover of the darkness.[33] Once hallucinating in his drink, her uncle reveals his secret to Mary:

> 'I've killed men with my own hands, trampled them underwater, beaten them with rocks and stones; ... when I'm drunk I see them in my dreams; I see their white-green faces staring at me, with their eyes eaten by fish; and some of them are torn, with the flesh hanging on their bones in ribbons, and some of them have seaweed in their hair ... There was a woman once, Mary; she was clinging to a raft, and she had a child in her arms; her hair was streaming down her back. The ship was close in on the rocks, you see, and the sea was as flat as your hand; they were all coming in alive, the whole bunch of 'em. Why, the water in places didn't come above your waist. She cried out to me to help her, Mary, and I smashed her face in with a stone; she fell back, her hands beating the raft. She let go of the child and I hit her again; I watched them drown in four feet of water. ... For the first time we hadn't reckoned on the tide. In half an hour they'd be walking dry-shod on the sand. We had to pelt at 'em all with stones, Mary; we had to break their arms and legs; and they drowned there in front of us, like the woman and her child, with the water not up to their shoulders ...'
>
> His face was close to Mary, his red-flecked eyes staring into hers, and his breath on her cheek. 'Did you never hear of wreckers before?' he whispered. (116-17)[34]

Within the value system of the novel, small-scale horse-thieving is a petty crime, almost a misdemeanor, while smuggling is bad but pardonable. Wrecking, by contrast, represents the ultimate horror. The reason for this particular quality of horror, I would argue, is not the element of slaughter alone, but its mythical dimension and its connection to the nautic metaphor - and this is where my argument comes full circle, back to Blumenberg. Reading *Jamaica Inn* as an exploration of a cultural myth makes it possible to set it in the context of the philosophical discourse on the nautic metaphor. The mariners who have risked a sea-voyage symbolizing the risk of existence, come back to find that the land and their fellow beings have turned hostile to them; the spectators' faces, far from expressing compassion or detachment, glow with greed. Mary Yellan herself seeks to understand her journey to Cornwall in terms of a sea-voyage: 'She wondered if this was how a ship felt when the security of harbour was left behind. No vessel could feel more desolate than she did, not even if the wind thundered in the rigging and the sea licked her decks' (15).

In du Maurier's novel, the loss of all certainties about fellow humans is paralleled with the loss of the land's security. Mary frequently walks the moors that surround Jamaica Inn. This treacherous region is completely soaked with water. She wades through burbling brooks and tries to avoid the tufts of grass that promise comfort but would not hold her weight. Her uncle's brother, she knows, was drowned in the marshes. The moors in winter are reminiscent of the sea, sudden fogs rise out of nowhere, and the frozen ground sounds like shingle under Mary's feet. Once, Mary is surprised by the darkness and loses herself in the moors, overwhelmed with despondency. She is 'rescued' by Francis Davey, the Vicar of Altarnun, who promises comfort and help but who is later revealed as the mastermind behind the wrecking business, the most unscrupulous and deadly of all. He is a long shot from the benevolent and often pompous country parsons who preached to the coastal population.

The philosophical dimension is underlined by several other elements which subvert the conventions of the wrecking tale. Authority does not look particularly good in *Jamaica Inn*: the Church is infiltrated by a rather satan-like figure while the local squire has a modest intellect and needs the help of a horse-thief to clear up the crime. This horse-thief, Jem Merlyn, is the other man apart from Francis Davey with whom Mary forms a relationship, and both are associated with the moors, the existential testing ground. Jem, of questionable character, lives low down in the marshes close to the brook, but he proves a 'gem', a true merlin, while Davey with his mesmerizing ways, always high up on a horse, in a trap or carriage, whisks Mary away ever deeper into trouble. Morality, *Jamaica Inn* appears to suggest, is

like a walk in the moors: try to keep to the high ground but remember that
things are often not what they seem. Connected with this is another element
of subversion: the hero of this tale of adventure is a heroine, hardy, independent, courageous and unsentimental. At this point, du Maurier sacrifices
socio-historical for psychological realism. She all but depopulates
Cornwall; there is hardly any mention of a poor working population, and
the huge crowds eager for coastal plunder are nowhere to be seen. Mary is
alone, and the novel concentrates on her perspective as well as her
reflections on existence and her fellow beings. This existential dimension is
rooted in the soaked mythical landscape of the moors. Mary responds to
this landscape, which predestines her for her part in the wreckers' quest for
gain, meaning and power.

> The air was strong and sweet-smelling, cold as mountain air, and strangely
> pure. It was a revelation to Mary, ... there was a challenge in the air that spurred
> [her] to adventure. ... Strange winds blew from nowhere; they crept along the
> surface of the grass, and the grass shivered; they breathed upon the little pools
> of rain in the hollowed stones, and the pools rippled. Sometimes the wind
> shouted and cried, and the cry echoed in the crevices, and moaned, and was lost
> again. There was a silence on the tors that belonged to another age; ... And
> there was a stillness in the air, and a stranger, older peace, that was not the
> peace of God. (32, 38)

The notion of the coast as a liminal space is extended to the moors, and
these liminal spaces reflect the erosion of self-evident moral standards in
their blurred boundaries.[35]

Having taken refuge at the Vicar's house, Mary discovers a caricature
where Davey has drawn himself as a wolf preaching in his church to a congregation of sheep. 'I live in the past', he tells her when she has learnt the
truth about him, 'when men were not so humble as they are today. Oh, not
your heroes of history in doublet and hose and narrow-pointed shoes - they
were never my friends - but long ago in the beginning of time, when the
rivers and the sea were one, and the old gods walked the hills.' (243) Davey
knows that he is discovered and forces Mary to escape with him:

> 'We go by the moors and the hills, and tread granite and heather as the Druids
> did before us.' ... There was an old magic in these moors that made them
> inaccessible, spacing them to eternity. Francis Davey knew their secret, and cut
> through the darkness like a blind man in his home. ... 'The time will come when
> officers of the law will walk the coasts of Cornwall', he said. ... 'But tonight
> and tomorrow we shall meet no such interference; only the gulls and the wild
> birds haunt the cliffs from Boscastle to Hartland. The Atlantic has been my

friend before; savage perhaps and more ruthless than I intended, but my friend nevertheless.' (247-9)

Davey appears to guess Mary's every thought, and her fear of him is claustrophobic because he represents a primeval, oceanic oneness that threatens the boundaries of the self, clearly reminiscent of the Freudian notion of 'oceanic feeling'. Appropriately, Davey wants to make his escape via the sea: 'After today the Vicar of Altarnun must cast himself adrift from Holy Church and become a fugitive again. You shall see Spain, Mary, and Africa, and learn something of the sun; you shall feel desert sand under your feet, if you will.' (249) This renewed voyage, a new *plus ultra*, does not take place, however, since Davey is thwarted by the fog, trapped on a granite rock and hunted down, wrecked before he reaches the coast.

Allowing for differences of time and genre, there is a strange similarity between the Vicar of Altarnun and Shakespeare's Prospero. Both are wreckers, and wreckers of souls at that, overreachers masquerading as wise men. However, Prospero's Christian virtue is depicted as his saving grace. He turns rescuer, even as he himself needs to be rescued. His own forgiveness at the end of the play is to secure him pardon for all the suffering he has inflicted - 'As you from crimes would pardoned be, / Let your indulgence set me free' (epilogue, lines 19-20). For the Vicar of Altarnun there is no saving grace:

> I do not belong here, and I was born with a grudge against the age, and a grudge against mankind. ... When you know me better ... I will tell you how I sought refuge from myself in Christianity, and found it to be built upon hatred, and jealousy, and greed - all the man-made attributes of civilization, while the old pagan barbarism was naked and clean. (243-5)

Jamaica Inn offers a powerful account of the cultural myth of wrecking because it fuses philosophy and social practice within the realm of fictional representation. The residue of historical fact, charged with the emotional energy of a popular tale of romance, adventure and gothic horror, gains a symbolic quality. The mythopoeic dimension of the narrative is enhanced by the frequent evocation of archaic times. Conversely, the element of specificity and realism which makes the wrecking myth political in this novel is the aspect of gender. *Jamaica Inn*, as a *Bildungsroman*, focuses on the trials and the psychological development of its heroine. As Mary negotiates the rules of her world and learns to tell wreckers from rescuers, the wrecking myth is revealed to be gendered. In the role of spectator, Mary is morally incapable of the detachment of the philosopher, nor can she embrace the depravity of the criminal, but at the same time she is prevented from taking a rigorous moral stand by her fascination with the events and by her own emotional ties, her loyalty to her aunt and her desire for Jem Merlyn whom she believes to be implicated in the wrecking business. At one point, Mary squeezes through the window of the locked coach in which she is held captive and lies bleeding and drenched on the shingle. This symbolic rebirth marks her entrance into the adult world of responsibility and action. Thus, her position within the wrecking myth is not the traditionally female one of victim, or tacit accomplice, but she comes down on the side of the rescuers, choosing empathy and relationship.

Francis Davey, on the other hand, stands alone. He is a perversion of the Christian fisher of men, a Nietzschean *Übermensch* who, in his heroic nihilism, would not only scorn to evade a single cliff in order to postpone the inevitable shipwreck, but who also deduces from his purportedly superior insight the justification to lead others to destruction. Davey is an albino, and his extraordinary appearance figures the uncanniness of the wrecker masquerading as rescuer. Although he appears monstrous, he is a logical product of the nautic metaphor - an overreacher who seeks to emancipate himself from the ordinary patterns of existence. The myth of wrecking tells the story of the human desire to reduce contingency, to supplement and contradict the workings of both natural and metaphysical power, to load the dice, to spin the wheel of fortune in a deeply uncanny project of negative creativity.

Notes

1   Laurence Coupe, *Myth*, The New Critical Idiom (London and New York: Routledge, 1997), 1-3. I will make no attempt here to engage with the vast and complex field of myth criticism. Coupe's account is useful but should be supplemented with Ernst Cassirer's important notion of myth as a 'symbolic form'. Cassirer was among the first to see the specific structural quality and productive value of myth. See Ernst Cassirer, *Language and Myth*, trans. Susanne K. Langer (London: Harper and Brothers, 1946).

2   Coupe, *Myth*, 4, 5.

3   *Ibid.*, 4.

4   '"[M]ythology", the body of inherited myths in any culture, is an important element of literature, and ... literature is a means of extending mythology. That is, literary works may be regarded as "mythopoeic", tending to create or recreate certain narratives which human beings take to be crucial to their understanding of their world.' *Ibid.*

5   Hans Blumenberg, *Schiffbruch mit Zuschauer. Paradigma einer Daseinsmetapher* (Frankfurt: Suhrkamp, 1979). English edition: *Shipwreck with Spectator. Paradigm of a Metaphor for Existence*, trans. Steven Rendall (Cambridge, MA, and London: MIT Press, 1996). With respect to Blumenberg's thinking on myth, see also his *Arbeit am Mythos* (Frankfurt: Suhrkamp, 1979).

6   It is interesting that Coupe also chooses *The Tempest* as his paradigm for the literary myth, observing in passing that 'if literary myth takes the form of drama, it cannot escape the suggestion of ritual.' Coupe, *Myth*, 5. The mythopoeic character of literature, combined with the ritual dimension of drama, explains the importance of theatre in the context of cultural memory. The paradigmatically mythopoeic character of *The Tempest* might also go some way towards explaining the notable lack of imagery in the play. Rather than employing imagery - which is often taken from classical mythology - the play itself is the myth, and its own image, 'such stuff as dreams are made on'.

7   All *Tempest* quotations are taken from *The Norton Shakespeare*, ed. Stephen Greenblatt *et al.* (New York and London: Norton, 1997).

8   For an influential critical reading of this scene see Francis Barker and Peter Hulme, 'Nymphs and Reapers Heavily Vanish: The Discursive Con-Texts of *The Tempest*', John Drakakis (ed.), *Alternative Shakespeares* (London and New York: Routledge, 1985), 191-205.

9   For a historically specific engagement with the contexts of geography, travel and colonialism see Peter Hulme and William H. Sherman (eds), *'The Tempest' and Its Travels* (London: Reaktion, 2000).

10   Margarette Lincoln identifies the 'earliest collection of narratives of shipwrecks' as '*Mr James Janeway's legacy to his friends, containing twenty-seven famous instances of God's Providence in and about sea-dangers and deliverances* (London 1675)'. Lincoln, 'Shipwreck Narratives of the Eighteenth and Early Nineteenth Century', *British Journal for Eighteenth-Century Studies* 20 (1997), 155-72, 159.

11   *Ibid.*, 155.

12   A.K. Jenkin, *Cornish Seafarers: The Smuggling, Wrecking & Fishing Life of Cornwall* (London and Toronto: Dent, 1932), 75, 79.

13   *Ibid.*, 79.

14   *Ibid.*, 85.

15   Robert Heath, *A Natural and Historical Account of the Islands of Scilly* (London: R. Manby and H.S. Cox, 1750), 88; quoted in Jenkin, *Cornish Seafarers*, 87.

16   Jenkin, *Cornish Seafarers*, 90.

17   John G. Rule, 'Wrecking and Coastal Plunder', Douglas Hay *et al*, *Albion's Fatal Tree. Crime and Society in Eighteenth-Century England* (New York: Pantheon, 1975), 167-88, 167-8.

18   Tom Bennett, *Shipwrecks Around Anglesey* (Holmws: Happy Fish, 1995), 5.

19   *Ibid.*

20   *Ibid.*

21   George Charles Smith, *The Wreckers, or, a Tour of Benevolence from St. Michael's Mount to the Lizard Point* (London: J. Hill, 1818), 13.

22   Charles Crump, *The Morte Stone: A Tale of the Coast, Based on Facts. (With a Remonstrance Against the System of Wrecking; and an Appeal for Shipwrecked Seamen)* (London: Simpkin, Marshall & Co., 1850), 5. Crump, however, cannot resist including a footnote in defense of the clergy, stating that '[t]his censure is, perhaps, too severe, as regards the Inhabitants of Morthoe, whose character has improved under the praiseworthy exertions of the present Reverend Incumbent, who resides among them.' *Ibid.*

23   Jenkin, *Cornish Seafarers*, 109.

24   *Ibid.*, viii.

25   *Ibid.*, 119, 124.

26   *Ibid.*, 133.

27   Alain Corbin, *The Lure of the Sea: The Discovery of the Seaside in the Western World 1750-1840* [French original 1988], trans. Jocelyn Phelps (Berkeley and Los Angeles: University of California Press, 1994), 223, 225.

28   Anon., 'The Wrecker. A Tale of the Sixteenth Century', William Hazlitt (the Younger) (ed.), *The Romancist and Novelist's Library*, New Series, vol. 3 (London: John Clements, 1841), 1 (each text is paginated separately).

29   *Ibid.*, 2.

30   Rosa Mackenzie Kettle, *The Wreckers* (London: Thos. Cautley Newby, 1857); H.B. [Brewster], *The Wreckers. Cornish Drama in 3 Acts*, music by E.M. Smyth (London: R. Barrett, 1909[?]).

31   J. Macdonald Oxley, *The Wreckers of Sable Island* [1894] (London *et al.*: T. Nelson & Sons, 1904), 80, 82. See also Henry Frith, *The Wrecking of the Samphire. A Tale of Adventure* (London and New York: Frederick Warne and Co., 1886); R. Dixon Box, *The Wreckers of Havenford Bay. A Children's Operetta in Two Acts*, music by E.D. Beaumont Shepheard (London: n.p., 1901); Michael D. Gibson, *The Wreckers of Pengarth* (London and Glasgow: Collins, 1949). The similarities between Gibson's story and Alfred Hitchcock's 1939 screen adaptation of Daphne du Maurier's novel *Jamaica Inn* [1936] are striking enough to suggest plagiarism.

32   On Daphne du Maurier see Alison Light, *Forever England: Femininity, Literature and Conservatism Between the Wars* (London: Routledge, 1991), chapter 4; Margaret Forster, *Daphne du Maurier* (London: Chatto & Windus, 1993); and Avril Horner and Sue Zlosnik, *Daphne du Maurier: Writing, Identity and the Gothic Imagination* (Basingstoke: Macmillan, 1998).

33   The name of the house, Jamaica Inn, suggests that these cargoes are mostly the fruits of a prior injustice, namely the colonial trade. This is, however, more a historical than a critical footnote since du Maurier did not invent the name, and the implications of colonial trade are not explored in the novel. During an excursion with a friend, she visited the real 'Jamaica Inn' where she was inspired for her story, having also read Stevenson's *Treasure Island*. It is tempting but, I think, unwarranted to argue for more than a small element of 'exotic' *frisson* in this context. Du Maurier prefaces her book with the following note: 'Jamaica Inn stands today, hospitable and kindly, a temperance house on the twenty-mile road between Bodmin and Launceston. In the following story of adventure I have pictured it as it might have been over a hundred and twenty years ago; and although existing place-names figure in the pages, the characters and events described are entirely imaginary.' Daphne du Maurier, *Jamaica Inn* [1936] (London: Pan Books, 1976). In the context of narrative theory, this is a typical authorial distancing device which paradoxically serves to make the related events more real.

34   All *Jamaica Inn* quotations are taken from Daphne du Maurier, *Jamaica Inn* [1936] (London: Pan Books, 1976).

35   For an analysis of the coast as a liminal space see Corbin, *The Lure of the Sea*.

7 The Sea Is History: Historicizing the Homeric Sea in Victorian Passages

Tobias Döring

The broad survey over a thousand years of sea writing in English that Jonathan Raban offers in the introduction to his anthology[1] concludes with an example by the Caribbean poet Derek Walcott. First published in 1979 and programmatically entitled 'The Sea is History', this poem explores the ocean as an enigmatic site of memory which contains as much as it conceals mythological and material remnants of the past:

> Where are your monuments, your battles, martyrs?
> Where is your tribal memory? Sirs,
> in that grey vault. The sea. The sea
> has locked them up. The sea is History.[2]

As suggested by this opening stanza, Walcott's text sets out to question the potentials of the ocean to function as a storehouse of historical remains and their cultural reconstructions. Throughout this poem, Raban notes, 'the sea itself is the metaphor' of cultural experience.[3] Whereas previous writers of the sea regularly tried to find new descriptive and expressive metaphors as a mode to speak about their otherwise unspeakably sublime oceanic experience, Walcott seems to have reversed this process. To him, the ocean offers a powerful and concrete language to bespeak history and to engage with the material and political problems of historical representation.[4] In this way, his text may be seen as an incentive to think about the sea not simply in terms of mythical concepts nor treat it as mere socio-economic fact, but to search for links between these two traditional paradigms.

This paper tries to follow the agenda so suggested. My project is to trace some cultural strategies by which the sea is made a site of political activity while, at the same time, operating as an agent also of historical reviews in the Victorian era. I shall not draw on maritime fiction or the popular sea romances that played such a prominent role in the literature of the period (discussed elsewhere in this volume), but confine myself to lesser known, though not less influential texts that engage in contemporary reconstructions of the Homeric sea. Parts II and III each present and problematize a pertinent example, before Part IV, drawing on David Quint's theorizing of the epic genre,[5] tries to come to a conclusion as to the social functions of the Victorian discourse about Homer and the sea. Let me begin, however, with a cultural event in London, early in the Victorian period.

I

On 6 May 1839, the Royal Academy Exhibition opened and presented a painting that soon emerged as one of the most acclaimed and characteristic works of the period, J.M.W. Turner's 'The Fighting "Temeraire", tugged to her Last Berth to be broken up, 1838' (Figure 7.1).[6] An outstanding example of both his artistic and his patriotic standing, the painting ranks among Turner's best known pieces; he seems to have himself regarded it with such affection that he declined all offers to sell it in his lifetime and only bequeathed it to the National Gallery as part of his posthumous gift to the nation. The picture is remarkable for many reasons, not least for its topicality. Though otherwise given to remote historical subjects or, especially in his famous seascapes, to broad naturalizing visions, Turner here depicts a clearly recognizable and recent scene that had taken place the previous year. On 6 September 1838, the *Temeraire*, a 98-gun fighting ship of the Second Rate, after forty years of service in the Royal Navy, was auctioned to a London ship-maker and tugged upriver from Sheerness to his wharf at Rotherhithe. There she was to be finally dismantled. The event, much publicized in the contemporary media, was a routine and, from the Admiralty's point of view, expedient operation to discard of old and rotting ships as long as they could still be sold for the value of their timbers. But Turner's painting places this event into a specific cultural history of the sea that has occasioned enthusiastic responses from generations of viewers, writers and admirers. At the same time, it compels us to consider how historical mythologies relate to economic factors in the formation of maritime memories and their social functioning. As a central English icon, Turner's 'Temeraire' is fighting an epic battle against cultural oblivion.

This was evident already in the immediate context of its first exhibition. During the period when Turner's painting was shown at the Royal

FIGURE 7.1

J.M.W. Turner, 'The Fighting "Temeraire" tugged to her Last Berth to be broken up, 1838'

Academy, the real *Temeraire* - or rather, what was left of her - could still be seen and visited a few miles down-river at Beatson Wharf. This was such a popular pastime for Londoners that the huge, empty hull of the man-of-war became a favourite destination for crowds of visitors and connoisseurs. In actual fact, there was not much to see; but even with her fittings all removed, the once-proud and famous vessel still attracted visitors from afar. Launched in 1798, the *Temeraire* had seen her greatest day as early as 1805 when she fought next to Nelson's flagship in the Battle of Trafalgar and so attained a lasting aura of victory and naval glory. A generation later, after long years of peace, visitors now came in search of by-gone heroism to her last berth. Indeed, they came not just to look at her, but also to buy small pieces of her oak as souvenirs and tokens. As soon, therefore, as the ship was officially discharged from naval service and used for a more basic economic function, as material for recycling, she entered a cultural process of myth-making. Through social circulation her physical remains became national relics.

Turner's painting was instrumental in initiating and consciously shaping this process, as a number of pointed oppositions and reversals in his visual design suggest. For all its apparent documentary quality, the picture is clearly no example for Turner's 'truth to nature', later so prominently celebrated by Ruskin, but a carefully composed political statement of ominous symbolic import. The sense of contrast between the sun and the moon or the juxtaposition in colour and stature between the ghostly-golden *Temeraire* and the black-red steam-tug serve as powerful pictorial devices to establish the message implied in the title and already spelled out by the reviewers who first saw and described the image:

> The old Temeraire is dragged to her last home by a little, spiteful, diabolical steamer. A mighty red sun, amidst a host of flaring clouds, sinks to rest on one side of the picture, and illumines a river that seems interminable, and a countless navy that fades away into such a wonderful distance as never was painted before. The little demon of a steamer is belching out a volume (why do I say volume? not a hundred volumes could express it) of foul, lurid, red-hot malignant smoke, paddling furiously, and lashing up the water round about it; while behind it (a cold gray moon looking down on it), slow, sad and majestic, follows the brave old ship, with death, as it were, written on it.[7]

As in these lines, from Thackeray's famous letter in *Frazer's Magazine* (June 1839), the tone of both contemporary and later reviews of the painting is highly moralizing and elegiac. With the blame placed on the 'demonic' steamer, rather than the Admiralty who sold her in the first place, the painting thus becomes an epitaph to England's naval pride. But the emphasis on the 'foul, lurid, red-hot malignant smoke' suggests a more embittered reading: in Thackeray's response, the image of the glorious navy does not just fade away into a wonderful and distanced past, it is rather actively obliterated and upstaged by the effects of industrial modernity. The majestic warship has become an article of merchandise.

This reading clearly follows the artist's agenda. In the construction of the picture Turner purposefully subjected the established facts to his cultural design with no regard to the inconsistencies that this incurred. The sunset on the painting, for instance, is pointedly displaced. Not only was the tug, historically, carried out by daylight only, but its entire route up the Thames went from East to West - so, given the direction of the ships on Turner's canvas, the sun here sets in the East. Other details show an equally decisive if less glaring disregard for facts. The real *Temeraire*, at this stage of her career, would no more have carried masts because all riggings were removed before her auctioning and re-used by the Navy; there would have been strong cables between her and the steamer; and, most tellingly, the funnel of the painted tug is placed before the mast, instead of after it, as in real ship construction. All these are signs of Turner's powerful and pointed statement against the modern age. Epitomized in the rise of steamboats and the decline of sailing vessels, the transport media of the industrial age no longer allow for heroic associations. Steam and smoke deface epic grandeur.

The terms of contrast established with this image dominated English cultural debates and fictions of the sea for many decades to come - at least up to the late-Victorian age and Joseph Conrad. When in his *The Nigger of the 'Narcissus'*, published in 1892, the eponymous ship leaves Bombay harbour she is also hauled out by a steam-tug - in the very year that the diesel engine was invented.[8] Throughout the long Victorian period, Turner's 'Temeraire' prompted several literary responses that were, like his painting, directed against the rise of maritime industrialism. Among the many popular poems so inspired there is a ballad by Herman Melville, published in 1866 in his *Battle Pieces and Aspects of War*. It culminates in an apostrophe to the dethroned ship:

> O, Titan Temeraire,
>   Your stern-lights fade away;
> Your bulwarks to the years must yield,
>   And heart-of-oak decay.
> A pigmy steam-tug tows you,
>   Gigantic, to the shore -
> Dismantled of your guns and spars,
>   And sweeping wings of war.

> The rivets clinch the iron-clads,
>   Men learn a deadlier lore;
> But Fame has nailed your battle-flags -
>   Your ghost it sails before:
> O, the navies old and oaken,
>   O, the Temeraire no more![9]

What these nostalgic lines suggest most strongly is a powerful and pervasive sense of disenchantment. The elegy on the decline of sailing ships, retrospectively identified with the fate of the *Temeraire*, seems to function like a symptom that indicates a fundamental feeling of loss or bereavement. In this perspective, Victorian representations of the ocean can perhaps be seen as mournful attempts at re-enchanting sea-travel and reinvesting contemporary maritime culture with a romance lost. Rather than featuring recent technical achievements in establishing steam traffic across the seas - such as Brunel's *SS Great Western* launched a month before the *Temeraire* was tugged - many Victorian fictions of the sea were, to a great extent, set on historicization, modelled on familiar means of transport and in this way, as Raban has observed,[10] often aggressively reactionary. In cultural terms, the 19th-century ocean was thus defiantly kept up as an alternative to the machinery and regulations of the modern world, a sublime realm of elemental forces, heroic battles and masculine probation - a space, in sum, to escape from civilization's discontents.

How could this refuge be maintained? With the undeniable rise of new technologies to rule the waves, how could heroic powers of the sea be reinvented? In what ways was the nation's noble history of seafaring available or adaptable to the industrial age?

It is my claim in this paper that cultural reconstructions of the Homeric sea were used to recruit maritime memories as a transformative force against modern disenchantments. Against the background of the *Temeraire* mythology and history, I shall explore two different versions of Victorian Homer to argue that historicizing the ocean, in this context, offers a strategy to react against, if not actually withdraw from, the pressing realities and unsettling social changes of the time. When Melville's *Temeraire* ballad, in conclusion, claims: 'Your ghost it sails before', it pointedly reminds us of the survival, or revival, of cultural memories that continue to haunt the modern world, ghost-like substitutes for what seems to have been lost. I suggest examining such ghosts through a reading of two interesting, but little studied texts by key protagonists from either side of the Victorian political divide: William Gladstone, the Liberal Prime Minister, and James Anthony Froude, the Tory historian. Their texts - dating from the mid-

Victorian and late-Victorian period, respectively - invite comparison in that they both engage in ocean readings and sea mappings in order to engage with myths of Englishness and English masculinity, while trying to retrieve epic power for present purposes. And for both, Homer and the Homeric sea figure as the major vehicle of their projects.

To be sure, neither Gladstone nor Froude were active in the seafaring professions. Unlike, say, Melville or Conrad, they were Oxford men and scholars, who seem to have stayed on shipboard just as occasional passengers. Unlike Turner, who is said to have risked his life on board in stormy weather to study cloud formations, they engage just textually with the experience of the sea. And yet, I would like to consider their texts also for pragmatic uses and what Said once called the 'wordly' effects of writing.[11] Exploring their rhetorical manoeuvres, I shall argue that they combine philological, historical and political concerns to establish the Homeric sea as a space of national desire in adverse times of steam, trade and imperial rivalry.

II

During the summer of 1855, while out of office and on holiday in Wales, William Gladstone embarked on what a biographer describes as 'one of the most bizarre of all his intellectual exercises',[12] a monumental three-volume book entitled *Studies on Homer and the Homeric Age*. Published by Oxford University Press in 1858, the project shows a curious combination of philological empiricism with imperial desire. In a staggering series of comprehensive analyses and minute readings of the classic epics, Gladstone here dissects the old texts for what he takes to be the factual, encyclopedic information they contain about the remote world of archaic heroism.

In this context, he is especially interested in the wealth of geographical knowledge they offer: 'Nowhere is Homer's precision more remarkable', he explains in volume one, 'than in the numerous passages where he appears before us as a real geographer or topographer. Indeed, by virtue of this accuracy, he enables us to define with considerable confidence the sphere of his knowledge and experience.'[13] In the course of the inquiry we learn that such geographical precision pertains in particular to Homer's information about sea-distances and, based on this, the maritime topography of the world he shows:

> The distances of which I now speak are sea-distances. It is a somewhat remarkable fact, that Homer scarcely gives us land-distances at all. ... This

circumstance is illustrative of a trait, which assumes great importance in Homer's Outer Geography, namely, the miniature scale of his conceptions as to all land-spaces; a trait, I may add, to which we shall have occasion to return. The sea-distances of Homer are performed in no less than six different modes. 1. By ordinary sailing. 2. By ordinary rowing. 3. By rafts. 4. By drifting on a timber. 5. By floating and swimming. Sixthly, and lastly, the ships of the Phaeacians perform their voyages by an inward instinct, and with a rapidity described as marvellous.[14]

In this way venturing into intricate calculations and elaborate reconstructions, Gladstone uses the best part of volume three - more than six hundred pages - to conduct a topographical analysis of the *Iliad* and the *Odyssey*, so as to establish precisely in what spatial order they proceed. The result is documented in an actual map (Figure 7.2), a large illustration added at the end to represent the totality of the Homeric world. As Gladstone emphasizes, the chart contains precise locations for the convoluted plot and indicates the routes of all the maritime passages between them. With this final product of philological endeavour, Homer's epics are transformed into cartography.

Gladstone's map was not the first of its kind. As early as 1597, in the great age of map-making, Abraham Ortelius published a chart of 'Vlyssis Errores' in which he projected the putative course of Odysseus' voyage onto the available representation of the Mediterranean sea.[15] The opposite approach was taken in the first edition of the German Homer translation by J.H. Voß in 1797, offering a reconstruction, from textual clues and contextual information, of what Homer's idea of the Mediterranean might have been.[16] This corresponds, in method, to Gladstone's study. But where his project goes beyond such earlier versions is not only his quasi-religious faith in Homer, but also his densely contextualized and anthropological approach, claiming an unquestioned realism for the ancient songs and their spatial figurations. In a long and incredibly detailed argument, he spares no effort to measure sea-distances through the time of sailing, rowing, floating, swimming, drifting and rafting; to hypothesize the speed of travel and, hence, the distance covered by calculating the speed and direction of the four Homeric winds; to examine waterways and currents; to survey coastlines and landmarks - all on the basis of critical hermeneutics and with the avowed aim to provide a concrete and correct representation of Homer's maritime geography. What may have been the motivation for this passionate project?

Gladstone maps the Homeric sea in an attempt at recuperating heroic powers for the purposes of national education, for, in his view, the old epics should serve as manuals of contemporary masculine schooling. His

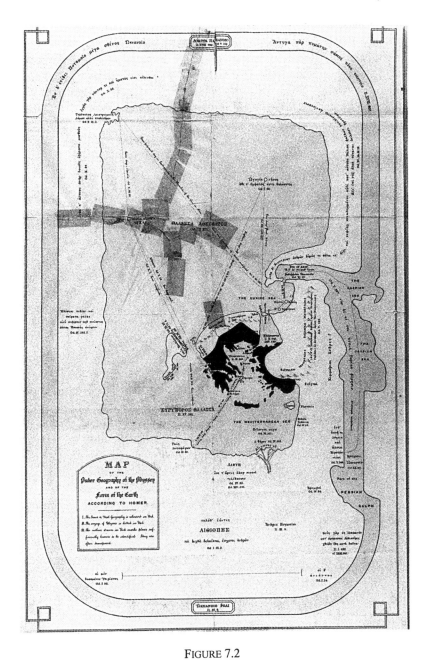

FIGURE 7.2
'Map of the Outer Geography of the Odyssey and the Form of the Earth, according
to Homer', W.E. Gladstone, *Studies on Homer and the Homeric Age* (1858)

philological desire to define and document the spatial order of the Homeric world, I contend, should therefore be seen in close connection to the con- current political project to define and shape a spatial order for the imperial world at large. For Gladstone, the world of Homer rather than of Roman statecraft contains the 'real first foundations of political science'[17] and, hence, the model also for the colonial empire of the English.[18] In his read- ing, Homer's ancient warriors are so strongly Anglicized that they operate as prefigurations of England's rise to power and colonial success. Glad- stone's liberalist ideology of Empire is modelled on the association of city states in ancient Greece, as opposed to Troyan Oriental tyranny or Roman centralism. Such immediate applications of Homer to topical concerns sug- gest the reason why, for him, Homeric study must lie at the core of national education and why he tries to construct a real link, even in geographical terms, between the ancient epics and the contemporary world. Gladstone's map delineates both Homer and contemporary imperial politics.

'Worked on Homer: finished the Iliad, say, 35th or 30th time; & every time richer and more glorious than before.'[19] This entry in Gladstone's diary, in November 1886, shows clearly that his Homeric preoccupations were no passing fad of early years, but formed a life-long passion and obsession, whose bearings on practical matters did not go unnoticed. When his *Studies* came out in autumn 1858, Gladstone happened to be on a delicate political mission to Corfu and the neighbouring Greek islands,[20] which since 1815 had been British protectorates. With his brief to maintain this status and his head full of Homeric echoes, he discharged this duty with a sense of felicitous conjunctions between philological and colonial interests. Two decades later, when he reviewed his Mediterranean voyage, he paid tribute to the contemporary Greeks, 'a race of hardy mariners',[21] in whom he saw the heroic spirit reawaken and align itself with the kindred spirit of the English.[22]

In fact, the final paragraph of *Studies on Homer and the Homeric Age* already emphasizes the beneficial effects that such academic activities may have on political affairs:

To pass from the study of Homer to the ordinary business of the world is to step out of a palace of enchantments into the cold grey light of a polar day. But the spells, in which this sorcerer deals, have no affinity with that drug from Egypt, which drowns the spirit in effeminate indifference: rather they are like the Φαρμακου Εσθλον, the remedial specific, which, freshening the understanding by contact with the truth and strength of nature, should both improve its vigi- lance against deceit and danger, and increase its vigour and resolution for the discharge of duty.[23]

However, this conclusion does not just posit the Homeric map as guide through the contemporary world. The imagery of the first sentence ('out of a palace of enchantments into the cold grey light') strongly reflects the more desperate sense of disenchantment which I suggested earlier is characteristic of the Victorian cultural condition. Gladstone's epic ocean map, like the Homeric pharmacy he speaks of, is proffered as a means to remedy such difficulties in coming to terms with the cold grey light of modernity. For, significantly, the map contains both the contours of the recognizable and real Mediterranean world - represented in red, i.e. the same colour as the British colonies in popular imperial world maps - and, directly neighbouring on, the realms of wonder and the marvellous of which Ulysses speaks in the account of his adventures.

The map therefore realizes what Gladstone concludes from his maritime calculations when he claims to have 'secured for Ulysses ... what sea-men call a good or wide berth; room enough for the disposition of his marvels, and the mystery of the distances between them'.[24] The point can best be understood, I think, as an attempt at offering comfort and cultural compensation. In the polar night of the mid-19th century, the map of the Homeric sea is to provide a 'good or wide berth' to accommodate remnants of the mythical and revivals of the heroic.

In this perspective, Gladstone's ambivalent charting of the Ulyssean adventures corresponds to a contrast between two earlier and rather more famous English representations of this ancient epic hero of the sea. On the one hand, Turner's 1829 canvas, painted ten years before the 'Temeraire', presents Ulysses' voyage in strong colours as a glorious image of promise and grand success, dominated by a brilliant sunrise (which Ruskin later juxtaposed to the gloomy sunset vision of the 'Temeraire'). On the other hand, Tennyson's 1833 well-known 'Ulysses'-poem sets the grim voice of the ageing and yet restless sailor, calling upon the former spirit of adventure in his crew, against a background of rapidly approaching dusk:

> The long day wanes; the slow moon climbs; the deep
> Moans round with many voices. Come, my friends,
> 'Tis not too late to seek a newer world. ...
> To sail beyond the sunset, and the baths
> Of all the western stars, until I die. ...
> Though much is taken, much abides; and though
> We are not now that strength which in old days
> Moved earth and heaven, that which we are, we are -
> One equal temper of heroic hearts,
> Made weak by time and fate, but strong in will
> To strive, to seek, to find, and not to yield.[25]

For all their call to perserverance and relentless urge, these lines are underwritten by a diagnosis of exhaustion. Most clearly this applies to the geography they mark. The comparative form of the adjective used here - 'a newer world' - points us to the dilemma that the Victorian voyager must face: in the totally mapped space of the modern maritime world, where are new worlds to be found? What oceans can still be explored? And what seas are left to answer the masculine imperative of a 'strong will / To strive, to seek, to find, and not to yield'?

It is as a response to such pressing and enduring questions, and with explicit reference to Tennyson's as well as Gladstone's vision of the Empire, that James Anthony Froude in the late 1880s embarked on a voyage to the New World in order to seek memories of England's naval glory that could be rendered in Homeric terms.

III

While Gladstone mapped the Homeric sea, on the basis of classical learning and philology, as a berth for the marvellous in contemporary English projects, Froude's interest in the sea, a generation later, is clearly historical: he regards the ocean first and foremost as a site of great naval battles. This is, of course, entirely in keeping with his professional duties as a historian. But we must also note that his interest in national and naval history is not simply archival, but equally strongly motivated by a current political agenda. Whether in his 1893 Oxford lectures on *English Seamen in the Sixteenth Century* (published in 1897), or in his notorious travelogue *The English in the West Indies, or The Bow of Ulysses* (published in 1887), on which I shall focus for the purposes of this paper, Froude's main concern lies with the future of the Empire and the shaping of connections between the mother country and her colonies overseas - a tie he wants to tighten and defend against Gladstonian liberalist misrule.

This is why the ocean plays a key role in his argument. For him, the sea never constitutes a wild, open space, undefined or untouched by contemporary politics, but on the contrary a powerful political reality. Suffice it here to cite one of his most popular books, the imperial bestseller *Oceana* published in 1887;[26] the title refers to Australia, New Zealand and South Africa, i.e. the English settler colonies which Froude proposed to unify under this common name and under strong British leadership.[27] In his vision, then, the ocean translates directly into imperial practice.

However, Froude was painfully aware that such translations in the late-Victorian world were fraught with serious difficulties and that the vital ties of oceanic politics were submerged. This is why he, at a late stage in his long career, embarked on a transatlantic passage to go in search of English naval glories, monuments of colonial success that his travelogue plans to bring home from the West Indies as an antidote against encroaching *fin-de-siècle* gloom in England. In *The English in the West Indies*, Froude tries to persuade his readers, in the words of Simon Gikandi, 'that his tour will serve to affirm the integrity of empire as a *symbolon* that unifies English people across diverse geographical spaces and endows them with a privileged identity.'[28] With this agenda, then, Froude travels to the colonial periphery as if to travel back in time: into a period where English power and maritime dominance were still unquestioned and intact.

To begin with, the plan seems to work well enough and his expectations are well met. When he comes to Barbados, the first destination of his voyage, he remarks with satisfaction that the market square at the centre of Bridgetown is graced with a statue of Lord Nelson - the symbolic presence of the great Admiral thus forms the focal point in the public space of the island. Just one feature in the colonial version of the hero of Trafalgar remains odd and irritating: as Froude notes, 'for some extraordinary reason they have painted it a bright pea-green.'[29] It is for these small but extraordinary differences between English cultural models and their West Indian replicas that Froude's travelogue makes rather more interesting reading than previous critics like Rob Nixon[30] seem to have thought.[31]

However, Froude's main historical focus is not Admiral Nelson and Trafalgar, important though they clearly are, but Admiral Rodney and the sea battle of Dominica in April 1782, when the Royal Navy destroyed the French fleet under De Grasse, won British supremacy in the Caribbean and, in Froude's own words, secured the survival of the Empire:

So on that memorable day [12 April 1782] was the English Empire saved. Peace followed, but it was 'peace with honour'. The American colonies were lost; but England kept her West Indies; her flag still floated over Gibraltar; the hostile strength of Europe all combined had failed to twist Britannia's ocean sceptre from her: she sat down maimed and bleeding, but the wreath had not been torn from her brow, she was still sovereign of the seas. The bow of Ulysses was strung in those days.[32]

These lines are not just remarkable for predicating the identity that Froude's journey set out to define entirely on naval dominance ('Britannia's ocean sceptre'), but also for framing the historical account, as the final comment indicates, in Homeric parallels.

Rodney's resounding victory, the story of which Froude finds occasion to retell several times in his travelogue, is so significant for him because it revives the glory of the Elizabethan sailors and adventurers, who laid the first foundations of the Empire, and invites renewed comparison to the Ulyssean heroic model that Froude establishes with the subtitle of his book. Whereas Gladstone's stringent realism sought Homeric legacies in the contemporary Mediterranean, Froude can only trace such memories displaced to the geography of the West Indies. He goes on his voyage to rediscover the New World and retake the islands in the name of English Homer. This project becomes evident early in the book when he declares that the 'Caribbean Sea was the cradle of the Naval Empire of Great Britain' and hence concludes: 'If ever the naval exploits of this country are done into an epic poem - and since the Iliad there has been no subject better fitted for such treatment or better deserving it - the West Indies will be the scene of the most brilliant cantos.'[33] The Homeric parallels here suggested form a conscious and consistent strategy throughout his text, culminating in the final chapter where Froude argues for a genuine affinity between ancient Greek and modern English culture - an affinity which he, not unlike his opponent Gladstone, explains through shared maritime experience:

> Our thoughts flow back as we gaze to the times long ago, when the earth belonged to other races as it now belongs to us. The ocean is the same as it was. Their eyes saw it as we see it. ... The sea affected the Greeks as it affects us, and was equally dear to them. It was a Greek who said, 'The sea washes off all the ills of men;' the 'stainless one' as Aeschylus called it - the eternally pure. On long voyages I take Greeks as my best companions.[34]

In this way, Froude establishes the sea as a *tertium comparationis* in order to use the language of classical battles as a repertoire of tropes to narrate English history, while Greek literature functions as a reservoir of topoi to describe contemporary colonial conditions.

Such rhetorical devices that the travelogue employs throughout are all the more important because Froude's text cannot avoid the impression that, in actual fact, there is not much to see on this New World tour. Touristic sights and natural beauties apart, the English West Indies have little to offer to the eye and are certainly not forthcoming with the historical significance they promise. This lack of substantial historical markers is acutely felt at many points of the journey, but never more prominently than in Froude's descriptions of the sea. Here, all the details that can be observed and visually rendered fall short of the grand epic visions they are expected to communicate, and must therefore be supplemented with historical narration, as in the following portrayal of the bay of Dominica, the actual scene of Rodney's victory:

> The situation of Roseau is exceedingly beautiful. The sea is, if possible, a deeper azure even than at St. Lucia; the air more transparent; the forests of a lovelier green than I ever saw in any other country. ... To a looker-on at that calm scene it was not easy to realize the desperate battles which had been fought for the possession of it, the gallant lives which had been laid down under the walls of that crumbling castle. These cliffs had echoed the roar of Rodney's guns on the day which saved the British Empire, and the island I was gazing at was England's Salamis.[35]

This passage illustrates the fundamental problem Froude must face in his attempt to historicize the Caribbean Sea. The fine rhetorical phrase 'England's Salamis', a condensation of 18th-century English and classical Greek naval victories, serves only to signify the dramatic absence of the desired spectacle. Whatever can be actually observed, as the introductory comments note, is entirely picturesque, a 'calm scene' totally out of keeping with the sublime meaning sought. So the observer must consciously inscribe such peaceful scenes with the heroic figures he is after.

The same problem, although at times with different premises, concerns the illustrations in his travel book. For instance, he presents us with a picture of Port au Prince on Haiti (Figure 7.3), a place where colonial rule has long been overthrown by black republicans and hence, as Froude obsessively points out, a realm of greatest horrors. The image, however, does not betray a single trace of the political abominations that supposedly must happen on this island. When Froude defies all warnings and himself ventures on land to stroll around a Haitian market, he takes special note of the butcher's meat on slabs: 'I looked inquisitively at these last; but I acknowledge that I saw no joints of suspicious appearance.'[36] In the same way, the picture of the black-governed island does not manifest any of the brutish practices his historical narration would suggest. Instead we see the maritime idyll of a peaceful harbour scene that cannot be visually distinguished from the hallowed scenery of Roseau. This is why Froude here must resort to literary and classic precedents: 'The island I was gazing at was England's Salamis.' As readers we bear witness here to the rhetorical manoeuvres by which the gaze of the imperial beholder must produce the sublime vision of naval history because, strictly speaking, there is nothing to see except a serene and deeply azure water surface.

This may also suggest the reason why Froude's narrative constantly resorts to Homeric parallels and so continuously displaces the West Indies into the Mediterranean. 'On long voyages', he tells us, 'I take Greeks as my

FIGURE 7.3
'Port au Prince, Hayti', J.A. Froude, *The English in the West Indies, or the Bow of Ulysses* (1887)

best companions.' This companionship, however, works by absence; just as the title reference to the bow of Ulysses cites an authority missing: no one can string the bow except the true lord and master, who, for the time being, has not yet returned.[37] The political analogy we learn lies in the fact that 'Penelope Britannia', after the long misrule of the Whigs, still awaits the return of a strong authority as her imperial husband.

What emerges from this reading of Froude's *The English in the West Indies, or The Bow of Ulysses* is an interesting and ambiguous relation to Gladstone's use of the Homeric sea. Gladstone constructs a comprehensive map on which the empirical topography of the Mediterranean can nevertheless accommodate realms of the marvellous - a strategy, as I suggested, to re-enchant mid-Victorian political realities by re-enacting roles of ancient heroism. Froude, on the other hand, inscribes the observable topography of the Caribbean Sea with Homeric meanings, against visible evidence and against a background of acute late-Victorian anxiety, to revive the flagging imperial spirit of the nation. For their purposes, both engage with the sea as the central site where mythic meanings intersect with political realities. The question remains, however, why Homer and his ancient epics are recruited for this project. This is what I would finally like to address in the concluding section.

IV

West of Lisbon in Belém, where the estuary of the River Tejo opens into the Atlantic, a great monastery was built in the 16th century. It was given to the Order of St Jerome, whose members traditionally provide spiritual comforts to sailors and seafarers. King Manuel I is said to have ordered the enormous architectural project in 1499 in memory of Vasco da Gama's recent discovery of a sea route to India. Appropriately, the great explorer and maritime pioneer himself lies buried in the monastery's church, the Igreja de Santa Maria, where his richly decorated sarcophagus is placed left of the main portal, for every visitor to see. The church also contains the tombs of several Portuguese kings and queens and other members of the royal family. But right opposite Vasco da Gama's burial place, on the south side of the portal, we find another symmetrically constructed sarcophagus, set there clearly as a parallel and adorned with carefully juxtaposed images. Where the one tomb shows a caravel and a globe, instruments of the seafarer's activity, the other shows a lyra and a quill, tools and symbols of the poet's craft. This sarcophagus serves as a monument for Luís de Camões, the epic writer, who was born the year after Vasco da Gama died and who later immortalized his fame in the great epic of the *Lusiads*.

The significant and honourable placing of their tombs suggests an equally contiguous relation of their legacies in the national memory: the maritime discoverer side by side with the epic poet, the seafarer and the singer as complementary contributors to a common project - material and literary empire building. As a matter of fact, Camões' presence here is entirely symbolic; he died in 1580 as a plague victim and was, supposedly, buried in a mass grave. This makes the move to inter his memory in the Mosteiro dos Jerónimos, opposite and next to the explorer who helped initiate Portugal's rise to global power, all the more significant. The building of the monastery was financed through a special tax known as 'pepper money' levied on all income from the spice trade. The great cultural monument, in which also the national epic poet is commemorated, is therefore materially based on the beneficiary domestic effects of imperial trade connections in the wake of maritime discoveries.

In *Epic and Empire*, David Quint has given an interesting reading of the *Lusiads* to support his general argument that the Renaissance voyage of discovery was often strategically redescribed as an epic project in order to distinguish it as an aristocratic pursuit rather than a mercantile enterprise. In terms of its narrative structures, the epic genre is steeped in the ideology of a martial aristocracy and so must cultivate disdain for trading, and disassociate itself from mere activities of money-making. In Camõens' heroic version, therefore, Vasco da Gama claims 'that Portugal's aim in opening up new trade routes, the general goal of all the voyages of discovery, is the acquisition not of wealth that traders normally seek but of fame.'[38] But the heroic voyages of maritime heroes are not so easily differentiated from their commercial doubles. Even the *Odyssey*, Quint notes, carefully tries to contrast the travels of Ulysses from less heroic maritime adventures such as those by Phoenician traders, but still, 'when the actions of the Odyssey ... are transferred to the sea, the domain of traders and sailors, epic fiction collides with social reality, and uncertainties arise about their heroes' motives and behaviour.'[39]

This argument seems to have special relevance for the Homeric passages I have traced through texts and images from the Victorian period - a period in which Hakluyt's *Principal Navigations* was propagated as a national epic while the Empire, in real terms, emerged ever more clearly as the 'bread and butter' question of economic rivalries. In an act of maritime archaeology, therefore, the Homeric sea was charted and contemplated by political writers and philological politicians in order to turn the collision of epic fiction with social reality, identified by Quint, to current political uses. Both Gladstone's and Froude's writings bear reconsideration in terms of this contrast. The Gladstone family, for instance, is well known to have procured its wealth and commercial stature through large investment in West Indian plantations and long-standing involvement in the slave trade.[40] Froude served as adviser to the colonial office, even while he, in his lecture series, celebrated English naval history as a 'high epic story'.[41] Drake and Hawkins seem to him English versions of Ulysses, and their achievements worthy of the greatest poet: 'I, for my part, believe a time will come when ... these sea-captains of Elizabeth will then form the subject of a great English national epic as grand as the "Odyssey".'[42]

But when he himself sets out, on his voyage to the West Indies, to contribute a great chapter to this project, the great epic design is submerged and the Homeric meanings lost. Froude's and Gladstone's texts are not least interesting because they seem to offer literal readings of the maritime metaphor that Derek Walcott has employed in the poem quoted at the outset. Whether Gladstone's mapping of Homeric marvels or Froude's gazing at the Caribbean Sea trying to salvage their historical significance - with such efforts both writers can be seen to respond to Walcott's question

'Where are your monuments, your battles, martyrs' with the desperate answer: 'In that grey vault. The sea. The sea / has locked them up. The sea is History.'

Notes

1   Jonathan Raban (ed.), *The Oxford Book of the Sea* (Oxford: Oxford University Press, 1992).
2   Derek Walcott, *Collected Poems, 1948–1984* (London: Faber, 1992), 364.
3   Raban, 'Introduction', *Oxford Book of the Sea*, 1-34, 33.
4   For a discussion of these issues, cf. Tobias Döring and Bernhard Klein, 'Of Bogs and Oceans. Alternative Histories in the Poetry of Seamus Heaney and Derek Walcott', Bernhard Klein and Jürgen Kramer (eds), *Common Ground? Crossovers between Cultural Studies and Postcolonial Studies* (Trier: Wissenschaftlicher Verlag, 2001), 113-36.
5   See David Quint, *Epic and Empire* (Princeton: Princeton University Press, 1993).
6   Much of the following information is indebted to Judy Egerton, *Turner, The Fighting Temeraire* (London: National Gallery Publications, 1995).
7   Quoted in *ibid.*, 88.
8   Cf. Raban, 'Introduction', *Oxford Book of the Sea*, 20.
9   Quoted in Egerton, *Turner, The Fighting Temeraire*, 139.
10   Raban, 'Introduction', *Oxford Book of the Sea*, 18.
11   Edward W. Said, *The World, the Text, and the Critic* (Cambridge, MA: Harvard University Press, 1983), 4.
12   Roy Jenkins, *Gladstone* (London: Macmillan, 1995), 181.
13   William Ewart Gladstone, *Studies on Homer and the Homeric Age*, 3 vols (Oxford: Oxford University Press, 1858), vol. 1, 217.
14   *Ibid.*, vol. 3, 276.
15   Cf. Armin Wolf, *Hatte Homer eine Karte? Beobachtungen über die Anfänge der europäischen Kartographie* (Karlsruhe: Fachhochschule Karlsruhe, Fachbereich Geowissenschaften, 1997), 9.
16   *Ibid.*, 10.
17   Gladstone, *Studies on Homer*, vol. 3, 8.
18   Cf. C.C. Eldrige, *Victorian Imperialism* (London et al.: Hodder & Stoughton, 1978), 92.
19   William Ewart Gladstone, *The Gladstone Diaries*, vol. 11, ed. H.C.G. Matthew (Oxford: Clarendon, 1990), 625.
20   Cf. Jenkins, *Gladstone*, ch. 12.
21   William Ewart Gladstone, *The Hellenic Factor in the Eastern Question with Other Tracts* (Leipzig: Bernhard Tauchnitz, 1877), 23.
22   *Ibid.*, 29.
23   Gladstone, *Studies on Homer*, vol. 3, 616.
24   *Ibid.*, 286.
25   Alfred Lord Tennyson, *The Poems of Tennyson*, ed. Christopher Ricks (London and Harlow: Longmans, 1969), 565-6.

26   James Anthony Froude, *Oceana or England and Her Colonies* (Leipzig: Bernhard Tauchnitz, 1887).

27   Cf. Ilse Grossklaus, *James Anthony Froude und seine politische Ideenwelt im Spiegel der Entwicklung des Britischen Empire, 1870–1880* (Frankfurt am Main: Lang, 1981).

28   Simon Gikandi, *Maps of Englishness. Writing Identity in the Culture of Colonialism* (New York: Columbia University Press, 1996), 87.

29   James Anthony Froude, *The English in the West Indies, or The Bow of Ulysses* [1887] (London: Longman, Green & Co., 1909), 38.

30   See Rob Nixon, *London Calling: V.S. Naipaul, Postcolonial Mandarin* (New York and Oxford: Oxford University Press, 1992).

31   Cf. Tobias Döring, *Caribbean–English Passages: Intertextuality in a Postcolonial Tradition* (London: Routledge, 2002), ch. 1.

32   Froude, *The English in the West Indies*, 31.

33   *Ibid.*, 9-10.

34   *Ibid.*, 321.

35   *Ibid.*, 125-6.

36   *Ibid.*, 165.

37   Cf. *ibid.*, 14.

38   Quint, *Epic and Empire*, 257.

39   *Ibid.*, 259.

40   Edgar J. Feuchtwanger, *Gladstone* (London: Allen Lane, 1975), 2-3.

41   James Anthony Froude, *English Seamen in the Sixteenth Century* [1893] (London: Longman, Green & Co., 1897), 260.

42   *Ibid.*, 104.

8 'As I wuz a-rolling down the Highway one morn': Fictions of the 19th-Century English Sailortown

VALERIE BURTON

As I wuz a-rolling down the Highway one morn,
I spied a flash packet from ol' Wapping town,
As soon as I seed her I slacked me main brace,
An' I hoisted me stuns'ls an' to her gave chase.

I hailed her in English, she answered me clear,
'I'm from the Black Arrow bound to the Shakespeare',
So I wore ship wid a what d'yer know her,
An' I passed her me hawser an' took her in tow.

I entered her little cubby-hole, an' swore damn yer eyes,
She wuz nothin' but a fireship rigged up in disguise,
She had a foul bottom, from sternpost to fore,
Tween wind and water she ran me ashore ...

Here's a health to the gal wid the black, curly locks,
Here's a health to the gal who ran me on the rocks;
Here's a health to the quack, boys, who eased me from pain,
If I meet that flash packet I'll board her again.

'Ratcliffe Highway'[1]

The pestilent lanes and alleys which, in [the seafarer's] vocabulary go by the names of Rotten-row, Gibraltar-place, and Booble-alley, are putrid with vice and crime; to which, perhaps, the round globe does not furnish a parallel. The

141

sooty and begrimed bricks of the very houses have a reeking, Sodom-like, and murderous look ... These are the haunts from which sailors sometimes disappear forever; or issue in the morning, robbed naked, from the broken door-ways.[2]

Herman Melville

When the hero of Melville's novel *Redburn* came ashore eastbound on a North Atlantic voyage the youngster was already equipped with a printed guide to Liverpool and from that he took his bearings on the town.[3] Redburn's shipmates disembarked with less preparation and made directly for the brothels and beerhouses of the port's sailortown. At no place in the novel was the social distance between the middle-class officer-apprentice and his shipmates quite so pointedly observed. On their coming ashore the egalitarian relations of shipboard life were fractured, and the problem as Melville saw it was that women were present in the seafarers' on-shore world. Women galvanized men's passions and were the subject of proprie-torial rivalries which divided men from men. Melville took a dim view of the ordinary seaman: 'with the majority of them, the very fact of their being sailors, argues a certain recklessness and sensualism of character, igno-rance, and depravity', he observed. Later he described how the respectable inhabitants of Liverpool crossed the street to avoid passing too close to a sailor on the same side.[4] The Victorian novelist gave expression to the social and cultural geography of the port. Nowhere were his descriptions more vivid than in respect of its sailortown. A cameo of 'Booble Alley' was a centrepiece in the novel. It established the archetypal references for a sailortown. But seafarers' accounts of sailortown were no less important: their recollected visits to brothels, lodging places and drinking houses inspired their bawdy songs.

This paper concerns sailortowns in the largest of English ports in a period of rapid commercial and imperial expansion. It deals with Liverpool's Paradise Street and, more particularly, London's Ratcliffe Highway. My plan is to explore the sailortown and its place in the changing lives of seafarers during the 19th century. There can be no understanding of sailortowns as cultural phenomena without taking account of the lived relations of production, consumption and reproduction which a seafaring life entailed. But the paper will also consider the processes of signification and the historical legacies which were at work in producing 'maps' of the port city. It will make reference to state-building; the power of the market and patterns of capital accumulation and in these connections explore some of the differences between disciplinary and subjugated knowledges of the sailortown.

When, in the 1920s, a would-be chronicler of sailortowns, C. Fox Smith, set out for Ratcliffe Highway she claimed it was unrecognizable as 'the Highway'. 'Gone long ago are "Paddy's Goose", the "Hole in the Wall" and the "Mahogany Bar"', she explained.[5] Her account continued: 'it was here that all sorts of evil-doers lived who devoted themselves to robbing and enticing sailors ... [but] nowadays seamen are more wide-awake, the crimps and bloodsuckers have disappeared and "Poor Jack" is better paid.' Seafarers' lives had indeed changed, and as for Ratcliffe Highway, maps of London now showed it as St George's Street; yet still seafarers visited the place which they knew as the Highway. They continued to do so as long as their vessels berthed at the docks and wharves nearby. Only after container berths were constructed well downstream in the 1950s did the old dock areas become inaccessible to their crews. The speed of turn-around in container operations allowed seafarers little if any time to come ashore. Indeed containerization ended the facility with which seafarers had for a very long time moved between sea and shore. In Wapping and Shadwell the streets and premises which had survived name changes were cleared in docklands re-development. Since this did not happen until the second half of the 20th century, Fox Smith's announcement of the demise of the places frequented by seafarers was premature by several decades. This can only be explained if the sailortown which beguiled her was of the kind which Redburn had spied in mid-19th-century Liverpool: but now, in the early 20th century, she looked for it through different eyes.

When Fox Smith named premises in the sailors' vernacular she professed to an intimacy with the common seaman which Melville had not allowed his hero. Her counterparts, folklorists, anthropologists and others, were embracing a new interest in seafaring culture as they awoke to the demise of the sailing ship and its crew. In the three decades before the First World War sailormen declined from the majority to a small minority of the British merchant marine.[6] But not at all did the circumstances of the crews of sailing vessels warrant their treatment as working at sea in a golden age.[7] *Low* wages prevailed and vessels were old, leaky and undermanned. Shipowners' determination to make profits at the margins of the market had them deployed away from British shores for long periods, much longer than was customary in previous times.[8] In this generation sailors intersected with shore society in quite different ways from their contemporaries in steam-ship employment, and still more important was the difference from earlier generations in sail. Turning inward to the fo'c'sle, these crews found consolation in an escapist world of male bonding and they took to minimizing their emotional, financial and psychological engagement with women by rejecting what was considered feminine in the social world.⁹ There was a difference between the 'bachelor' culture which gave rise to tales of whoring, drinking sailors around the mid-19th century and an equally ebullient, but more aggressively misogynist culture of seafarers in the early 20th century. That distinction should be kept in mind because much of what we think we know about life at sea before the last century comes, atypically, from the final days of sail.¹⁰

Fox Smith's book, *Sailor Town Days*, was a product of anti-modernism, yet it relays the influence of those who in the 19th century would see life and labour in the port city transformed. She credited sailors' missions with the largest influence in the sailortown. Their 'good work helped banish those who preyed on sailors', she declared. It is likely that Fox Smith knew of the memoirs which the Reverend Rowe had published in 1875 after several years of missionary work on the Highway. In *Jack Afloat and Jack Ashore* Rowe called it 'one of the most rowdyish, rollicking quarters of London' but claimed that in his day it was 'much improved'.¹¹ Rowe was following in the footsteps of the Reverend Harris who in 1837 published his account of the Highway.¹² The assumptions made in the 19th century that the sailortown and its under-class would eventually vanish under modernizing influences accounts for Fox Smith's willingness in the 20th century to pronounce them gone. Melville's and like visions which portrayed the sailortown as a site of excitement and danger were reaffirmed for they established that the sailortown had once existed. Bourgeois commentators writing about life in Victorian cities and towns did so in linear discourses. They moved between cultural formations and social processes in narratives of social life which underlined the differences (as they conceived them) between society's proprietors, producers and non-producers. As we shall soon see, hierarchies of class, status and function were elucidated via distinctions of character and behaviour in the demonologies which mythologized cultural living in the 19th-century port.

Space and time separated sea and shore: modernity on land was played out against the primitive and elemental at sea. In the mid-18th century no simple aversion to sea-going persuaded Samuel Johnson to make his celebrated comparison between the vessel and a gaol.¹³ Nor was it accidental that two centuries later incarceration suggested itself to sociologists when total institution theory gave them a new reason for looking at what happened to men at sea.¹⁴ The sense of social displacement entailed in leaving land was a reflection of a psychological fragmentation which began with capitalism. As the hierarchy of proprietors, producers and non-producers emerged on shore, people looked differently at the sea which was never so separate from the new arrangements of productivity and power as landsmen began to believe. In the mid-Victorian period the primacy accorded to market forces found its mark in sailortown. Moving between sea and shore, there was a thickening of time, history and plot around the seafaring man.

In shipping, the state, labour and capital met along an extensive boundary. The sense of the industry's economic and ideological importance to the nation was never far away.[15] When Thomas Gray occupied the office of Assistant Secretary to the Marine Department of the Board of Trade in the mid-1860s, this was not long after the Department had been created.[16] In one of the most important reallocations of resources in the Victorian state, it replaced the Admiralty in the task of regulating seafaring labour. It worked with a remit to consolidate free market structures, and over the next twenty years, under Gray's control, the Department did perhaps its most important work.[17] The period was one of rapid technological renewal in steam and shipowners looked to recoup large investments from extracting more of the surplus product of labour. The Board in its task of facilitating the supply of workers focused attention on seafarers' competency. Gray was called to give evidence to the Royal Commission on Shipwreck in 1873 and there he chose to elucidate on the 'personal peculiarity which *once* bespoke the sailor'.[18] 'He could not come ashore and walk quietly down the street', said Gray, 'he could not speak without a string of oaths', and perched upon his head was a hat 'much like of a Dutch fishwoman'. The artefact, arcane and effeminate, was an inspired piece of iconography. Evidently this old-time sailor hailed from the 17th century; a period when the military and trading functions of the merchant marine were more closely intertwined. He illuminated a growing sophistication of the workforce and he symbolized the difference made by the change from adversarial commercial relations to market rationality (that which was said to have secured the supremacy of British shipping across the world). The unmanliness of the figure had a purpose too: it detracted from seafarers' self-representations wherein the buccaneering and privateering adventures which the state had previously supported squared up to demonstrate male agency. The refashioning of notions of authentic manhood was part of the transformative power of capitalism, and it is significant that Gray's sailor was spotted not at sea but on shore.

A class who lived by exploiting seafarers existed on shore, or so it was said. Boarding-house runners, more commonly known as crimps, were one of three groups whose practices were increasingly censured in the Victorian period. It was said they intercepted seafarers back from the sea securing the wages the men were owed and which they obtained in advance of future work.[19] Accommodation, food and drink were made available in return, but at the first opportunity crimps delivered their clients to the master of an outward-bound vessel, making up the numbers of seasoned seafarers with greenhands and involuntary recruits.[20] Crimping became a byword for practices which brought unsuitable men to the market. Ship owners in sail complained most about of the activities of crimps - low wages and deteriorating working conditions in sailing ships accounted for their increasing difficulties in securing crew - but the logistics of the supply and organization of labour were mostly to do with steam and the opening up of new market sectors. On the Thames from the late 1860s police boarded incoming vessels to prevent crimps joining them.[21] Official influence was exerted in other ways, notably through the persuasion that in a market free of crimps seafarers would exercise greater autonomy.[22] The language of institutional integration, liberalization and market rationality did not have much resonance amongst the workforce, until a trade union, set up first in the North East ports in the 1880s, established a national presence through accommodation with shipowners.[23] With arguments shaping up that union supply would improve the quality of seafaring labour, crimps had few defences against their characterization as interlopers.

The second set of characters in sailortown were its prostitutes. Supposedly they parted seafarers from their money and clothes and left them infected with disease. Reverend Rowe included especially vivid portraits of Ratcliffe Highway's prostitutes in his memoirs. He showed them in 'mud-splashed, liquor-stained, greasy silks', with their eyes 'blackened', and conversing in 'utterances [which] call to mind the eruption of a mud-volcano'.[24] Long-standing clerical prejudices against 'painted women' found an opening in this vision, but closer to Rowe in time was the furore surrounding the Contagious Diseases Acts. Applied in just a few non-naval ports, the influence of the Acts went much further.[25] A set of conventions identifying the prostitute emerged from the debates and as the historian of the Acts, Judith Walkowitz, has observed, the result was a new visibility to prostitution.[26] The outcome which most concerns us here are the diminished opportunities for women to move into and out of casual prostitution because it was said that seafarers' wives turned occasionally to the trade.[27] This meshes with what we know from other sources about the expedients these women used to cope financially. Ports were places with only casual work for women and any partner of a seafarer knew not to depend on receiving money from him regularly. While he was away deep-sea, there was little opportunity for him to send money home.[28] The distinction drawn between virtuous wives and fallen women compromised these women in many of their wage-earning activities outside the home.

The other key figures in sailortown were its money-lenders cum slop-shop dealers. Those of Ratcliffe Highway set up their stalls as Rowe envisaged it, 'beneath drooping banian groves of garments', and they posted a notice to advertise their business: 'Seamen's Advance Notes Cashed'. He described how they 'tout[ed] for custom in an affectionate "Will you walk into my parlour said the spider to the fly" tone'.[29] The implication was that these were Jewish money-lenders and his middle-class readers would have recognized it through their increasing familiarity with ideas of race degeneration. Turning sex into money and money into sex linked the prostitute and the money-lender.[30] And it is relevant here to highlight the ambiguities of mid-Victorian concepts of circulation. Political economists had taken to explaining how capital accumulation was conducive to the 'health' of the nation using the analogy of circulation.[31] The scarcity precept of liberal political economy extended to capital circulating in a closed system and led to the understanding of spending as waste. While the activities of sailortown lodging-house keepers, hawkers and traders were known to be important in the circulation of the products of capital, their business was done on the margins of the market and at what were thought of as the borders of legitimate exchange. The Jewish money-lenders signified the instability of credit in these quarters. More broadly based though was an attack on the credit basis of the popular economy and the patterns of consumption which it funded. The transformation of public life most surely involved the private domain. Shipping officials cautioned the seafarer away from sailortown and commended him to the safety of his home.

In his memoirs Rowe suggested that disorder from Ratcliffe Highway spilled over 'during business hours'.[32] The concerns of his class were to see arrangements conducive to prosperity and progress secured in a functional separation of space. Over the century a process of functional differentiation and structural integration had been going on in the areas adjacent to Ratcliffe Highway. The phenomenon of a sailortown underclass - Henry Mayhew's 'class who prey upon the earnings of the more industrious part of the community' - which was first created, and then destroyed, is better understood from tracing this process however briefly.[33]

It had begun during the Revolutionary wars with Patrick Colquhoun's plans for secure warehouses and a river police.[34] An entry in the mid-19th-century edition of J.R. McCulloch's *Dictionary of Commerce* made a point of noting the success of the scheme. It had cut down on pilfering to the extent of over half a million pounds every year.[35] The original plan was backed by the shipowners and merchants of the City. In his proposals Colquhoun made plain that the chief threat to property arose from the light-finger inhabitants of the waterfront whom he supposed were long accustomed to help themselves from cargoes in ships and on the docks.[36] When making his proposals Colquhoun suggested to the city authorities that it would be prudent to separate drinking places from the premises of pawnbrokers. This was a move in defence of property though canvassed as one against the seductions of pastimes funded from illicit activities. But we need to recognize the link to the collective dynamics of a popular economy which was fluid in its reciprocities, involved market and non-market activities and which, indeed, was open-ended to goods purloined from cargoes in ships and on the docks. The criminalization of cargo-broaching was thus linked with curtailing the practices by which additional resources were brought into the maritime community. An imaginary barrier drawn around sailortown and rationalized in the connection made with the indulgence of dissipation and vice marked the boundaries between the economies of legal and of illicit exchange. Having, spending and selling on the margins were controversial, contested activities in circumstances where political economy advanced market integration, defended the security of private property and limited the definition of economically useful activity to what realized a market value.

Fantasies of life in the city can take hegemonic or subversive forms. My discussion thus far has privileged the terms of hegemonic discourse with its emphasis on denotation and truth. But it is time to switch to another fiction of sailortown. Seafarers' sailortown songs and legends used the dislocations of urban life to some effect. The rationalizing agenda of government and industry and of sailortown reformers reified a particular kind of experience and established a fluid behavioural field on shore for the seafarer back from the sea.[37]

Throughout the 19th century the wharves and docks close by Ratcliffe Highway were crowded with vessels. Thousands were moored on the river at any one time. The thoroughfare was in daily use by dockers, shipwrights and labourers as well as seamen. In their comings and goings they conducted themselves quietly enough, but the Highway's drinking places and dancing halls were made famous in seafarers' songs and tales as the particular haunts of a sea-going clientele.[38] The songs involved a mixture of fantasy, reality and wishful thinking and often revolved around the seafarers' lump-sum pay.[39] For it was the unusual feature of deep-sea employment that wages accumulated during the course of the voyage and were paid later, after the seafarer came back from the sea. This rendered disposable income into the seafarers' hands. The idea that he returned with a windfall was an idea of some importance in the working-class community where there were few individuals who had resources to treat and share around. The songs survive in the form of contemporary broadsheets or as transcriptions from recordings made almost a century later at a time when deep-sea sailing vessels were few. The source for 'Ratcliffe Highway' in the version reproduced above is a collection of shanties and forebitters edited by a former seafarer, Stan Hugill, and published in 1977.[40] Its most striking feature is a trope which brings the sea to the shore and makes the seafarer-narrator into a privateer on land. His capture of a vessel - a prostitute on Ratcliffe Highway - is the subject for playing between the parts of a vessel and sexual anatomy in a set of ribald puns.

In Melville's tale of Liverpool's sailortown Redburn lingered on its margins fearful for his health and wealth, and ambivalent about its pleasures. His shipmates had no such reservations. Yet their own songs and tales also showed sailortown as a place of danger. There were prostitutes waiting to rob the hapless sailor and boarding-house keepers who connived to ship him back to sea. Seafarers called them 'landsharks' and with that they brought the derring-do of seafaring onto land. Sailortown was a place of adventure as well as danger. There was scope in this setting for table-turning on the neophyte seafarer or the timorous landsmen who hung back from sailortown. On the streets of port towns seafarers met reformers (religious and official) in a literal and figurative contest over ground. Sailortown was a place which exercised the libidinal imagination. The passage in *Redburn* made that much plain; and though Melville himself found the space for his own erotic imaginings in the fo'c'sle among men, seafarers' bawdy songs took the heterosexual inclinations of the sailor for granted. They suggested his appetites were all the greater for his being fresh back from the sea. In boasting about his sexual conquests, they turned the tables on a reticent bourgeoisie.

'Admiration for physical prowess and sexual adventuring did not simply disappear in the face of middle-class proselytizing', an historian of 19th-century Britain has observed.[41] Indeed middle-class proselytizing when it concerned male sexuality was double-edged. A dual-standard morality extended men freedoms to be men in what were thought to be natural ways. When the seafarers of the legend came ashore as transgressors of the rules of sobriety, prudence and sexual restraint, they did so with a confidence which spoke of men whose daily battle with the elements left them unintimidated by man-made things. Jack's predilections were indulged as belonging to men in a pre-ordained, natural state. Ideas rooted in Enlightenment thinking gave a specific form of validity to the expression of 'natural' needs and desires.[42] The sailortown legend set out an essentialist masculinity and identified privileges which belonged to men by virtue of their sex. It accessed a privileged arena within the beliefs of industrial society: one in which libidinal energies could be reclaimed for pleasure and enjoyment against the persuasion of political economy to harness them to work.

It was common enough in the 19th century for seafarers to think, speak and write of their ships as 'she'. Although scholars have made little of this phenomenon, with verses from 'Ratcliffe Highway' in hand the subject presses here. Seafarers used vessel anthropomorphism as a device of relational positioning and in this song the device is extended by means of the privateering trope. Privateering was a collective act of predation.[43] A share in the prize taken rewarded privateering crews. Ever since pioneering work in the 1970s, anthropologists have been aware of the symbolism of male-female proprietorial relations. The 'traffic in women' has been observed in different cultures to be related to the production of culturally coherent sexualities. Expressive acts involve a network of material practices and understandings which are historically specific. In this light the significant point about 'Ratcliffe Highway' is that it uses an arcane commercial vernacular. By the probable time of the song's composition (the 1830s or 40s) privateering was over and its peak too distant in time for any practising seafarer to remember.[44] It is to be noted that Gray's image of the old-time sailor came from this period too, but it did not work with the same persuasions: indeed there is an antimony between the two.

In 'Ratcliffe Highway' privateering is a fiction of the process whereby determinate relations of gender domination and subordination were generated in society. In this regard the sailor's vow to 'have that flash packet again' is crucial. It indicated that all women were potentially subject to men's attentions and drew the assembled company of male listeners (the privateering gang) into a confederacy of 'prize-takers'. When the new order of competitive market capitalism came into being in shipping, it involved the separation of the naval from the merchant branch of the marine, and except perhaps in wartime seafaring did not again present iconographic opportunities to show seafarers quite so full of bravado. On shore new divisions of labour were shaping up by the mid-19th century. The emergence of the domestic female distanced from wage-earning and the market was part of this. The refashioning of authentic womanhood made its impact on sailortown where, as we have already seen, prostitution supported a weightier discourse about what women should not be and where they should not be seen. Authentic manhood was less easily defined: what it was to be a man was left open-ended and was subject to contest.[45] The rational market agent of bourgeois political economy was, to be sure, a breadwinning male.[46] He saw to his family's needs by hard work and saving and complemented the 'angel in the home'. But life in the urban working-class household, and more so the seafarers' household, did not have this idealized symmetry: masculinity was not to be resolved in 'bringing home the bread'.

The sea appealed as a place where women were never thought to have worked. It rendered seemingly unchanging truths about what it was to be male. In privateering those qualities were on display but privateering also exemplified a different economic mode. Like other workers, seafarers experienced increasing separation from the point of production, subordination to the capitalist wage relation, and they were vulnerable to deskilling when steam technology was introduced to the industry.[47] Did 'Ratcliffe Highway' cause seafarers and their audiences to reflect on the vanished days of privateering when seafarers' rewards had come in prize shares? If so, these reflections were not intended as a simple vision of times now passed and regretted in their passing. They were involved in bringing prize-taking into their present in a symbolic elaboration of the wage form. What they implicated was male wage control. Male prerogatives to have and spend were secured in the notion of a windfall. The dangers and isolation of work at sea played into the characterization of sailortown Jack but the character was only fully realized when he described a privileged spender in the consumer relations of shore society. Spending in its literal sense turned political economy's prescriptions to save around: 'spending' in the metaphorical sense was the waste of resources political economists understood to be in closed circulation. The sexual connotations of 'spending' are surely involved in these songs and tales.[48] When Jack 'spent' liberally in sailortown he exploited the subversive possibilities inherent in the over-determined economists' analogy between the political and libidinal economy.[49]

Privateering referred back to an age when relations of production, consumption and reproduction were not organized by the precepts of the modern market economy. It was a period when seafarers had, for example, traded the handkerchiefs they imported for the sexual favours of women in sailortown. Then port life was more fluid and unfettered of movement than was apparent in bourgeois plans to create social and economic order in the city. 19th-century seafaring workers and their communities refused the accumulationist imperatives of liberal political economy. Their defence of different ways of relating to the market was also a defence of different ways of relating to each other. Into the 20th century an open-ended economy continued to exist in the seafaring community. Women's particular part in the arbitrage of goods and services, inside and outside the market, went on undiminished, though not necessarily undisturbed, by capitalist reformulations of space in the city. The boundaries between sailortown and the rest of the port were crossed by women and men in their daily dealings. They sold sex or second-hand clothes, dealt in beer or in lodging-house beds, found berths for seafarers down on their luck and received goods scavenged from cargoes; all as opportunity arose and need obliged. They refused the material values of competitive individualism, but these men and women knew too that sailortown had its own set of priorities and privileges inhering in the world of goods.

In 1885 a handbill was prepared to issue to seafarers at the Mercantile Marine Offices where they were paid. It advised: 'When you come back to port after a long voyage and have to receive wages amounting to £3 or more it is a pity and it is your own fault if you and your wife, children, mother or sister or whoever may be keeping your home together do not have the use of your money. If you stop in a strange port you may get into debt, lose your well-earned money [and] get disease.'[50] Seafarers for their part did not need officials of the Board of Trade to remind them that they were best off 'taking their money home'. The notion of 'safe' and 'unsafe' space evident in this formula was, however, a bourgeois rationalization of the public and private sphere. Most seafarers took family provision seriously and it is unfortunate that, even now, they are thought of as men who evaded responsibilities: they did not. But the one-wage, male-wage family form had no ideological purchase nor made practical sense and by middle-class standards they fell short. Home, indeed, was the best resort when the seafarers' pay ran out.[51] Unlike the sailors' boarding house it was an open-ended source of support. Seafarers were less constantly at sea than we might think. Outside a very few trades, voyages of six months or more were uncommon and as more voyages were made in steam, long voyages became rarer still. In the normal run no wages were paid between voyages, and when tonnage markets were depressed, ships were laid up and their crews were discharged to manage as they could. Employers depended on these arrangements to maintain their labour in casual supply. What it meant in the seafarer's home is evident from a chance account. In Liverpool in 1876 the Reverend Nugent recorded the case of a seafarer's cohabitee (Nugent called her a 'dissolute partner') who put her clothes into pawn so he could be equipped to go back to sea.[52]

Credit was the basis of the household management in the port and middle-class attempts to have women match income and expenditure by regular budgeting were defeated in a practical way by the irregularity with which seafaring wages were paid.[53] On receiving their pay, however, seafarers were possessed of larger sums than any artisan had at the end of a week or fortnight's work, and more indeed than the archetypal breadwinner perhaps ever contemplated taking home. These were valuable resources in the port community where dock work - the most common alternative for men - meant short terms of employment and correspondingly small sums of pay.

The ability to raise loans and obtain credit depended on the earnings of the community's best-paid males. So women and older men watched and waited anxiously for returning vessels to put into port. The idea that seafaring wages constituted a 'windfall', a chance gain, suggested that once debts were paid off there was money for treats and to spread around. The seafaring household was not a site of capital accumulation, though neither was money used imprudently: what seafaring wages supported was a meaningful social life. This is not to say that the understandings and goals that the community reached were arrived at without conflict, nor did those goals incorporate women's equality with men. Seafarers gathered in public houses amongst male company and sung of setting out for Ratcliffe Highway with a gold watch in their pockets and dressed in their finest clothes. Women, it should be remembered, had no such songs.

Encountering a sailor's woman on Ratcliffe Highway in 1860 one of Mayhew's investigators, Bracebridge Hemyng, inquired into her life. 'I have many husbands', she said, 'six, ten oh! more.'[54] Each, as she told him, gave her their discharge pay: it was the only sensible thing to do. 'It [is] not good for Jack to keep his money', she observed with irony, for this was the phrase used by the middle-class reformers who set up their missions on the Highway. Mayhew called her a prostitute and included her story in the volume of his *Life and Labour* given to 'Those Who Did Not Work', but in an important sense she had the last word, for sailortown was a knowing part of a working-class burlesque.

Notes

1   Stan Hugill, *Sea Shanties* (London: Barrie and Jenkins, 1977), 136-7.
2   Herman Melville, *Redburn: His First Voyage. Being the Sailor-boy Confessions and Reminiscences of the Son-of-a-Gentleman, in the Merchant Service* [1849], ed. Harold Beaver (Harmondsworth: Penguin, 2nd ed. 1977), 265.
3   *Ibid.*, 208, 217.
4   *Ibid.*, 202, 220.
5   C. Fox Smith, *Sailor Town Days* (London: Methuen, 2nd ed. 1924), 28-9. Still she described how 'all the dregs and offscourings of male and female humanity swarmed in the foul and filthy dregs of the Ratcliffe Highway'. *Ibid.*
6   Valerie C. Burton, 'Counting Seafarers: the Published Records of the Registrar of Merchant Seamen, 1849-1913', *Mariner's Mirror* 71 (1985), 305-20.
7   For an instance of the glorification of sail technology in its passing, see another of Fox Smith's publications: *The Return of the 'Cutty Sark'* (London: Methuen, 1924), 12: 'There is to my thinking a great pathos about the ousting of the queens of sail from their own special realm by the despised "steam kettle" ... They were the thoroughbreds of the sea, never its beasts of burden.'

8   These things are explored in my major research project 'Spanning Sea and Shore' which uses the statutory Agreements and Accounts of Crew and vessel reports in the shipping press to track vessel deployment and voyage length in the period 1850 to 1914.

9   Thus Knut Weibust, the enthnographer of *Deep-Sea Sailors*, commented on the swearing which accompanied ship-board work: 'Profanity reflects ... social values such as strength, masculinity and freedom from the restraint of society at large'. *Deep Sea Sailors: A Study in Maritime Ethnology* (Stockholm: Nordiska Museet, 1969), 244. See also the comments on p. 138: '[T]he crew tend to dwell on the various adventures they have had - they do so in language that is not suitable for feminine company.'

10 Valerie Burton, '"Whoring, Drinking Sailors": Reflections on Masculinity from the Labour History of Nineteenth-century British Shipping', Margaret Walsh (ed.), *Working Out Gender* (Aldershot: Ashgate, 1999), 84-101.

11 Richard Rowe, *Jack Afloat and Jack Ashore* (London: Smith, Elder, 1875), 92.

12 John Harris, *Britannia: or, the Moral Claims of Seamen Stated and Enforced. An Essay in Three Parts* (London: Thomas Ward and Co., 1837).

13 Journal entry, 19 March 1776 in *Boswell's Life of Johnson*, 6 vols, ed. George Birk-beck Hill (Oxford: Clarendon Press, 1934), vol. 2: The Life, 1766-1776, 438.

14 Peter H. Fricke (ed.), *Seafarer and Community: Towards a Social Understanding of Seafaring* (London: Croom Helm, 1973).

15 W.S. Lindsay, *History of Merchant Shipping and Ancient Commerce, Vol. IV* (London: Sampson Low, Marston, Low, and Searle, 1876), chapters v-xv; T.H. Farrer, *The State in its Relation to Trade* (London: Macmillan, 1883), 120-31.

16 P.G. Parkhurst, *Ships of Peace: A Record of Some of the Problems Which Came Before the Board of Trade in Connection with the Mercantile Marine* (New Malden: P.G. Parkhurst, 1962), 140-83; J.S. Bromley, *The Manning of the Royal Navy: Selected Published Pamphlets, 1693-1873* (London: Navy Records Society, 1974), esp. xxxi.

17 Thomas Gray, 'Fifty Years of Legislation in Relation to the Shipping, Trade and the Safety of Ships and Seamen', *Shipping Gazette*, 11 March 1887, 148.

18 Thomas Gray in evidence to the 'Royal Commission Appointed to Inquire into the Alleged Unseaworthiness of British Registered Ships', *British Parliamentary Papers 1873, XXXVI*, 277.

19 Thomas Brassey, *The Advance Note: What It Is and Why It Ought To Be Abolished* (London: Longman, 1875), 55; *British Parliamentary Papers, 1893-4, LXXX*, 'Report of the Committee Appointed to Consider the Question of the Extension to Ports Abroad ... of the Arrangements Now in Force in the U.K. for the Transmission of Seamen's Wages, 1893', 3.

20 W.B. Manser, *How Ships Are Lost* (London: n.p., 1877), 25; Conrad Dixon, 'The Rise and Fall of the Crimp', Stephen Fisher (ed.), *British Shipping and Seamen, 1630-1960* (Exeter: University of Exeter Press, 1984), 49-67.

21 'Crimping in the Port of London', Public Record Office MT/9, 42, M. 4392/1868.

22 F.W. Beechy, *A Letter to the Master Mariners and Seamen of the Ports of Shields and Sunderland on the Subject of the Mercantile Marine Act* (South Shields: Hugh M'Coll, 1851).

23 Arthur Marsh and Victoria Ryan, *The Seamen: A History of the National Union of Seamen* (Oxford: Malthouse Press, 1989), 17-35.

24 Rowe, *Jack Afloat*, 81-2.

25 Anon., 'The Contagious Diseases Acts: Ought They to be Extended to All Seaports', *Nautical Magazine* (January 1876), 12; *Liverpool Daily Courier*, 9 Sept. 1874.
26 Judith Walkowitz, *Prostitution in Victorian Society: Women, Class and the State* (Cambridge: Cambridge University Press, 1980).
27 Frederick W. Lowndes, *Prostitution and Venereal Disease in Liverpool* (London: J. & A. Churchill, 1886), 17.
28 I deal with seafaring households and the concerns of seafarers to provide for families notwithstanding the difficulties caused by the employer's withholding of their wages in 'The Myth of Bachelor Jack: Masculinity, Patriarchy and Seafaring Labour', Colin Howell and Richard J. Twomey (eds), *Jack Tar in History: Essays in the History of Maritime Life and Labour* (Fredericton, New Brunswick: Acadiensis Press, 1991), 193-5.
29 Rowe, *Jack Afloat*, 92.
30 Sander Gilman, *The Jew's Body* (New York: Routledge, 1991), 124-7.
31 Reginia Gagnier, 'On the Insatiability of Human Wants', *Victorian Studies* 36 (1993), 125-51.
32 Rowe, *Jack Afloat*, 92.
33 Henry Mayhew (ed.), *London Labour and the London Poor. Those That Will Not Work* (London: Grifin Bohn and Co., 1862), 228.
34 Charles Capper, *The Port and Trade of London: Historical, Statistical, Local and General* (London: Smith, Elder and Co., 1862), 147-51.
35 J.R. McCullough, *A Dictionary of Commerce and Commercial Navigation* (London: Longman, Brown, Green and Longman, 1844), 468.
36 Patrick Colquhoun, *A Treatise on the Commerce and Police of the River Thames; And Suggesting Means for Preventing the Depredations thereon by a Legislative System of River Police* (London: Joseph Mawson, 1800), 41.
37 Peter Bailey, *Popular Culture and Performance in the Victorian City* (Cambridge: Cambridge University Press, 1999), 7.
38 Other printed versions of 'Ratcliffe Highway' are given in Stan Hugill, *Shanties and Sailors' Songs* (New York: Praegar, 1969), 208-33; Hugill, *Shanties from the Seven Seas* (London: Routledge and Kegan Paul, 1961), 1-44; William Main Doerflinger, *Shantymen and Shantyboys* (New York: Macmillan, 1951), 114-7; Terry L. Kinsey, *Songs of the Sea* (London: Robert Hale, 1989), 137-9.
39 W.B. Whall, *Sea Songs and Shanties* (Glasgow: Brown, and Ferguson, 6th ed. 1948).
40 Hugill, *Sea Shanties*, 136-7; Stan Hugill, *Sailortown* (London: Routledge and Kegan Paul, 1976).
41 Leonore Davidoff, '"Adam Spoke First and Named the Orders of the World": Masculine and Feminine Domains in History and Sociology', Helen Corr and Lynn Jamieson (eds), *The Politics of Everyday Life* (London: Hutchinson, 1989), 247.
42 'Naturalization' is the term which has been used to identify that process of ascribing socially constructed ideas (of sexuality) to a natural or pre-ordained state so that they gain a 'specific form of validity'. See the pioneering work of Ludmilla Jordanova, *Sexual Visions: Images of Gender in Science and Medicine between the Eighteenth and Twentieth Century* (Hemel Hempstead: Harvester Press, 1989), esp. 5.
43 David J. Starkey, *British Privateering Enterprise in the Eighteenth Century* (Exeter: University of Exeter Press, 1990).
44 Research in the Vaughan Williams Memorial Library [VWML], London, revealed two generic versions of 'Ratcliffe Highway'. Broadsheet sources indicate that the form

quoted above was in circulation by the mid-19th century. See Madden Collection VWML microfilm 81, no. 265 and microfilm 76, no. 327. The James Maddison Carpenter Collection (originals held at the Library of Congress, Washington, D.C. AFC 1972/001) includes transcriptions from recordings made by Carpenter in the 1920s.

45   Anna Clark, *The Struggle for the Breeches: Gender and the Making of the British Working Class* (Berkeley: University of California Press, 1997).

46   Keith McClelland, 'Masculinity and the Representative Artisan in Britain, 1850-80', Michael Roper and John Tosh (eds), *Manful Assertions: Masculinities in Britain since 1800* (London: Routledge, 1991), 74-91; Wally Seccombe, 'Patriarchy Stabilized: the Construction of the Male Breadwinner Wage Norm in Nineteenth Century Britain', *Social History* 2, no. 1 (1986), 53-76.

47   Marcus Rediker, *Between the Devil and the Deep Blue Sea. Merchant Seamen, Pirates and the Anglo-American Maritime World, 1700-1750* (Cambridge: Cambridge University Press, 1987); Eric W. Sager, *Seafaring Labour: The Merchant Marine of Atlantic Canada 1820-1914* (Kingston: McGill Queen's University Press, 1989).

48   The social organization of work impinged on the definition of erotic desire in this society and the biology of male sexuality was itself understood by reference to political economy. As Thomas Laqueur explains, 'spending' was a metaphor doubly vested with meanings. See his 'Sex and Desire in the Industrial Revolution', Patrick K. O'Brien and Roland Quinault (eds), *The Industrial Revolution and British Society* (Cambridge: Cambridge University Press, 1993), 101.

49   'Passion and desire were integral to the new economic order' suggests Thomas Laqueur, but there was, he observes, 'no clear conceptual boundary between the sexual kind and that which fuelled consumption'. 'Sex and Desire', 101.

50   Board of Trade hand-bill, dated 1885, number 25: uncatalogued holding in the Library of the Department of Transport, London.

51   Valerie C. Burton, 'Household and Labour Market Interactions in the Late Nineteenth Century British Shipping Industry: Breadwinning and Seafaring Families', T.W Guiannane and P. Johnson (eds), *The Microeconomic Analysis of the Household and the Labour Market, 1880-1939* (Seville: Universidad de Sevilla, 1998), 99-109.

52   'Second Report of the Select Committee on Habits of Intemperance', *British Parliamentary Papers, 1877, XI*, 8216.

53   E. Mahler and E.F. Rathbone, *The Payment of Seamen: How the Wives Suffer* (Liverpool: Liverpool Courier, 1911).

54   Bracebridge Hemying, in Mayhew (ed.), *London Labour and the London Poor*, 230.

9 Conrad's Crews Revisited

JÜRGEN KRAMER

Introduction

Josef Teodor Konrad Korzeniowski (1857-1924) lived 'three lives': as a child and young man in Poland until 1874, as a seaman first on French, then on British ships until 1894, and as the writer Joseph Conrad publishing thirteen novels, twenty-eight novellas and tales, as well as two volumes of memories and reminiscences between 1895 and 1924. Between October 1874 (when he left Cracow) and January 1894 (when he was discharged from his last ship) Korzeniowski worked on 18 ships, including long periods in ports, for almost eleven years. He served for over two-and-a-half years as a member of the crew, eight months as third mate, almost four years as second mate, two years and three months as first mate and one year and two months as captain.[1] As a writer Conrad first and foremost chronicled and responded to the climax and decline of two historical developments: the age of sail and the British Empire.[2] Both of these developments had found their pre-eminent literary expressions in the travel writing and adventure fiction of the Victorian Age and, coincidentally, had succeeded in securing a popular forum for propagating the ideals of the British Empire and the imperial subject. But while Conrad was profoundly influenced by these two different, if complementary, genres, he also challenged many assumptions of their conventions, affording and necessitating new ways of viewing and dealing with their objects. Although he was steeped in the 19th-century realist tradition, Conrad confronted political, cultural and moral issues in increasingly complex narrative constructions whose disrupted chronology, polyphonic voices and powerful irony precluded any 'conclusive message'. Moreover, the fact that he wrote in his third language made him acutely aware of both the challenge of exhausting the linguistic possibilities of English and the limits of any language as a means of creating anything more than an approximate representation of the world.

Reading selected texts of Conrad's oeuvre against reconstructions of the historical voyages and incidents they were based on, as well as in the light of his artistic credo, this essay will interrogate the ways in which Conrad deals with the problem of relations between different nationalities on board of 'his' ships, analyse his (alleged) attempts at portraying his service at sea more English in character than it really was, reassess in this particular context his commitment to particular ideas of work, manliness and solidarity and, thereby, contribute to a re-evaluation of Conrad's contribution to Britain's sea literature.

Three Voyages: Biographical Evidence and Literary Transformations

According to the most recent research, Korzeniowski's ships and voyages between 1874 and 1894 were the following:[3]

NAME OF SHIP	DATES OF VOYAGE	DESTINATION	KORZENIOWSKI'S POSITION
MONT-BLANC	8 December 1874-23 May 1875	Caribbean	Passenger
	25 June 1875-23 December 1875	Caribbean	Ship's Boy
SAINT-ANTOINE	10 July 1876-15 February 1877	Caribbean	Steward
MAVIS	24 April 1878-10 June 1878	Mediterranean	Unofficial Apprentice
SKIMMER OF THE SEA	11 July 1878-23 September 1878	Lowestoft-Newcastle	Ordinary Seaman
DUKE OF SUTHERLAND	12 October 1878-19 October 1879	Australia	Ordinary Seaman
EUROPA	11 December 1879-30 January 1880	Mediterranean	Ordinary Seaman

28 May 1880: Korzeniowski passed his second-mate's examination.

LOCH ETIVE	21 August 1880-25 April 1881	Australia	Third Mate
PALESTINE	**19 September 1881-3 April 1883**	**Bangkok**	**Second Mate**

RIVERSDALE	10 September 1883- 17 April 1884	India	Second Mate
NARCISSUS	**28 April 1884-** **16 October 1884**	**Bombay-** **Dunkirk**	**Second Mate**

17 November 1884: Korzeniowski failed his first-mate's examination; on 3 December 1884 he re-took and passed it.

TILKHURST	24 April 1885- 16 June 1886	Singapore	Second Mate

28 July 1886: Korzeniowski failed his master's examination; on 11 November 1886 he re-took and passed it.

18 August 1886: Korzeniowski was granted British nationality.

FALCON- **HURST**	28 December 1886- 2 January 1887	Penarth	Second Mate
HIGHLAND **FOREST**	16 February 1887- 1 July 1887	Java	First Mate
VIDAR	20 August 1887- 4 January 1888	Singapore- Borneo	First Mate
OTAGO	**19 January 1888-** **End of March 1889**	**Bangkok-** **Australia**	**Master**
ROI DES **BELGES**	Second half of 1890	[Congo]	
TORRENS	19 November 1891- 2 September 1892	Australia	First Mate
	22 October 1892- 27 July 1893	Australia	First Mate
ADOWA	26 November 1893- 17 January 1894	London- Rouen	Second Mate

I shall focus on three ships and their voyages in particular (as indicated above): the *Palestine* whose ill-fated voyage formed the basis for 'Youth' (1898) where it is re-named *Judea*, the *Narcissus* which appears under its name in *The Nigger of the 'Narcissus'* (1897) and the *Otago*, whose voyages provided the basis for *The Shadow-Line* (1917) and other tales. I shall deal with the first two voyages in reverse order following the sequence in which the texts based on them were written and published. And although *The Shadow-Line* was written in 1915 (and published in 1917), it should be borne in mind that its original idea belonged to the same phase of Conrad's writing as *The Nigger of the 'Narcissus'* and 'Youth' because he mentioned it in a letter to William Blackwood as early as 14 February 1899.[4]

The Nigger of the 'Narcissus' (1897)

Korzeniowski joined the *Narcissus*, a full-rigged iron sailing ship of 1,336 gross tonnage, built in 1876, in Bombay on 28 April 1884. When the *Narcissus* departed for Dunkirk via the Cape of Good Hope on 5 June it mustered a crew of twenty-four (including a master, a first and a second mate).[5] The voyage itself was relatively uneventful if one discounts the facts that the new mate suffered from severe depressions for quite some time, but later recovered,[6] and that one of the sailors, Joseph Barron, died near the Azores on 24 September. On 16 October 1884 the *Narcissus* reached Dunkirk; Korzeniowski signed off the next day.

In Conrad's novel the crew of the *Narcissus* number twenty-six.[7] Starting with the obvious we may note that, although there are some real persons (and, perhaps, even their names) resembling their fictitious counterparts, the text is a piece of fiction and *not* a more or less thinly disguised autobiography. According to his first biographer, Jean-Aubry, Conrad maintained shortly before his death (in June 1924):

> The voyage of the *Narcissus* was performed from Bombay to London in the manner I have described. As a matter of fact, the name of the Nigger of the *Narcissus* was not James Wait, which was the name of another nigger we had on board the *Duke of Sutherland*, and I was inspired with the first scene in the book by an episode in the embarkation of the crew at Gravesend on board the same *Duke of Sutherland*, one of the first ships the crew of which I joined. I have forgotten the name of the real Nigger of the *Narcissus*. As you know, I do not write history, but fiction, and I am therefore entitled to choose as I please what is most suitable in regard to characters and particulars to help me in the general impression I wish to produce. Most of the personages I have portrayed actually belonged to the crew of the real *Narcissus*, including the admirable Singleton, (whose real name was Sullivan), Archie, Belfast, and Donkin. I got the two Scandinavians from associations with another ship. All this is now old, but it was quite present before my mind when I wrote this book. ... As to the conclusion of the book, it is taken from other voyages which I made under similar circumstances. It was, in fact, at Dunkirk, where I had to unload part of her cargo, that I left the *Narcissus*.[8]

Central to the passage above, I think, is not so much Conrad's attempt at linking bits and pieces of his actual experiences with certain persons of (and incidents on) particular ships and their voyages (most probably prompted by the questions of his biographer rather than his own interest), but his claim to write fiction and the freedom of choice 'in regard to characters and particulars' he associates with it. Consequently, speculations about who in the book 'is' who in reality are not very satisfying: most of 'Conrad's characters are composites of many figures from his past'.[9] Moreover, as he clearly stated in his 'Preface', Conrad did not intend to 'reflect' reality but, rather, 'represent' (i.e. construct) it: 'My task which I am trying to achieve is, by the power of the written word to make you hear, to make you feel - it is, before all, to make you *see*.'[10] However, some critics, although they accept Conrad's freedom of choice and construction, feel entitled to ask *why* he *chose* to have no foreign officer and fewer foreign sailors (than there had actually been) on board his fictitious *Narcissus*: on the real vessel there were eleven foreigners, while on board the fictitious one we are given the impression that there are only four. Najder's answer to this question, for example, begins by pointing out the fact that, according to careful estimations, in Korzeniowski's seafaring days 'about 15 percent of all merchant service crews were foreign, but on the ships he sailed the proportion was usually higher, between 30 and 60 percent', and comes to the conclusion that, apparently, Conrad wanted 'to present his service at sea as unequivocally English',[11] or, at least, as more English in character than it had really been.

Indeed, this could be an understandable means of 'self-fashioning' employed by a writer of Polish extraction trying to find his English-speaking audience in the context of a largely conservative and nationally minded publishing business.[12] And as *The Nigger of the 'Narcissus'* was eventually serialized in W.E. Henley's ferociously Tory and imperialist *New Review*, there is a certain 'logic' in this reading: in his tale, Conrad uses varying narrative perspectives to praise the sailors' endurance (and Singleton's singular achievement in particular), to extol the officers' characters and competence and last, but not least, to preach the redemptive power of the late-Victorian ethic of work. It looks as if he wanted to create a world (with the ship, 'a small planet',[13] representing society as a whole) according to the ideological desire(s) of his envisaged (British) readership. As the perpetrators, who question the values of this particular microcosm, are also duly punished, it makes sense to call *The Nigger of the 'Narcissus'* 'Conrad's most conservative political fable'.[14]

However, a closer look at the text itself allows for a more ambivalent reading. For Conrad, the tale was about 'the crew of a merchant ship, brought to the test of ... the moral problem of conduct'.[15] The crew are tested in three ways: the storm and its consequences bring physical hardship which is professionally (but not easily) mastered, while Wait's feigned illness and Donkin's subversive agitation strike at the psychological roots of the crew's self-confidence. In both cases, however, the central significance does not lie in the quantitative relationship between British and non-British seamen but in the qualitative relationship between individual seamen and the crew as a whole.

In his address 'To My Readers in America' Conrad asserted: 'A negro in a British forecastle is a lonely being. He has no chums.'[16] However, in making the 'nigger' Wait 'the centre of the ship's collective psychology'[17] and, thereby, focusing on 'a smudge'[18] in the late-Victorian unconscious, Conrad chose to confront the crew of the *Narcissus* with a particular catalytic Other. On the one hand, he made the peripheral Wait 'the pivot of the action':[19] Wait's feigned illness (which, in this particular context, equals uncompromising self-love) subverts the unity of the sailors; his narcissism produces and reflects that of the crew.[20] On the other hand, Wait's erstwhile exclusion is confirmed in (and by) the course of the action: as he not only deceives the others but also himself (by adopting a pretence of dying in order to 'forget' that he is actually fatally ill), he becomes culprit and victim in one. Putting it differently and more radically, one could say that by making a black African the pivot of the action Conrad stages a confrontation between the imperial Other and the (predominantly British) crew to unmask the latter's inability to deal with this conflict and its repercussions. The inescapable logic is that the 'nigger' has to die so that the ship can reach her home port. And it is not without deep irony that the English-Cockney Donkin longs for (and accelerates) his death while Belfast, the Irishman, mourns it excessively.

Donkin's subversive agitation is of a different kind. He is a member of the crew (although Conrad welcomed a reading which found it difficult to accept him as such[21]), but also their (as well as the officers') antagonist. Donkin hates those 'damned furriners [who] should be kept under',[22] he swears, he cheats, he steals from the dying Wait. And although he almost succeeds in inciting a mutiny, in the end he reaps more disapproval than approval from the crew.

It has been claimed that *The Nigger of the 'Narcissus'* can 'safely be called Conrad's first English novel: not only is the *Narcissus* sailing home to England, but the novel's celebration of life at sea is simultaneously a celebration of the traditions of its creator's adopted homeland.'[23] However, the fact that a predominantly British crew is susceptible to Wait's and Donkin's subversive actions (although they withstand them in the final resort), demonstrates more ambivalence than can be allowed for in the text of an author who allegedly wanted to ingratiate himself with his readers. Moreover, by making a foreigner, a black African, the test case of the crew's psychology *and* by finding *them* wanting, Conrad's scathing criticism is only topped by allowing Donkin, the racist and violent xenophobe, to proudly proclaim his nationality: 'I am an Englishman, I am.'[24] No attempt at making the crew more multicultural in character would have added anything substantial to this supreme irony.

'Youth' (1898)

When, four years before his voyage on the *Narcissus*, Korzeniowski passed his second mate's examination in May 1880, his hopes of gaining an adequate berth immediately came to nothing; he had to make do with that of third mate on the *Loch Etive*, a full-rigged iron sailing ship of 1,287 gross tonnage, built in 1877. Perhaps the fact that the *Palestine*, a much smaller wooden barque of 427 gross tonnage, built in 1857, offered him his first berth as second mate about a year later, made Korzeniowski stick to this relatively old and leaky ship. The facts of this particular voyage are well-known:

> Under Captain Elijah Beard and with a crew of thirteen, the *Palestine* departed from London on 21 September bound for Bangkok. Stopping over at Gravesend until 1 October, she almost took three weeks to reach Newcastle after meeting violent gales (18 October) and remained there six weeks to load her cargo of coal. Departing from Newcastle on 29 November, the ship lost her sails and sprang a leak in the English Channel (24 December) and, with the crew refusing to continue, put back to Falmouth, where she underwent repairs for eight months. ... She departed from Falmouth for Bangkok with a new crew of twelve on 17 September 1882. Spontaneous combustion led to the ship's catching fire (12 March) and caused a coal-gas explosion (14 March), forcing the crew to abandon ship in Bangka Strait, off Sumatra. The crew took to boats and next day reached Muntok on Bangka Island. From there (21 March) they were taken in the SS *Sissie* to Singapore, where, on 2 April, a marine court of inquiry exonerated the master, officers, and crew from all blame.[25]

At the time of the shipwreck, the crew of the *Palestine* were 'a mixture of nationalities, of ages and origins':[26] 'Five men came from Cornwall, one from Ireland, and the remainder were foreigners - an Australian, a Negro from the Antilles, a Dutchman, and a Norwegian.'[27]

At least two aspects of 'Youth' have to be considered: first, this 'narrative' was Conrad's second contribution to *Blackwood's Edinburgh*

Magazine (and the first deliberately conceived as such). *Maga*, as it was affectionately called by its readers, originally founded as a Tory alternative to the liberal *Edinburgh Review*, was a Conservative and imperialist monthly magazine 'with a long reputation and a steady readership in the Establishment ..., people who liked seriously intoned reading on royalty and the aristocracy, on the problems of the army and the navy ... and about other countries in the world'.[28] Thus, it is hardly surprising that Conrad tried to meet his readers' expectations by combining a particular 'Englishness of the storytelling occasion'[29] - 'This could have occurred nowhere but in England, where men and sea interpenetrate, so to speak'[30] - with an exotic yarn.

Second, 'Youth' is a frame-narrative in which a group of four men - 'a director of companies, an accountant, a lawyer'[31] and a nameless I-narrator - listen to the tale of a fifth man, 'Marlow (at least I think that is how he spelt his name)',[32] of his first voyage to the East: Bangkok. These five men 'all began life in the merchant service' and between them 'there was the strong bond of the sea, and also the fellowship of the craft'.[33] Obviously, Marlow's auditors 'may be seen to reproduce a typical cross-section of a *Blackwood's* audience'.[34]

In his tale Marlow extols the crew of the *Judea*: '[T]hey all worked. That crew of Liverpool hard cases had in them the right stuff. It's my experience they always have.'[35] On the original *Palestine*, however, as we have seen, there was not a single Liverpudlian. Somewhat later Marlow contends:

[I]t was something in them, something inborn and subtle and everlasting. I don't say positively that the crew of a French or German merchantman wouldn't have done it, but I doubt whether it would have been done in the same way. There was a completeness in it, something solid like a principle, and masterful like an instinct - a disclosure of something secret - of that hidden something, that gift of good or evil that makes racial difference, that shapes the fate of nations.[36]

Certainly, this is highly patriotic, and as a small but hardly irrelevant indication of how far Marlow may have been prepared to conform to and, thereby, confirm his audience's nationalist prejudices we should note that in the *Maga* version Conrad had him even speak of 'the crew of a *vulgar* French or German merchantman'.[37] But as much as there cannot be any doubt that Conrad's original audience could (and would) easily identify with Marlow's group of auditors, their world-view, values and attitudes,[38] it would be rash and wrong to assume that Marlow is both a unified figure and Conrad's mouthpiece. Lest we forget: the voyage described in 'Youth' consists of a series of catastrophes, and it acquires its positive (if elegiac) evaluation only in a survivor's memory of 'a moment of strength, of romance, of glamour - of youth!'[39] In the beginning, Marlow introduces it as one of 'those voyages that seem ordered for the illustration of life, that might stand for a symbol of existence. You fight, work, sweat, nearly kill yourself, sometimes do kill yourself, trying to accomplish something - and you can't. Not from any fault of yours. You simply can do nothing, neither great nor little - not a thing in the world.'[40] This is borne out step by step throughout the voyage, culminates in the explosion of the ship's cargo and finds its ultimate expression in an almost apocalyptic vision:

> A portion of several boards holding together had fallen across the rail, and one end protruded overboard, like a gangway leading upon nothing, like a gangway leading over the deep sea, leading to death - as if inviting us to walk the plank at once and be done with our ridiculous troubles.[41]

But this is not all: the prospect which originally enticed Marlow to stick to the ship - the chance to see, hear and feel the East ('Bangkok!'[42]) - proves to be of doubtful value. Although he avers that he 'can never forget' the 'first sigh of the East'[43] on his face, he perceives the 'mysterious East' as 'perfumed like a flower, silent like death, dark like a grave'.[44] However, when he hears the East, it speaks to him 'in a Western voice' raging 'aloud in two languages':[45] a European ship's officer mistakes him for a 'native' in the dark. And the people of the East themselves, when Marlow eventually meets them, remain silent:

> And then I saw the men of the East - they were looking at me. The whole length of the jetty was full of people. I saw brown, bronze, yellow faces, the black eyes, the glitter, the colour of an Eastern crowd. And all these beings stared without a murmur, without a sigh, without a movement.[46]

So, young Marlow's adventure is nearly thwarted: he survives, but only by the skin of his teeth; he reaches the East, but has to come to terms with its enigmatic silence and the fact that his inquisitive gaze is returned; he feels 'the glamour of youth' and 'the fire of it',[47] but has to accept, twenty-two years later, the limited nature of his experiences. In this sense, 'Youth' is a story of initiation: to responsibility (the *Judea* offers Marlow his first berth as second mate and, after the ship's explosion, his first command of a small boat), to the East and its otherness and, finally, in the process of telling the story, to middle-age, its difference and limitations in comparison with youth. And in this context, I would suggest, the apparently quite straightforward extolling of the virtues of British seamen should be read as part of Marlow's subjective recollection of his particular initiation whose memory is, at one and the same time, glorified by his enthusiasm and qualified by his wistful but nevertheless pervasive scepticism.

And even if we accept that in 'Youth' Marlow (and through him, perhaps, Conrad as well) did voice patriotic sentiments, we also have to note that, for example, in 'Typhoon' (1902) these sentiments are seriously subverted when the prototypical English master mariner Captain MacWhirr neither understands nor shares his first mate's nationalistic indignation at the fact that the ship they serve on runs under the Siamese flag and not the Red Ensign.

Conrad, the Foreigner

How, then, do we evaluate our readings of *The Nigger of the 'Narcissus'* and 'Youth'? Undoubtedly, the crews in these (fictitious) ships are more English than in the ships Conrad (as Korzeniowski) really sailed in. But does this mean that he tried to make his sea service appear 'unequivocally English in character'?[48] If so, why did he (want to) do that? Did he want to forget about the fact that, in most ships, probably he was regarded as an outsider - not so much because of his foreign nationality and language but, rather, because he did not drink but, instead, spent his free time reading books?[49] We simply do not know. Or did he want to make his tales more readily acceptable for English readers? Perhaps, but if Conrad had really wanted to secure his success as a writer by ingratiating himself with a conservative publishing business and its equally conservative readership, this would have been much easier if he had written less complex and demanding texts.

First, I should like to suggest that in many of Conrad's texts a more radically ambivalent attitude towards his adopted country can be found than has hitherto been suggested (even if this ambivalence does not find its primary expression in the ratio between the British and the foreign people in his tales). Secondly, I would argue that a reading which assumes that those of his tales in which Conrad drew on personal experiences should be 'true to life' as he experienced it, is a *misreading* (which disregards not only Conrad's artistic credo but almost everything we know about the autobiographical and realist modes of writing). But what are the implications of such a misreading? Do the critics tacitly assume that Conrad, the Polish émigré who became a British master mariner and a writer, could not but wish that his process of being accepted and integrated in his chosen community had *always already* taken place? Do they assume that this wish determined (i.e. reductively limited) his writing? And do they, in some absurdly post-imperial move, criticize him for not depicting the multi-national reality on his ships 'faithfully' so that they can confront him with his own foreignness all the better (and more unashamedly crudely)? The first paragraph of Virginia Woolf's obituary is a telling example of such a 'critical policy':

> Suddenly, without giving us time to arrange our thoughts or prepare our phrases, our guest has left us; and his withdrawal without farewell or ceremony is in keeping with his mysterious arrival, long years ago, to take up his lodging in this country. For there was always an air of mystery about him. It was partly his Polish birth, partly his memorable appearance, partly his preference for living in the depths of the country, out of ear-shot of gossips, beyond reach of hostesses, so that for news of him one had to depend upon the evidence of simple visitors with a habit of ringing doorbells who reported of their unknown host that he had the most perfect manners, the brightest eyes, and spoke English with a strong foreign accent.[50]

This is malice masquerading as sensitivity: Conrad, who had been granted British nationality in 1886, at his death, 38 years later, was still regarded as a 'guest' (definitely not 'one of us') with 'an air of mystery about him', who took up his 'lodging' (not residence) in Britain and after all these years still spoke 'English with a strong foreign accent'. Reading this it seems impossible that Conrad not only enriched the themes and topics of English literature but also its language and narratological means.

Related to the criticism that Conrad made the crews of his fictitious ships more English than those he sailed with is the point that he was alleg-edly 'consistently silent on the problem of relations between the nationali-ties'[51] in the British Merchant Service. This definitely is not true. *The Nigger of the 'Narcissus'*, as I have indicated above, deals with this topic *in extenso*, and another telling example can be found in part VI of *A Personal Record* (1912) where Conrad describes his examinations. Although the way in which Conrad represented or, rather, mis-represented them (giving false details about his actual service at sea, leaving out his failures to pass the first-mate's and the master's exam at the first sitting) have been closely scrutinized, critics have seldom paid close attention to other telling details Conrad uses in describing his experiences.

Korzeniowski took his second-mate's examination in 1880, two years after his arrival in Britain. Some thirty years later, Conrad wrote that his examiner 'must, I am forced to conclude, have been unfavourably impressed by something in my appearance'.[52] Either he did not know or did not want to write what it exactly was, but a guess that it may have been

Korzeniowski's English is as good as any. The examination lasted for
almost three hours which, according to the doorkeeper Conrad mentions,
had never happened before. And what were Conrad's feelings? 'Had I been
a strange microbe with potentialities of deadly mischief to the Merchant
Service I could not have been submitted to a more microscopic examination.'[53] This imagery tells a clear story: the foreign applicant feels himself
treated as a dangerous intruder (invading the British Merchant Service like
a germ the human body), who has to be kept out if possible.

Conrad described the examiner of his next, the first-mate's examination
(1884) as 'motionless, mysterious, remote, enigmatical' who 'began by
trying to make me talk nonsense'.[54] Although this phrase has certainly to be
read metaphorically, its reverberations also signal the possibility that the
examiner tried to confuse him by making use of his disadvantage as a non-
native speaker of English. However, the task he set him is even more
telling:

> You must understand that the scheme of the test he was applying to me was, I
> gathered, a homeward passage - the sort of passage I would not wish to my
> bitterest enemy. That imaginary ship seemed to labour under a most
> comprehensive curse. It's no use enlarging on these never-ending misfortunes
> ... Finally he shoved me into the North Sea (I suppose) and provided me with a
> lee-shore with outlying sandbanks - the Dutch coast presumably. Distance,
> eight miles. The evidence of such implacable animosity deprived me of speech
> for quite half a minute.[55]

Although we can be sure that such a procedure was quite normal, this particular task - a homeward passage peppered with endless difficulties and
misfortunes - may have touched nerves in the foreign applicant which sig-
nalled meanings lying well beyond this particular examination.

The final master's examination, which Conrad characterized as com-
paratively 'easy-going',[56] took place two years later. However, this time the
examiner explicitly (although not in an unfriendly way) discussed Korzeniowski's foreignness. His answer is straightforward:

> I told him, smiling, that no doubt I could have found a ship much nearer my
> native place, but I had thought to myself that if I was to be a seaman then I
> would be a British seaman and no other. It was a matter of deliberate choice.[57]

Certainly *this* answer was a matter of deliberate choice, although it
probably was not true. When Korzeniowski went to France in 1874 he still
was 'a Russian subject without official permission to live and work abroad'
- a fact which rendered 'his employment in French ships ... problematic by

new regulations in the French merchant navy requiring crew members to have completed national service in their own countries'.[58] To evade this service, however, had been one of the reasons why he had gone to France in the first place because, in Russia, as the son of a political prisoner, he could be forced to serve up to twenty years, while in British merchant ships 'no special permits were required for the enlistment of foreigners'.[59]

I think the way in which Conrad negotiated the question of his national difference clearly illustrates his ambivalence: on the one hand, he craved to belong - and he felt adopted, not only by the British Merchant Service but also by the English language;[60] on the other, he unflinchingly registered the obstacles he had to (and could not) overcome. Even if we assume that this chapter of *A Personal Record* contains as much fiction as autobiographical detail, this does not erase the impression that Conrad sensitively felt, reacted to and wrote about the problem of relations between the nationalities.

The Shadow-Line (1917)

Korzeniowski commanded the *Otago*, an iron barque of 367 gross tonnage, for a little more than fourteen months. He was engaged in Singapore on 19 January 1888 and joined the ship in Bangkok five days later 'for her voyage to Australia. Departure being delayed until 9 February, the ship with a crew of ten took three weeks to reach Singapore, where she stopped over for fresh medical supplies and new crew members.'[61] From there he took the *Otago* to Sydney, Melbourne and, again, to Sydney. Voyages to Mauritius (and back to Melbourne) and Port Elizabeth in South Africa (and back to Minlacowie in South Australia and, from there, to Adelaide) followed. At the end of March 1889, Korzeniowski resigned his command and returned to England.

Some ten years later, Conrad mentioned the idea of a story under the title 'First Command' in a letter to William Blackwood[62] but, although he continued to allude to it for about a year and a half, it did not materialize. Sixteen years later, however, Conrad returned to his topic in a different mood and context: the First World War seems to have provided him with the necessary perspective for what he wanted to say. His letters from the early war years convey a stark picture of his 'steadily darkening mood' and a 'sense of frustrated uselessness';[63] the following lines to Ralph Wedgewood (15 November 1914) are paradigmatic: 'I am painfully aware of being crippled, of being idle, of being useless with a sort of absurd anxiety, as though it could matter to the greatness of the Empire.'[64] Fifteen months later, when he had already finished *The Shadow-Line*, he wrote to John Quinn (27 February 1916) in the same vein:

I have been affected mentally and physically more profoundly than I thought it possible. Perhaps if I had been able to 'lend a hand' in some way I would have found this war easier to bear. But I can't. I am slowly getting more and more of a cripple - and this too preys on my mind not a little.[65]

In writing *The Shadow-Line* (a reworking of his engagement and first spell as master of the *Otago*), Conrad, to the best of his ability, 'lent a hand': by creating a story which depicts 'the change from youth, carefree and fervent, to the more self-conscious and more poignant period of maturer life', he could not only *write about* something he intimately knew but also *speak to* a certain 'feeling of identity, though with an enormous difference of scale'[66] between his and his son's generation (to whom the book is dedicated) by universalizing his subject.

Like 'Youth', *The Shadow-Line* is a story of initiation. At the centre of this tale (told very straightforwardly by a first-person narrator) are the experiences of a young man who has to cross the 'shadow-line' between different kinds of responsibility: after somewhat rashly throwing up his berth as first mate because of the 'obscure feeling of life being but a waste of days',[67] a command is unexpectedly offered to him which puts him to the test of his professional and individual qualities. The ship is becalmed, the crew fall sick, his first mate suffers from fever, depression and paranoia, and the second mate is not 'of that invaluable stuff from which a commander's right hand is made',[68] either. Little wonder that the young commander increasingly feels the strain.[69] When he eventually finds out that his predecessor tampered with the medical chest so that nothing is left of the vital quinine, severe self-doubt as well as overwhelming feelings of incompetence and guilt nearly render him unable to act. What, paradoxically and wonderfully, allows the ship and her crew to survive, is a combination of weaknesses which turns into strength: a master sceptical of his competence, more impeded than aided by a mentally sick first mate, succeeds in sailing on a 'sick' sea with a sick crew because these weaknesses are perceived and acknowledged as part of the human condition and mastered by common effort. While the master takes 'the lead in the work', the men, mere ghosts and shadows, toil 'like Titans'.[70] And this adherence to an implicit but, nevertheless, 'distinct ideal',[71] makes them 'so wonderful, so worthy of my undying regard'.[72]

Interestingly, we do not learn any details about the crew's ethnic composition in *The Shadow-Line*: the few names (Burns, Ransome, 'Frenchy', Gambril) contain only an equivocal message. Of the *Otago*, however, although there are slight differences in the crew listings between Allen[73] and Najder,[74] we know that her British members were in the minority. Quite obviously, Conrad wanted to make a point about the war without appealing to jingoistic sentiments. The *Otago*'s first mate, for example, was a German called Charles Born. The first mate's name in *The Shadow-Line* is Burns; as far as we can gather, he is an Englishman. If Conrad had wished to play with the nationalistic feelings of his readers, he could have easily let this unlikeable and temporarily insane man be of German nationality (as he did in *Lord Jim*, when he 'turned' Captain Joseph Lucas Clark, responsible for the *Jeddah* scandal, into 'a sort of renegade New South Wales German'[75]). But this, I should like to argue, he would have regarded as a distraction from his more important theme: the crew's spirited attitude, endurance and solidarity symbolizing a nation's struggle for survival.

'Tradition' (1918) - 'Well Done' (1918) - 'Confidence' (1919)

This attempt at revisiting Conrad's crews and the meanings he attached to them in his tales and novels would be incomplete without a brief look at three propaganda pieces he wrote towards the end of the war. 'Tradition' appeared in the *Daily Mail* (4 March 1918), and 'Well Done' in the *Daily Chronicle* (22 to 24 August 1918). Both are tributes to the efforts of the men of the British Merchant Service during the war; the former includes a report of heroism at sea, while the latter turns into 'a eulogistic prose poem extolling the work ethic, spirit of service, seamanship, and national sentiment that have gone into the making of the Merchant Service's unspoken historical tradition'.[76] The third piece, 'Confidence', was commissioned by the *Daily Mail* on the occasion of the signing of the Treaty of Versailles and appeared on 30 June 1919 expressing Conrad's 'unshaken confidence' in the values represented by the British Merchant Service, which 'rests on the hearts of men who do not change'.[77] Although he privately confided his doubts,[78] we cannot disregard the fact that in these pieces Conrad practised a kind of (unified, eulogistic, propagandist) 'voice' which was prefigured in certain passages of *The Mirror of the Sea* (1906) and *A Personal Record* (1912) and elaborated in his 'Memorandum on the Scheme for Fitting Out a Sailing Ship for the Purpose of Perfecting the Training of Merchant Service Officers Belonging to the Port of Liverpool [1920]',[79] but which he assiduously avoided in his fiction.

Concluding Remarks

In my concluding - but deliberately inconclusive - remarks I should like to make three points. First, I should like to argue that Conrad as a writer did not speak with one voice. Not only do his fictional texts (spanning a writing career of thirty years) markedly differ with regard to their topics, *dramatis personae* and ideas, but they also differ from his essays, articles and letters. Although it is possible to use them for mutual elucidation, this does not imply congruence in meaning. Any attempt by biographers or literary critics to detect, distil or define some unified vision in his work cannot but fail *vis-à-vis* this heterogeneous output. Thus, we have to accept that although in most of his essays and other casual writings he praised 'sea life as a life of service' informed by 'an unshakeable code of professional duty, solidarity, and a keen sense of the value of work', his fictions 'tend with unremitting honesty to reveal human failures to meet this ideal standard'.[80]

Second, if we want to sketch the individual context in which this particular - disjunctive - writing originated we could do worse than remind ourselves of a number of imbricated factors influencing Korzeniowski's life and personal development: (i) as a young Polish *szlachcic* in 19th-century Ukraine he was exposed to 'the experience of being both a colonial and a colonialist, since the Polish gentry who were politically and culturally oppressed by Russia and Prussia in turn exercised domination over the Ukrainian serfs on their estates';[81] (ii) the mourning of his parents' early death (indirectly caused by their participation in the struggle for Polish independence) was contained and, perhaps, at the same time, transfigured in his specific perception of Poland's colonial status: 'I look at the future from the depths of a very dark past, and I find I am allowed nothing but fidelity to absolutely lost cause, to an idea without a future.'[82] Perhaps it is possible (iii) to read Korzeniowski's escape to the sea at the age of seventeen as his particular 'work of mourning'[83] which enabled him to replace one (lost) 'object' of love and devotion (his family and native country) by a new one (the sea, ships, and the community of sailors). However, (iv) the tragedy of Korzeniowski's particular choice was that his new 'object' also represented a 'lost cause': for almost sixteen years, he served in 'the dying world of sail'[84] of the British merchant marine, with more than three-quarters of this time as officer or master. (v) When the number of foreign-going vessels sharply decreased in the final third of the 19th century even as tonnage rapidly increased and, as a consequence, employment for masters fell,[85] Korzeniowski, who could not find a berth, became Conrad: the master mariner became a writer whose texts - instances of another 'work of mourning', I should like to suggest - became affirmative enunciations of the official ethos, on the one hand, *and* subversive memorials of 'lost causes', on the other.

Having said this it, third, does not make much sense to regard the fact that Conrad's fictitious crews do not match the number of foreigners in the ships in which Korzeniowski sailed as an attempt to let his service in the British merchant marine appear more English in character than it really was. What *is* striking, though, is the attempt at unifying and, thereby, misreading a very diverse and disjunctive oeuvre in such a way. Perhaps Henry Havelock Ellis was right in assuming that, on the one hand, the 'Englishman ... is an essential sailor' because each successive 'people that from prehistoric days onwards invaded and conquered England came as sailors, facing all the dangers of an unknown coast and its hostile population',[86] but that, on the other hand, English writers from Hakluyt to Masefield had immense difficulties in adequately incorporating these experiences in the collective cultural memory by creating artistically convincing texts. In this context, the fact that eventually a foreigner succeeded in doing just that - albeit in a more ambivalent way than many readers may have realized - could (however indirectly) be regarded as a particular offence which, in turn, had to be belittled as a move of over-adaptation.

Notes

1   Cf. Zdzislaw Najder, *Joseph Conrad. A Chronicle* (Cambridge: Cambridge University Press, 1983), 39-169.

2   Cf. Andrea White, *Joseph Conrad and the Adventure Tradition. Constructing and Deconstructing the Imperial Subject* (Cambridge: Cambridge University Press, 1993).

3   Owen Knowles and Gene M. Moore (eds), *Oxford Reader's Companion to Joseph Conrad* (Oxford: Oxford University Press, 2000), 346-51.

4   Cf. *The Collected Letters of Joseph Conrad*, ed. Frederick R. Karl and Laurence Davies (Cambridge: Cambridge University Press, 1983-96), vol. 2: 1898-1902, 167 (henceforth referred to as *CL*, volume, page).

5   Allan Simmons, 'Note on the Crew', Joseph Conrad, *The Nigger of the 'Narcissus'*, ed. Allan Simmons, Everyman Centennial Edition (London: Dent, 1997), 146-53, 149.

6   Morgan writes that 'the new mate went mad with melancholy (earning places for his name, and malady, in *The Shadow-Line*)'. Gerald Morgan, 'The Book and the Ship *Narcissus*', Joseph Conrad, *The Nigger of the 'Narcissus'*, ed. Robert Kimbrough, Norton Critical Edition (New York: Norton, 1979), 201-12, 203.

7   Conrad, *The Nigger of the 'Narcissus'*, 27. Throughout this essay my references to Conrad's works are to the respective volumes of Dent's Collected Edition (1946-55) if not otherwise stated.

8   G. Jean-Aubry, '[Conrad on the *Narcissus*]', Conrad, *The Nigger of the 'Narcissus'*, ed. Kimbrough, Norton Critical Edition, 200.

9   Simmons, 'Note', 150.

10   *The Nigger of the 'Narcissus'*, ed. Kimbrough, Norton Critical Edition, x.

11   Najder, *Joseph Conrad*, 82.

12   Cf. Peter McDonald, 'Men of Letters and Children of the Sea: Conrad and the Henley Circle Revisited', *The Conradian* 21, no. 1 (1996), 15-56; cf. also Knowles and Moore, *Companion*, 295-6.

13   *The Nigger of the 'Narcissus'*, ed. Kimbrough, Norton Critical Edition, 29.
14   Knowles and Moore, *Companion*, 93.
15   *Last Essays*, 95.
16   Joseph Conrad, 'To My Readers in America', Conrad, *The Nigger of the 'Narcissus'*, ed. Kimbrough, Norton Critical Edition, 167-8, 168.
17   *Ibid.*
18   *The Nigger of the 'Narcissus'*, ed. Kimbrough, Norton Critical Edition, 17.
19   Conrad, 'To My Readers in America', 168.
20   Cf. *The Nigger of the 'Narcissus'*, ed. Kimbrough, Norton Critical Edition, 139.
21   Cf. his exchange of letters with W.H. Chesson, a reader at T. Fisher Unwin, in Conrad, *The Nigger of the 'Narcissus'*, ed. Kimbrough, Norton Critical Edition, 187-9.
22   *The Nigger of the 'Narcissus'*, ed. Kimbrough, Norton Critical Edition, 13.
23   Knowles and Moore, *Companion*, 246.
24   *The Nigger of the 'Narcissus'*, ed. Kimbrough, Norton Critical Edition, 12.
25   Knowles and Moore, *Companion*, 348-9.
26   Jerry Allen, *The Sea Years of Joseph Conrad* (London: Methuen, 1967), 159.
27   Najder, *Joseph Conrad*, 78.
28   Ivo Vidan, quoted in Knowles and Moore, *Companion*, 39.
29   Knowles and Moore, *Companion*, 39.
30   *Youth*, 3.
31   *Ibid.*
32   *Ibid.*
33   *Ibid.*
34   Knowles and Moore, *Companion*, 39. This first Marlow tale was followed by three more: *Heart of Darkness* (1899), *Lord Jim* (1900) and *Chance* (1913-14).
35   *Youth, Heart of Darkness, The End of the Tether. Three Stories*, 25.
36   *Youth*, 28-9.
37   *Blackwood's Edinburgh Magazine* 164 (1898), 323 (my italics).
38   Cf. Todd G. Willy, 'The Call to Imperialism in Conrad's "Youth": An Historical Reconstruction', *Journal of Modern Literature* 8 (1980), 39-50.
39   *Youth*, 42.
40   *Ibid.*, 4.
41   *Ibid.*, 26.
42   *Ibid.*, 5 et passim.
43   *Ibid.*, 37.
44   *Ibid.*, 38. And somewhat later he adds: 'I have known its fascination since; I have seen the mysterious shores, the still waters, the lands of brown nations, where a stealthy Nemesis lies in wait, pursues, overtakes so many of the conquering race, who are proud of their wisdom, of their knowledge, of their strength.' (*Ibid.*, 41-2)
45   *Ibid.*, 39.
46   *Ibid.*, 40.
47   *Ibid.*, 30.
48   Najder, *Joseph Conrad*, 82.
49   Allen, *The Sea Years*, 108-9.
50   Virginia Woolf, 'Joseph Conrad', *Joseph Conrad. Critical Assessments*, ed. Keith Carabine, vol. 1: *Conrad's Polish Heritage, Memories and Impressions, Contemporary and Early Responses* (Mountfield: Helm Information, 1992), 420-24, 420.
51   Najder, *Joseph Conrad*, 82.

52 *A Personal Record*, 113.
53 *Ibid.*
54 *Ibid.*, 114.
55 *Ibid.*, 115.
56 *Ibid.*, 117.
57 *Ibid.*, 119.
58 Knowles and Moore, *Companion*, 240.
59 *Ibid.*
60 *A Personal Record*, v.
61 Knowles and Moore, *Companion*, 350.
62 *CL*, 2, 167.
63 Knowles and Moore, *Companion*, 117-18.
64 *CL*, 5, 427.
65 *CL*, 5, 559-60.
66 *The Shadow-Line*, vi.
67 *Ibid.*, 22-3.
68 *Ibid.*, 73.
69 *Ibid.*, 86, 92, 93, 95, 106-7.
70 *Ibid.*, 109.
71 *Ibid.*, 126.
72 *Ibid.*, 100.
73 Cf. Allen, *The Sea Years*, 247, 253, 322-3.
74 Cf. Najder, *Joseph Conrad*, 105-6.
75 *Lord Jim*, 14; cf. Allen, *The Sea Years*, 122-50.
76 Knowles and Moore, *Companion*, 399.
77 *Notes on Life and Letters*, 206-7.
78 Cf. Knowles and Moore, *Companion*, 70.
79 *Last Essays*, 66-80.
80 Knowles and Moore, *Companion*, 47-8.
81 Benita Parry, 'Conrad and England', Raphael Samuel (ed.), *Patriotism. The Making and Unmaking of British National Identity, Vol. 3: National Fictions* (London: Routledge, 1989), 189-98, 194.
82 *CL*, 2, 161.
83 Cf. Sigmund Freud, 'Trauer und Melancholie [1917]', Freud, *Studienausgabe*, vol. 3 (Frankfurt am Main: Fischer, 1989), 197-212.
84 R.D. Foulke, 'Life in the Dying World of Sail', *The Journal of British Studies* 3, no. 1 (1963), 105-36.
85 Cf. Valerie Burton, 'The Making of a Nineteenth-Century Profession: Shipmasters and the British Shipping Industry', *Journal of the Canadian Historical Association* 1 (1990), 97-118.
86 Henry Havelock Ellis, 'From "Mr. Conrad's World"', *Joseph Conrad. Critical Assessments*, ed. Carabine, vol. 1, 521-5, 521.

10 Cabin'd Yet Unconfined: Heroic Masculinity in English Seafaring Novels

SUSAN BASSNETT

In 1842 Robert Browning published two poems that were to enter into the national consciousness in a profoundly significant way. 'Home-Thoughts, from Abroad' with its famous opening lines 'Oh, to be in England / Now that April's there'[1] is still frequently anthologized and taught in schools, but the companion poem, 'Home-Thoughts, from the Sea' is less well-known today, for reasons that may become obvious when a contemporary reader encounters it. Here, for the benefit of that reader, is Browning's poem in full:

> Nobly, nobly Cape Saint Vincent to the North-west died away;
> Sunset ran, one glorious blood-red, reeking into Cadiz Bay;
> Bluish 'mid the burning water, full in face Trafalgar lay;
> In the dimmest North-east distance dawn'd Gibraltar grand and grey;
> 'Here and here did England help me: how can I help England?' - say,
> Whoso turns as I, this evening, turn to God to praise and pray,
> While Jove's planet rises yonder, silent over Africa.[2]

It would be easy, at the start of the 21st century, to dismiss this as a jingoistic relic from an imperial past. Nevertheless, I choose deliberately to begin with this poem, because it touches on what we shall call 'the matter of England', the mythical construction of an ideal of England and Englishness that is still very much present in contemporary discourse. For in Browning's short lyric, the myth of English greatness is connected both to geography and to historical circumstance, following a long-established tradition, perhaps most clearly exemplified in John of Gaunt's description of England in Shakespeare's *Richard II* as a 'sceptred isle':

176

> This precious stone set in the silver sea,
> Which serves it in the office of a wall,
> Or as a moat defensive to a house
> Against the envy of less happier lands ...[3]

Here the sea is depicted as a moat and as a wall, a defensive ring around the island home. It was a view that found support in the 1590s, in the uneasy final years of the reign of Elizabeth I, when the cult of Gloriana was being created, building upon the epic defeat of the Spanish Armada in 1588. That historical turning-point is suggested by Browning's reference to Cadiz, where Sir Francis Drake attacked the Spanish fleet in 1587 in an attempt to prevent the launching of the Armada, an action enshrined in folklore as 'singeing the King of Spain's beard'. Drake's triumph at Cadiz is then linked to Nelson's later victory at Trafalgar in 1805. English pride, Browning is suggesting, is bound up with English naval success and always has been. Not for nothing did the navy style itself the Senior Service: England's survival and England's greatness were the result of England's long-standing control of the seas. And Browning was well aware of the popular importance of that myth: the death of Nelson inspired national mourning; and prints depicting the dying Admiral sold in great numbers at fairs across the country, along with Staffordshire pottery figures purporting to represent him. The year that saw the publication of Browning's poem was also the year when a column celebrating the greatness of Nelson was erected in London's Trafalgar Square.

Commenting on Nelson's career in his history of the Royal Navy, William Laird Clowes points out that although he may have been a strategic genius, had he lived, Nelson would have had problems fitting in to the rapidly expanding, reformed navy that was developing all around him: 'Had Nelson survived Trafalgar, there would have been but little scope for his marvellous energy, his religious devotion to duty, and his wonderful military genius.'[4] Nelson, Clowes argues, was a man of a particular time, who would have had difficulty coping with life after Trafalgar, for 'neither his education nor his tastes fitted him to shine in civil life.'[5] This is a matter of opinion, but I raise it here because it will form part of the mythology of naval heroes that writers of fiction were to develop later on, that is, the gap between the hero's role at sea and that same hero's more ambiguous relationships on land. Clowes believed that Nelson died at the peak of his achievements, and that had he lived after Trafalgar, he would have been unable to continue in the same way for the navy itself was changing. Certainly, the navy increased phenomenally during Nelson's lifetime: between 1789 and 1812, numbers rose from 16,000 to 140,000,[6] necessitating organizational changes, while the same period was dominated by calls within the service for reform of abusive practices.

In 1836 a book appeared entitled *Nautical Economy, or the Forecastle Recollections of Events during the Last War. Dedicated to the brave Tars of Old England by a Sailor, politely called by the Officers of the Navy Jack Nasty-Face.*[7] The author claimed to have been a serving seaman between 1805 and 1811, and his intention was to expose the extent of malpractice at sea: the brutality of the regime, the incompetence of the officers, the appalling food, the corruption and the cruelty. Despite his account of the hardships suffered on board His Majesty's ships, the author nevertheless expressed his pride in the navy and his belief that there was none other comparable to it. A good captain could command the loyalty of his men and win great prizes, while a bad captain who ran an unhappy ship where floggings were frequent always ran the risk of failure. The contrast between the good captain and the cruel one is a motif that we shall see recur in the seafaring novels of all the writers considered in this paper.

I propose to look at three such writers, all best-selling authors at different moments in time. All three are linked in terms of continuity through their treatment of similar material, but each offers a very different version of the matter of England and the myth of naval supremacy. Captain Frederick Marryat's life spanned the age of revolutions from 1792 to 1848, C.S. Forester was born in 1899, the year in which the Boer War began, and died in 1966, while the third writer, Patrick O'Brian, was born in the year when the First World War broke out, in 1914, and died at the very end of the millennium in January 2000. From Marryat's birth-year to the present we can observe the whole story of the rise of the British Empire to its high point at the close of the 19th century, when Britain had annexed one quarter of the territories on the world's surface, through two world wars, a period of uncertainty and change, and the present moment of devolution, re-evaluation and repositioning. It is not accidental that books on the history, theory and pragmatics of Englishness should have sold so many copies in England in the 1990s, for debates about the identity of the English, once perceived unproblematically and synonymously as British, have risen to the forefront of public attention with the end of the millennium. We might even talk about a crisis of Englishness, though since the debate is so heavily gendered, it is more productive to focus on the crisis of the figure of the English hero. For with the end of empire has come a reassessment of the masculine values that served to support the structures that sustained that empire and a revision of the particular version of heroism that emerged in the middle of the 19th century and endured until well into the second half of the 20th century.

Captain Marryat, though a prolific writer, is best known for only a handful of books that were phenomenally successful in the 19th century. He wrote for both adults and children, and the best known of his novels that focus on naval life are *Peter Simple*, the most autobiographical of his books that appeared in 1834, *Mr Midshipman Easy*, published in 1836, and *Masterman Ready, or the Wreck of the Pacific*, that came out in 1841-42. His first novel, *The Naval Officer, or Scenes and Adventures in the Life of Frank Mildmay* established him as a novelist in 1829.[8]

Captain Marryat went to sea in 1806, as a First-Class Volunteer in *The Imperieuse*, commanded by the extraordinary Thomas, Lord Cochrane. The adjective 'extraordinary' is used advisedly here, because although he is far less well known than Nelson today, his life and exploits were the subject of huge contemporary public interest. Cochrane distinguished himself through several daring (some might say foolhardy) attacks on the French and became a highly popular public hero. Then in 1814 he was implicated in a stock exchange fraud, was struck off the navy list, expelled from his seat as a member of Parliament and condemned to be set in the pillory, a penalty later commuted to imprisonment. Following this disgrace, he went out to take command of the Chilean revolutionary fleet, later moving on to command the Brazilian fleet. He returned to England in 1825 and was granted a royal pardon. Robert Harvey, in a recently published study of the men who liberated Latin America from Spanish rule has this to say about him:

> If Nelson was unquestionably Britain's greatest admiral since Drake, Cochrane was her greatest single-ship captain; indeed, he was the last of his kind, as the grey age of steam he so forcefully championed came to replace the far more romantic age of sail. As a master of naval deception and trickery, he was in a class of his own. ... Cussed, bloody-minded and egotistical, his relentless pursuit of his own self-interest and liberties led him to fight for the self-interest and liberties of others.[9]

Cochrane's life was, it could be argued, stranger than fiction. Apart from the details mentioned above, we could refer to his public quarrels with other officers, Napoleon's nickname for him as 'le loup des mers', his elopement at the age of 34 with a 16-year-old orphan and his dubious financial profiteering from the Greek War of Independence. So it is not surprising to find Cochrane or Cochrane-like figures emerging in the novels of Marryat, who admired his captain greatly. Cochrane is clearly the influence behind Patrick O'Brian's Captain Jack Aubrey, who is also condemned to stand in the pillory accused of fraud. In O'Brian's *The Reverse of the*

Medal, the punishment is carried out, but so great is Jack's popularity that his men form a cordon round him, to offer their moral support and prevent anyone from insulting their hero. In the next novel, *The Letter of Marque*, Jack takes up the command of his old ship, *The Surprise,* as a privateer, having been struck off the navy list. This reflects what happened in Cochrane's case, when he left England to take up his Chilean commission. Those who follow the adventures of Jack Aubrey and his friend and shipmate, the surgeon and intelligence agent Stephen Maturin through O'Brian's naval *roman fleuve* will know how prominently the Chilean campaign features in many of the novels.

We have begun to move around rather freely in time here, passing per-haps too quickly from Marryat to O'Brian, but this shifting is also signifi-cant, for there is a clear line of continuity between Marryat's novels and O'Brian's, that passes through the novels of C.S. Forester. Marryat based his novels on his own experiences in the navy, but he also drew upon the conventions of his time and upon the mythology of the seafaring hero, from his own experience encapsulated in the controversial figure of Cochrane. In his recent study on the conflicting socio-political views in the novels of Marryat, Louis Parascandola discusses the significance of the naval hero, as exemplified by Cochrane for Marryat's contemporary readers:

> The period of the Napoleonic wars, one of the greatest in British naval history, was recent enough so that many readers had lived through it, yet it was far enough removed to detach it from the present age. His novels often feature noble deeds, dashing heroes, *esprit de corps* and exciting action. They extol force but force used to preserve order, not subvert it. The frequent hand-to-hand combat, a form of fighting learned by Marryat while on board the *Imperieuse* with Lord Cochrane, recalls medieval tournaments. ... It is natural that a nation yearning to hold onto its past would find comfort in its military glory ...[10]

Marryat was drawing both upon his own experience and on the nostalgia for past greatness that held strong national appeal. The hierarchical structure of naval life could also serve to remind readers of the need for social order in an age troubled by the constant threat of social unrest, while the heroic exploits of valiant individual characters provided models of bravery. Significantly, in many of his books Marryat takes a strong moral line, rewarding good deeds and stressing the importance of gentlemanly behaviour.

O'Brian, whose novels reflect assiduous historical research, also read Marryat and the hugely successful C.S. Forester and the connections are clearly visible. Indeed, in many respects his hero is the antithesis of Forester's protagonist, Horatio (after Nelson, of course) Hornblower: Jack

Aubrey loves music, Hornblower is tone-deaf; Aubrey loves women, Hornblower is reserved and sexually repressed; Aubrey is gregarious, Hornblower is shy and taciturn; Aubrey has excellent communication skills, Hornblower has difficulty communicating with anybody except when giving orders at sea.

Forester created the character of Horatio Hornblower, a young man whose career we follow from the age of seventeen, as a midshipman on the HMS *Justinian* when he is troubled by the seasickness that will plague him throughout his career and has his first taste of action on the *Indefatigable* when '[h]is higher faculties were quite negatived by his lust for blood',[11] through the curiously ambiguous *Lieutenant Hornblower* (1952) in which we see him primarily through the eyes of his fellow Lieutenant, William Bush. In this novel, Bush and Hornblower have to contend with a demented paranoid captain, who mysteriously falls down a gangway. The suspicions of Bush about Hornblower's role in this event are shared by the reader, but we are repeatedly told of Hornblower's expressionless face whenever the question is raised of how the captain came to fall. Bush discovers facts about Hornblower's poverty, though not about the emotional insecurity that the narrator constantly hints at, which culminates in his disastrous, unthinking marriage to the plain, obsessive Maria, a marriage that is not destined to be his last. Hornblower is unlucky in love, and the novels trace his unhappy affairs and marriages which contrast with the sense of fulfilment that can only be realized when he is at sea.

Hornblower and the Hotspur (1962), the sequel to this novel, opens with Hornblower standing at the altar, when '[t]he thought came up in Hornblower's mind that these were the last few seconds in which he could withdraw from doing something which he knew to be ill-considered.'[12] He does not withdraw, though, and in subsequent novels the dismal marriage is contrasted with the freedom he experiences through his life at sea. As his naval career blossoms and his heroic exploits and human leadership win him friendship and respect, the failure of his personal life remains a constant shadow. It also serves to remind him of his own insecurity, for Maria comes from a lower-class background and Forester shows how her tastes, ethics and aspirations condemn Hornblower to feeling insecure with his improving social status. When he meets and falls in love with Lady Barbara, he is still shackled to the increasingly abject Maria. *A Ship of the Line* (1939) ends with him captured by the French, thinking of Maria who is pregnant again and wondering how Lady Barbara will judge him. Later, though he eventually marries Barbara, the relationship is not a success. Hornblower is as uncomfortable with women of all classes as he is at ease with men on board ship. Interestingly, Forester's novels were not written in biographical sequence as were O'Brian's, whose books follow one another in a sequence that requires the reader to have some knowledge of the previous volumes. The Hornblower books were written over a long period, with the first, *The Happy Return*, appearing in 1937 and the last, unfinished novel *Hornblower and the Crisis* published in 1967 after Forester's death, so that details of Hornblower's life emerge gradually and the reader fills in the gaps.

In *Mr Midshipman Easy*, Marryat's hero, Jack Easy, also has very different relationships between sea and land. When we first meet him, he is the only adored son of an eccentric father and a clinging mother. He is sent away to school, where the brutality of his treatment, though shocking to a contemporary reader, was meant to be humorous to Victorian readers, and following this period of toughening-up he goes to sea, where he continues to preach the doctrine of equality between all men that he has been taught by his philosophizing father. The novel is a picaresque account of his many adventures, culminating in his marriage to a beautiful Sicilian girl whose family he rescues. He returns to England, becomes a Conservative MP and lives out his days as a country gentleman. The sea serves as a framing device for showing the education of an unorthodox figure who, despite a difficult start in life, becomes a pillar of the community once he settles down. Life at sea is thus primarily a means of training unruly youths to become men, a process we see even more clearly in the heavily didactic *Masterman Ready*, in which a shipwrecked family are helped by the generosity and skill of the hero of the title. Two narratives intertwine: Ready's own life-story and the survival of the family on the island. Ready passes on his skills, his knowledge and his experience to young William, the boy-hero of the novel, who learns his lessons well.

Captain Marryat's career as a best-selling novelist began after he left the navy, but he had already published two pamphlets, one on a code of signals for merchant vessels in 1817 and another proposing the abolition of the system of pressing men into naval service in 1822. From these pamphlets, as well as from his novels, it becomes apparent that he was a man of some sensitivity who, like Nelson and Cochrane, had strong moral views on the state of the navy. In his works we can see another thread that recurs in the novels of the two later writers also: insistence on the need for electoral reform. Marryat, of course, witnessed at first hand the popular agitation that resulted in the first Reform Bill of 1832. Forester and O'Brian depict Hornblower and Jack Aubrey respectively witnessing the corruption in the upper ranks, along with the exploitation of the lower ranks, the evils of impressment and, in several of O'Brian's novels, the horrors of transportation, the convict colonies in Australia, and the slave trade, against which

Stephen Maturin is passionately committed. Both historical novelists weave their knowledge of the socio-political context of the early 19th century into their novels. Marryat, of course, takes that context for granted with his readers.

The success of the Hornblower novels and of Forester as the doyen of seafaring novelists remained intact throughout the post-war period. Then, in 1970, O'Brian published *Master and Commander*, the novel that introduces Jack Aubrey and Stephen Maturin and which was to be the first of 20 novels, all linked to one another as a *roman fleuve* that ended only with *Blue at the Mizzen* in 1999.[13] In the 1980s he became a cult success in the United States, where O'Brian appreciation societies flourished and a variety of O'Brian merchandise sold well, including a cookery book that offered recipes for dishes eaten at Aubrey's table - including the ubiquitous Drowned Baby, or Sunday suet pudding - and for dishes eaten by the Midshipmen - including stewed rats, or millers as they were known. By the time of his death in 2000, O'Brian had acquired a huge following and was beginning to be successful in Britain as well, where such figures as John Bayley, the late Iris Murdoch and A.S. Byatt declared themselves to be fans.

Why, we may ask, should an elderly writer of seafaring novels acquire such fame, amounting almost to cult status, at the end of the century, and what distinguishes him from his predecessors? The answer, I believe, is two-fold. First, O'Brian is simply a very fine writer, whose detailed historical research and shrewd sense of humour make him outstanding. The best way to think of his novels is to imagine C.S. Forester, with all his emphasis on action and military encounters, combined with Jane Austen's witty exposure of provincial bourgeois English life, told in a style reminiscent of the great Irish writer, J.G. Farrell. O'Brian creates detailed portraits of life ashore that run parallel to his portrayals of life at sea, so that readers are always aware of the dualism in the lives of his protagonists.

But another reason why O'Brian's novels should have emerged so significantly at the end of the 20th century is because he is the latest in a line of writers concerned with heroic English masculinity, and his treatment of that theme is more multi-faceted than either Forester or Marryat could ever have been, despite the fact that he builds upon a set of conventions that these writers, and others, established. By the time O'Brian came to create Aubrey and Maturin, the seafaring novel had become a distinctive genre, with its own conventions and a well-established readership. What was different, however, was the context in which O'Brian was writing. Marryat wrote with the confidence of a man who had both experienced at first hand naval life and who lived in an England that was expanding its colonial empire and moving to assert itself ever more prominently on the international stage; his was a didactic writing, with instruction filtered through entertainment, and if he tended to create grotesque characters both at sea and on land, this was merely a device to focus attention on his heroes. Right always triumphs in Marryat's universe and the forces of unrest and darkness are vanquished.

This kind of self-assurance is absent from Forester's works, for Forester was writing in a period when England was again sensitive to the threat of invasion, this time from Nazi Germany. Britain in the late 1930s was very different from the Britain of a hundred years earlier, and a note of uncertainty pervades Forester's novels. After the war, when the process of reconstruction of the 1950s depended on re-establishing national pride in an heroic past, the Hornblower novels became extremely popular, perhaps because Forester's hero struck a chord with readers. Hornblower, for all his bravery, his tactical skill and his ability to command a vessel is a flawed human being, a man like so many of the ex-servicemen returning to civilian life who is unable to settle outside the structures of his all-male naval world, a man devoted to duty but out of his depth with women and emotional attachments. In one of the oddest episodes in all the novels, in *Hornblower and the 'Atropos'* (1953), Hornblower is given the task of escorting Nelson's body up the Thames for the funeral, at the time when his wife Maria is about to give birth. The barge carrying the coffin springs a leak, and Hornblower manages with great difficulty to avoid the ultimate humiliation of having the dead hero sink into the Thames in full view of the crowds of mourners on the riverbanks. As he watches Nelson's body finally being unloaded, he realizes that he somehow left his precious watch dangling on the coffin, and Forester gives us an insight into his thoughts: 'Oh well, he could do nothing about that at the moment. And nothing about Maria. He went on standing in his icy breeches.'[14]

Forester's hero is a brave man, but emotionally inadequate. Hornblower standing in his icy breeches, acknowledging the impossibility of reconciling public duty and private needs, is a symbol of a particular type of Englishman, reflecting the values of a particular age. O'Brian's Jack Aubrey, in contrast, is a very different kind of man. Through the novels we follow the vicissitudes of his love life and his (relatively) happy marriage to Sophie. Jack constantly seeks some kind of reconciliation between his duty and his private life, and although O'Brian repeatedly points out that he feels himself most fully realized when at sea, especially when engaged in some form of action, we nevertheless follow his relationship with his wife, children and friends. We also follow Stephen Maturin, whose troubled marriage does not prevent him from working for the British government as a secret agent or from following his passion for ornithology and for science in general. Stephen is similarly split between public duty and private needs, and in the later novels his love for his daughter becomes a strong theme that demonstrates his capacity for profound emotional commitment.

What characterizes the O'Brian novels, however, is their depiction of male friendship. Hornblower is close to Bush, who is killed in action in *Lord Hornblower* (1946), but we are given few insights into the significance of this friendship for either man. The friendship between Jack Aubrey and Stephen Maturin, two very different men, is the bedrock on which O'Brian's novels are structured, from their initial unpropitious meeting in *Master and Commander*, through the vicissitudes of their rivalry for Diana Villiers to the moment at the close of *Blue at the Mizzen*, when Stephen brings Jack the longed-for news of his promotion to admiral. The relationship is bonded through a common love for music and much of the humour that O'Brian displays as he illuminates their respective weaknesses emerges from passages that recount incidents shared by both men. In *H.M.S. Surprise*, for example, Stephen is wounded fighting a duel over Diana and decides to operate on himself. Jack, whose bravery in battle or in open boats on tumultuous seas is never in question, volunteers to help with the operation but faints at the sight of Stephen's deliberate cutting of his own flesh. He is led out of the cabin by his men, who appear to be coping with the situation far better than their captain. This episode is typical of O'Brian's method of subtly flagging up personality traits, not by authorial comment but by letting the characters speak for themselves.

> Jack began to protest that he should stay, but M'Alister put his finger to his lips and led him on tiptoe to the door. More of the ship's company than was right were hanging about outside it. Discipline seemed to have been forgotten. 'The ball is out,' he said. 'Pullings, let there be no noise abaft the mainmast, no noise at all,' and walked into his sleeping-cabin.
>   'You look wholly pale yourself, sir,' said Bonden. 'Will you take a dram?'
>   'You will have to change your coat, your honour,' said Killick. 'And your breeches, too.'
>   'Christ, Bonden,' said Jack, 'he opened himself slowly, with his own hands, right to the heart. I saw it beating there.'
>   'Ah, sir, there's surgery for you,' said Bonden, passing the glass.[15]

The friendship between Jack Aubrey and Stephen Maturin hinges not only upon what they share, but also upon the great differences of personality, training, background and aspirations that divide them. Jack is the archetypal English sea captain in the tradition of Forester and Marryat, but Stephen is a figure who has no counterpart in earlier naval novels. He is half-Irish, half-Catalan, a man of strong principles whose involvement in some way with the doomed 1798 Irish rebellion is hinted at several times but never explicitly recounted. He is, however, a man who is a gifted espionage agent, who can speak many languages and whose stoicism even under torture is almost superhuman. Through his presence in the novels, the motif of English patriotism exemplified in the behaviour of a noble captain and his valiant men is mitigated. Marryat invites us to see Jack Easy as an ideal young Englishman, who learns how to behave from his experiences at sea and is able to escape from the cloying upbringing imposed upon him by well-meaning but incompetent parents. Forester depicts Hornblower as a man who keeps escaping to sea to get away from the insecurity he feels on land; the sea is the place where he can realize his masculinity and express his patriotism. But although Jack Aubrey is created in the Hornblower image, the presence of Stephen and the multicultural nature of the charac- ters and settings of the novels downplay the nationalistic thread that runs more prominently through the works of the other two novelists.

By giving Jack Aubrey a hybrid companion, a man who is an emotionally repressed, self-effacing natural philosopher, O'Brian opens out the genre of the seafaring heroic novel and, if obituaries are to be believed, wrote himself into the character of Maturin. For like Maturin, O'Brian was a man uncomfortable with his own identity: his grandfather came from Leipzig, he changed his name from Russ to O'Brian, invented an Irish rather than an English past, and hinted at a career as a British intelligence agent. Most significantly, though, the model for his English hero is not so much Horatio Nelson, who is quite clearly also the model for Hornblower, it is the wild, unpredictable Cochrane, about whom the First Lord of the Admiralty wrote to the Queen in 1854: 'Age [Cochrane was 79] has not abated the adventurous spirit of this gallant officer, which no authority could restrain.'[16]

From Marryat to O'Brian, the seafaring novel underwent radical changes that reflect changes in the world inhabited by each of the three novelists considered here. The confidence of an imperial England in the 19th century, the uneasiness of the Second World War and its aftermath and the more pluralistic post-imperial England of O'Brian's time are mirrored in the portrayal of the very different protagonists. On the surface, the formula appears to be similar: exciting naval action, relationships forged between men at sea, the social hierarchy of Nelson's navy are all basic elements in the works of each of the novelists. But it is only when we come to O'Brian, who splits his hero-figure into two distinct individuals, one English and one Irish, one open and one secretive, one physical and one intellectual, that it becomes clear that his version of the seafaring novel has moved on. In his novels there is less concern with exploring notions of English masculinity, nor does he ask the question that obsessed Browning as he sailed past ancient battle-grounds. Instead, he gives us insights into two men's minds, balancing the Tory Englishman with the Irish radical. The importance of his achievement is aptly summed up by John Bayley, in an essay that discusses O'Brian's innovative approach to the historical naval novel: '"[H]istory" as such does not seem greatly to interest him: his originality consists in the unpretentious use he makes of it to invent a new style of fiction.'[17]

Notes

1 Robert Browning, *The Poems. Volume One*, ed. John Pettigrew (Harmondsworth: Penguin, 1981), 412.

2 *Ibid.*

3 William Shakespeare, *Richard II*, 2.1.40, lines 46-9. *The Norton Shakespeare*, ed. Stephen Greenblatt *et al*. (New York and London: Norton, 1997).

4 William Laird Clowes, *The Royal Navy. A History from the Earliest Times to 1900*, vol. 5 [1900], facs. ed. (London: Chatham Publishing, 1997), 165.

5 *Ibid.*, 166.

6 Linda Colley, *Britons. Forging the Nation 1707-1837* [1992] (London: Pimlico, 1994), 287.

7 *Nautical Economy; or, Forecastle Recollections of Events during the last War. Dedicated to the brave Tars of Old England by a Sailor, politely called by the Officers of the Navy, Jack Nasty-Face* (London: William Robinson, 1836).

8 See Frederick Marryat, *Complete Works*, ed. and intr. William Leonard Courtney, 12 vols (Boston: Colonial Press, 1896-98). See also Oliver Warner, *Captain Marryat. A Rediscovery* (London: Constable, 1953).

9 Robert Harvey, *Liberators. Latin America's Struggle for Independence, 1810-1830* (London: John Murray, 2000), 516.

10 Louis J. Parascandola, *'Puzzled Which to Choose'. Conflicting Socio-Political Views in the Works of Captain Frederick Marryat* (New York *et al*.: Lang, 1997), 11-12.

11 C.S. Forester, *Mr. Midshipman Hornblower* (London: Michael Joseph, 1950), 178.

12 C.S. Forester, *Hornblower and the Hotspur* (London: Michael Joseph, 1962), 5.

13 Patrick O'Brian, *Master and Commander* (London: HarperCollins, 1970); *Blue at the Mizzen* (London: HarperCollins, 1999).

14 C.S. Forester, *Hornblower and the 'Atropos'* (London: Michael Joseph, 1953), 69.

15 Patrick O'Brian, *H.M.S. Surprise* [1973] (London: HarperCollins, 1996), 354.

16 Quoted in Donald Thomas, *Cochrane. Britannia's Sea Wolf* (London: Cassell, 2000), 339.

17 John Bayley, 'In Which We Serve' [1991], Patrick O'Brian, *The Ionian Mission* (London: HarperCollins, 1993), 369-78, 377.

11 The Sea Is Slavery: Middle Passage Narratives

Carl Pedersen

In the preface to his recent survey of the transtlantic slave trade, Herbert Klein remarks on a curious paradox: in spite of the obvious importance of the transatlantic slave trade in world history, it 'remained one of the least studied areas in modern Western historiography until the past quarter century.'[1] According to Klein, two factors have given rise to this paradox: the reluctance to deal with a morally difficult problem having so close an association with European imperialism, and a lack of methodological tools to properly analyse the complex and massive quantitative data available to historians. Barry Unsworth, in a review of Philippa Gregory's 1995 novel of the British slave trade from the port of Bristol, *A Respectable Trade*, makes a similar point about imaginative writing: 'Considering the impact of this terrible traffic between the Old World and the New, not much British fiction has been devoted to it.' Unsworth explains this state of affairs by evoking the conflict between the sheer enormity of the transatlantic slave trade and 'the natural ground for fiction, [which] lies in individual lives, specific involvements and relationships'. Unsworth proposes several solutions to this dilemma. He advocates transforming the transatlantic slave trade by making it symbolic, situating the trade in a contemporary context, or demonstrating a continuing pattern of man's exploitation and oppression of man by making the trade itself into a protagonist.[2] Unsworth reproaches Gregory for making the transatlantic slave trade a mere device for precipitating action instead of a protagonist.

However, one could make the argument that the transatlantic slave trade has not so much been subject to neglect, but rather that selected works dealing with the slave trade have been marginalized. African-American history, autobiography and fiction are replete with examples of writing on the slave trade. Klein dutifully cites some of the first studies of the transatlantic slave trade by English abolitionists like Thomas Clarkson and

188

William Wilberforce, and the systematic collection of statistical materials by the English Parliament.[3] But he neglects the presence of black writers of the 18th century like Olaudah Equiano, Quobna Ottobah Cugoano and Ignatius Sancho, who produced narratives, essays and letters that combined personal experience, contemporary accounts of the trade, and moral outrage in aid of the abolitionist movement in Britain.[4] This rich tradition of black British letters should be read alongside the work of Clarkson and Wilberforce as an integral part of the corpus of the abolitionist movement.

Klein's exclusive focus on mainstream historiography prompts him to argue that after the success of the abolitionist movement in abolishing the slave trade in 1807, there was little writing done on the trade until after World War I. Yet in the 19th century, Frederick Douglass and Herman Melville provided fictionalized accounts of slave-trading voyages that nevertheless, according to a recent study, can be seen as historical documents that 'entered into then-current debates regarding the place of rebellion and slavery - and slave rebellion - in US national identity'.[5] Douglass' *The Heroic Slave* (1853) and Melville's *Benito Cereno* (1855) provide fictionalized accounts of slaveship revolts that echo the revolts on the *Amistad* and *Creole* in the previous decade. Both works anticipate the emphasis on African agency in slave historiography in the 20th century and look at the slave trade from a diasporic perspective that would be elaborated upon by W.E.B. Du Bois in the 20th century. Unsworth's comment that the paucity of British fiction dealing with the slave trade can be attributed to the enormity of the trade overlooks the ways in which the history of British involvement in the slave trade was at once wilfully suppressed but nevertheless functioned as a subtext for much British fiction in the 19th century. For example, as Edward Said points out in *Culture and Imperialism*, the Bertrams in Jane Austen's *Mansfield Park* 'could not have been possible without the slave trade, sugar, and the colonial planter class'; nevertheless, the novel is rarely read with this 'global perspective' in mind.[6]

The body of writing on the slave trade continues on into the 20th century. At the very end of the 19th century, W.E.B. Du Bois published his PhD dissertation *The Suppression of the African Slave-Trade* (1896) which Hugh Thomas still regards as 'the best book on United States abolition'.[7] In the first decades of the 20th century, black historians and writers like Benjamin Brawley, Du Bois and Carter G. Woodson included detailed accounts of the transatlantic slave trade in their surveys of African-American history. As Robin D.G. Kelley puts it, 'Woodson, Brawley, and many early contributors to the *Journal of Negro History* were attempting to write transnational history before such terminology came into being.'[8] Ulrich B. Phillips, whose *American Negro Slavery* (1918) would become the standard work on the subject until the 1950s, included several chapters on the transatlantic slave trade. Unlike African-American historians, however, Phillips took pains to show that, on the whole, Africans experienced 'the then customary dangers and hardships of the sea', and, furthermore, 'the victims of the rapine were quite possibly better off on the American plantations than the captors who remained in the African jungle.'[9] Contrast Phillips' benign view of the Middle Passage with Carter G. Woodson's description of what he calls the 'horrors' of the Middle Passage in the chapter of his *The Negro in Our History* called, tellingly, 'Foreign Aggression':

> Sometimes forced into a crouching position, sometimes compelled to lie down, captives accepted as valuable were shackled and herded together like cattle in ships. The space generally allowed for the standing room of a slave was just a few square inches. Ventilation was usually inadequate, clothing was limited, the water was insufficient, and the food was spoiled. Crowded thus together in the lower parts of an unsanitary vessel, many of these unfortunates died of various complaints before reaching America.[10]

In the 1930s, the sociologist E. Franklin Frazier followed Phillips by conceptualizing the transatlantic slave trade in terms of an abrupt cultural break between the African and the American worlds. Melville Herskovits countered this view by emphasizing the extent to which Africans managed to sustain their culture despite the trauma of the Middle Passage.[11] Eric Williams' *Capitalism and Slavery* from 1944 presented the bold and controversial argument that slave-trade profits financed the Industrial Revolution and that the rise in industry rendered the slave trade obsolete. Williams' study is still the subject of heated debate in academic circles today.[12]

The last quarter century has witnessed a boom in the representation and historical study of the transatlantic slave trade, in part brought on by the impact of the American Civil Rights movement and the breakup of Europe's African empires and the rise of independent African republics on the development of African and African-American studies programmes. Philip Curtin's seminal *The Atlantic Slave Trade: A Census* from 1969 and Alex Haley's surprisingly popular and fatally flawed *Roots* from 1976 prompted a renewed interest as well as a paradigm shift in the interpretation of the transatlantic slave trade that nevertheless owed much to the tradition of writing about it. Curtin's study placed the slave trade in the context of Atlantic history, as black writers had done before him. His primary aim, however, was to seek to determine the volume of the trade. Haley's wildly popular saga, *Roots*, pursued the opposite course of starting with the life of a single individual, Kunta Kinte, from his capture in Africa to his life as a slave in the United States.[13] To take Unsworth's point, while Curtin's re-search put a number on the enormity of the trade, Haley's account, though marketed as non-fiction, took the individual lives of Kunta Kinte and his descendants, what Unsworth called the stuff of fiction, to portray the largely forgotten history of African America.[14] While the two books thus complement each other, the gap between them in terms of focus and poten-tial audience underscored the dual nature of contemporary knowledge of the slave trade. The popular version embodied in *Roots* was a moral tale of suffering and redemption framed as a twist on the classic immigration story. The academic interpretation became in the eyes of some a numbers game that threatened to anaesthesize the horrors of the slave trade. In their introduction to the *Trans-Atlantic Slave Trade Database*, David Eltis, Stephen D. Behrendt, David Richardson and Herbert S. Klein acknowledge the limitations of their database that builds on the work of Curtin: 'The data set contains thousands of names of shipowners and ship captains, but it contains no names of the millions of slaves carried to the Americas.'[15] Bar-bara Solow, in an essay published in the special issue of *The William and Mary Quarterly* on new perspectives on the transatlantic slave trade, recognizes that data compiled by Curtin and the *Trans-Atlantic Slave Trade Database* cannot provide 'an understanding of the human experience of the Middle Passage. For this there is no resource except the historical imagina-tion, and perhaps the best sources are tales and poems and novels.'[16] How-ever, if the transatlantic slave trade is in danger of being made banal by the unceasing deluge of statistics in quantitative studies on the one hand, it can also suffer from excessive aestheticization by writers on the other.

Recent studies of the transatlantic slave trade have followed Fernand Braudel's 1949 edict to study history integrated by the sea.[17] On the whole, the many scholarly works of history that have come out since Curtin's study have broadened the interpretation of the trade. The new historio-graphy of the transatlantic slave trade runs the gamut from non-scholarly descriptive works like Hugh Thomas' *The Slave Trade* and general histories like *The Oxford History of the British Empire* to quantitative studies like *The Trans-Atlantic Slave Trade Database*, and a variety of specialized works by, for example, Herbert Klein, Peter Linebaugh and Marcus Rediker and Robin Blackburn, important essays in journals like *Slavery and Abolition* and *The William and Mary Quarterly*, as well as theoretical meditations like Wilson Harris' 'History, Fable, and Myth in the Caribbean and the Guineas', and Paul Gilroy's *The Black Atlantic*.

This new scholarship contains several important elements that have both drawn on and elaborated past histories and representations of the transat-lantic slave trade. Foremost, perhaps, is the recognition of African agency, both as complicity in the trade that limited European incursions into the African continent, resistance during the Middle Passage from day-to-day resistance to outright ship revolts, and the development of methods of cultural survival in the Americas. The work of Peter Linebaugh and Marcus Rediker has highlighted class and ethnic conflict on the African coast and on the sea between officers, first and second mates and crew, as well as among slaves. Their *The Many-Headed Hydra* reconfigures early American and British history as part of Atlantic history. They construct a scenario in which what they call the Herculean process of globalization that promoted an Atlantic division of labour was driven by mercantile capitalism but at the same time created a multi-ethnic motley crew of sailors, slaves and indentured labourers, a many-headed Hydra which resisted exploitation. The Atlantic became at once a zone of capitalist accumulation and a potential zone of freedom. The ships criss-crossing the Atlantic within the lop-sided rectangle of the slave trade and indentured labour linked other sites of exploitation and resistance: the English commons, the slave labour camps of the Americas, and factories in England and the Northern American states.[18] More information on the ethnic origins of slaves has uncovered less homogeneous groupings than hitherto supposed which in turn affected relationships between slaves during the Middle Passage. Finally, the centrality of the trade for the formation and development of the Atlantic system and European imperialism has placed it at the cutting edge of Atlantic history.

In looking at histories and fictions of the transatlantic slave trade, I am attempting to seek out the ways that they enter into dialogue with each other. Historians of the transatlantic slave trade could perhaps take a page from so-called postmodernist histories like Simon Schama's *Citizens* on the French Revolution and Orlando Fige's *A People's Tragedy* on the Bolshevik Revolution - two works that take on big subjects by interweaving small incidents as subplots. For its part, the literary imagination is faced with a twofold project in taking on the slave trade: responding or entering into dialogue with the advances and revisions in slave trade historiography, by imagining gaps in historical knowledge, and overcoming the burden of romantic narratives of the sea that, according to Jonathan Raban and Marcus Rediker, focus on man against the sea instead of man against man on the sea.[19] Two recent novels that succeed in constructing another sea, the sea of slavery, are Barry Unsworth's *Sacred Hunger* from 1992 and the Guyanese writer Fred D'Aguiar's *Feeding the Ghosts* from 1997. Although both novels deal with the Liverpool slave trade, they take place during different periods in the 18th century, the century of trade. The centrality of Liverpool to the transatlantic slave trade during this period is undisputed:

of the over 11,000 slaving voyages during the 18th century, more than half originated from Liverpool.

Sacred Hunger is framed by a prologue and epilogue set in New Orleans in 1832. The main body of the narrative stretches from Liverpool to the West coast of Africa to Eastern Florida and spans the period from 1752 to 1765, from the height of the Liverpool slave trade to the very beginning of the abolitionist era. *Feeding the Ghosts* begins later, in 1781, and focuses on a single voyage, that of the infamous *Zong*, and the ensuing trial the year after, and ends with a coda, set in Jamaica in 1833. *Sacred Hunger* thus takes an expansive, transatlantic view of the trade, while *Feeding the Ghosts* is more narrowly focused on a specific incident in a shorter period of time. In many ways, the two novels complement each other and indeed overlap in the Middle Passage segments.

Sacred Hunger and *Feeding the Ghosts* also display a sensibility that places them in the context of recent slave historiography. In a review of Hugh Thomas' *The Slave Trade*, D'Aguiar singles out what he regards as the two defining slave histories of the 20th century: C.L.R. James' *The Black Jacobins* (1938) and Williams' *Capitalism and Slavery*. D'Aguiar argues that the two works supplement each other: James highlights the role slaves played in the struggle for freedom while Williams focuses on the economic imperatives of the slave trade and slavery that undergirded the Industrial Revolution.[20] In D'Aguiar's view, the two recent slave histories by Robin Blackburn build on these works: the first, *The Overthrow of Colonial Slavery* (1989) focusing in part on the role slaves played in their own emancipation, and the second, *The Making of New World Slavery* (1997), expanding on the Williams thesis linking slavery with the British economic growth.[21] *Sacred Hunger* and *Feeding the Ghosts*, on the other hand, constitute fictional representations of *both* aspects of slave historiography.

Unsworth's novel begins in 1752, at the height of the British slave trade and at the start of Liverpool's predominance. David Richardson has identified three major expansionary cycles of the trade, from circa 1650 to 1683, 1708 to 1725, and 1746 to 1771.[22] Liverpool overtakes London and dominates this last expansionary era. The Liverpool merchant William Kemp, who oversees the construction of the slaveship *Liverpool Merchant* (the name of the ship thus becomes the embodiment of the will of its owner) in the auspicious year of 1752, epitomizes the optimism of the Liverpool merchants during this era. 'The trade is wide open', he exults to guests at a dinner party. 'I tell you, sure as I sit here, the future of Liverpool lies with the Africa trade.'[23]

Not content to focus on the horrors of the Middle Passage, Unsworth takes on the entire trade, from the construction of the *Liverpool Merchant* and the recruitment of its crew, to its journey to Sierra Leone and the Gold Coast Castle, and to its final voyage across the Atlantic, aborted by mutiny. Unsworth conceptualizes the trade as a sacred hunger for profit which is controlled by the Liverpool merchant classes and infects and connects all strata of the Atlantic system. The captain, Saul Thurso, is described as the incarnation of the profit motive. The crew are literally kidnapped for service aboard the *Liverpool Merchant*. The Atlantic creoles along the African coast and interior who supply the Europeans with slaves, and the African captives themselves who remain largely voiceless until they mutiny and gain their freedom in a maroon community in Florida form the final link in this enormous commercial enterprise. Interspersed between this narrative of the trade is a subplot involving those left behind in Liverpool, including Kemp's son, Erasmus, and Erasmus' prospective fiancé Sarah Wolpert, who unconsciously play out their ignorance of the implications of the trade by acting in the bastardized Davenant/Dryden version of Shakespeare's *The Tempest*, appropriately titled *The Enchanted Island*. For Erasmus, participation in the play is just part of a courtship ritual. For all the players, the sanitized text of the Davenant/Dryden adaptation is a measure of how far removed the English merchant classes were from the realities of the trade.

Unsworth is at pains to link his particularized narrative with the larger trade:

> Day by day the *Liverpool Merchant* made progress southwards. Under full sail, propelled by fair winds, she dipped and rose through the heavings of the sea with a profound regularity. On the line of the horizon there would sometimes appear the brief stain of another ship, like a breath on a distant mirror; but most of the time she could feel herself alone on the ocean, the sole trader of the world, instead of what she was, a member of a vast fleet sent forth by men of enterprise and vision all over Europe, engaged in the greatest commercial venture the world had ever seen, changing the course of history, bringing death and degradation and profits hitherto unheard of.[24]

In this striking image the trade becomes part of a vast gulag archipelago, with the sea as a conduit, and ships as floating transport wagons bringing Africans to slave labour camps in North America, the Caribbean, and Brazil.[25] Peter Wood suggests substituting the term slave labour camps, with its resonance of 20th-century atrocities, for the more benign plantations that evoke antebellum social harmony. As the editors of the *Trans-Atlantic Slave Trade Database* argue, their data shows the 'pervasiveness' of the trade, which involved all Atlantic ports in Western Europe and the Americas.[26]

However, in keeping with the shift in slave historiography in general from looking at Africans as passive victims to potential agents of resistance, the captain and crew of the *Liverpool Merchant* continually express their concern about possible revolt. The ship itself is constructed 'high in the stern so that the swivel guns mounted on their quarter decks could be more easily ... trained down on their waists to quell slave revolt',[27] and in one of the most effective passages in the novel, an African foils his captors by refusing to eat and in a last gesture of defiance, spits rice in the face of the surgeon Matthew Paris before dying. The ultimate act of resistance is the shipboard mutiny and subsequent establishment of a maroon multi-ethnic community in the Florida swamps. Yet even this remote outpost provides no refuge from the sacred hunger of profit. Erasmus Kemp represents the next generation of profit-seekers, and travels to Florida to reclaim his father's lost goods. In 1765, Florida had been under British control for two years. The new British Governor of Florida tells Kemp that '[t]his could be a paradise, if settled with the subjects of King George and properly cultivated.'[28] The younger Kemp sees the reorganization of Florida under the British as a new opportunity to assuage his sacred hunger. Indeed, the British were quick to impose their absolute rule on their new possession. Before the British, what Ira Berlin calls the charter generations of Africans had a role in the institutions, militias, and churches of Spanish Florida. By 1770, however, the influx of planters had transformed the region to such an extent that many estates had 'no white face belonging to the plantation but an overseer.'[29] The vision of an interracial community of equals had been replaced by the sacred hunger for slaves and land. The legacy of the community survives as a pale shadow in the form of Paris' and the former slave Tabakali's son, Kenka, known by local residents as Paradise Nigger, in New Orleans in 1832, a site of African survivals expressed during Sunday Market in Congo Square.

Sacred Hunger can thus be characterized an an extended Middle Passage narrative. The journey from the West coast of Africa to the waters of the Americas takes up only a little over 30 pages in an over six-hundred-page narrative. In his effort to forge connections between the rise of capitalism in England and the slave trade, Unsworth traces the steps of the trade from the construction of the *Liverpool Merchant*, the voyage to Africa, the bargaining for slaves to the mutiny/rebellion and the establishment of a mixed-race maroon community in Florida. The large cast of characters, both European, African, and American, and the historical and geographical span of the novel evoke the concerns of contemporary slave historiography.

Feeding the Ghosts has a narrower focus than *Sacred Hunger* and compresses the history of the slave trade into the story of a ship that is also a matter of historical record. D'Aguiar draws on what is undoubtedly the most notorious example of the Liverpool slave trade: the case of the *Zong*, which sailed from Liverpool in September 1781. Destined for Jamaica, the ship lost its way and the water supply was depleted. The captain, Luke Collingwood, was faced with a choice. If the slaves on board died of natural causes, the owners of the ship would incur the loss. However, Collingwood argued that if the slaves were thrown alive into the sea, the loss would be covered by the insurance. The first mate, James Kelsal, objected to the latter solution, but Collingwood prevailed, and the crew proceeded to throw slaves overboard. A total of 132 slaves were jettisoned, but the final loss was put at 131. The incident received widespread publicity after Olaudah Equiano had recounted it to Granville Sharp.[30] The mystery of the one slave that seemed to have escaped death by drowning intrigued D'Aguiar. In *Feeding the Ghosts*, he adopts a familiar post-colonial strategy and expands the historical record with his rumination on the atrocity told from an African perspective.

Although set in the 1750s and 1760s, *Sacred Hunger* was in part inspired by the case of the *Zong*, which served as a catalyst for the abolitionist movement of the 1780s. Elizabeth Donnan's massive compilation of *Documents Illustrative of the History of the Slave Trade to America* contains but a brief prosaic excerpt from the memoirs of Granville Sharp recounting the particulars of the case of the slaveship *Zong* before a British court in 1782. The *Trans-Atlantic Slave Trade Database* includes a record of the *Zong*, detailing the facts of the voyage. Both records are distinguished by the absence of an African voice. It has been left to works of the imagination to capture the deeper meaning of the *Zong*, the cynical mass-murder of Africans for something as banal as an insurance claim that belies the sensibility of the Age of Enlightenment. J.M.W. Turner was one of the first to use this incident in order to offer a commentary on contemporary society in his painting *Slavers Throwing Overboard the Dead and Dying - Typhoon Coming On*. According to Paul Gilroy, '[t]he picture deploys the imagery of wrathful nature and of dying slaves as powerful means to highlight the degenerate and irrational nature of English society as it entered the 1840s.'[31]

In their imaginative renderings of the *Zong* tragedy, Unsworth and D'Aguiar employ different strategies. Unsworth uses the jettisoning of slaves as the culmination of the sacred hunger that precipitates the mutiny of the crew and the rebellion of the slaves against the officers of the *Liverpool Merchant*, particularly the despised Captain Thurso. D'Aguiar's novel is a meditation on the fate of the one slave who apparently survived the jettisoning. The fate of the *Zong* and the subsequent trial are at the heart of the novel. However, this tale is told from an African perspective and underscores the importance of African testimony. The denouement of *Sacred Hunger* emphasizes other concerns. Like D'Aguiar, Unsworth gives the Africans names and voices. From anonymous (though potentially rebellious) captives during the Middle Passage, they emerge as individual protagonists in the maroon community in Florida. This maroon community is described to Erasmus Kemp as 'a community of black and white living in the south part of the peninsula'.[32] Yet this potentially alternative society is in threat of being undermined by the sentiments of avarice that have been imbibed in the members of the community through their contact with the slave trade. For both D'Aguiar and Unsworth, the greed at the heart of the transatlantic slave trade is epitomized by the fate of the *Zong*.

Feeding the Ghosts confronts the *Zong* tragedy directly, following its chronology and keeping the name of the slaveship, the number of slaves cast overboard, and the broad contours of the subsequent insurance claim hearing. *Sacred Hunger* and *Feeding the Ghosts* thus frame the period of Liverpool's emergence as the predominant slave port for the most powerful slave-trade nation to a time when the trade was increasingly coming under question. D'Aguiar fills in the gap between documentary record and the literary imagination by creating the character of Mintah, an African captive who has been taught to read and write in English by missionaries, and who survives being cast overboard and provides written testimony that the captain of the *Zong* was throwing 'stock' (as the slaves are referred to in the novel) into the sea irregardless of illness, all for the sake of an insurance claim. Like Thurso, Captain Cunningham (whose name has been inexplicably changed from Collingwood) is suffused with cruel impulses and obsessed with profit. The first pages of the novel have him exhorting the crew to agree to his solution of casting slaves overboard and claiming their loss as an insurance claim. The choice for Cunningham is simple - profit or loss. It is less so for the crew, some of whom object to the characterization of the Africans as stock.[33]

The slaves on the *Zong* are nameless, except for Mintah. She is cast overboard not because of illness but because she exhibits defiant behaviour that Cunningham regards as a threat. She is the one survivor of this atrocity and sees as her mission recording the history of the *Zong* from her observations. Set against this narrative is Cunningham's ledger, the stuff of documentation available to historians. D'Aguiar's imagining of Mintah's testimony expands and recasts this dry history of numbers and economic calculation as a heinous act deserving of condemnation. Like the struggle for representation that takes place between Nehemiah and Dessa Rose in Shirley Anne Williams' *Dessa Rose* or between Baby Suggs and Schoolteacher in Toni Morrison's *Beloved*, Mintah's diaries form a hidden history of the African diaspora that is ultimately wilfully suppressed by Lord Chief Justice Mansfield at the insurance hearing. In the height of irony, Mintah's writing, which 'proves' to Europeans that she is in fact a thinking human being, is rejected because they regard her as illiterate, unthinking 'stock'.

Mintah's tale brings to mind other references from the history of the African diaspora as well. In 1927, Zora Neale Hurston published a short piece in Woodson's *Journal of Negro History* that combined oral history with historical research. The story of Cudjo came about as a result of an interview by Hurston, but, as the editor notes, she amplified her story with historical documentation.[34] At one point in *Feeding the Ghosts*, Mintah imagines an alternative to the horrors of the slave trade:

> From [planting and harvesting], and from seeing the offspring of unions between white men and black women, and the many tribes who trafficked in captive souls for riches, grew her conviction that if the whites had come and settled in Africa and hired Africans to work African soil and grow the very crops they deemed so valuable that they were willing to cast their humanity aside in order to procure them in abundance and gain riches fast, the whole encounter between black and white would have been pleasant and beneficial for all concerned.[35]

This passage not only echoes the vision of the interracial maroon community in Florida set up by the artist Delblanc and Paris, it resonates with sentiments expressed by Olaudah Equiano in the 1780s, who argued an open African market would bring prosperity to Britain: 'A commercial intercourse with Africa opens an inexhaustible source of wealth to the manufacturing interests of Great Britain, and to all which the slave trade is an objection.'[36]

D'Aguiar has an excerpt from Derek Walcott's poem 'The Sea Is History' as an epigraph to his novel. He restates Walcott in the first line of *Feeding the Ghosts*, which reads 'The sea is slavery' and makes the sea a protagonist. It provides a memory of slavery, an underwater 'road of bones', as well as salvation for Mintah, who literally emerges from the water to bear witness. It functions as a space-in-between where Mintah, hardened into wood, can prepare for her life in the new world. Mintah's is a story of survival in the Americas. The defeat at the metropolitan centre forces Mintah into the periphery. The end of the novel has her in Kingston, Jamaica, in 1833, teaching schoolchildren about the meaning of freedom. The year is significant. It is a year in between the Jamaican rebellion of 1831-32 and the first declaration of emancipation on 1 August 1834. Mintah's mission of 'feeding the ghosts' of the Africans lost to the slave trade with her memory is augmented by the knowledge of continuing slave resistance of the Jamaican rebellion.

In his study of the relationship between history and film, *Visions of the Past*, Robert Rosenstone makes the useful distinction between false invention, which ignores the discourse of history, and true invention, which engages it.[37] Steven Spielberg's *Amistad* (1997), which frames the effective and gripping scenes of the Middle Passage with a celebratory narrative that distorts the historical record and ultimately elides African agency, however much it strains to make a 'hero' out of Cinque, is a good example of false invention. Unsworth's and D'Aguiar's Middle Passage narratives, on the other hand, actively engage historical discourse. The two contemporary writers can be characterized as a latter-day Melville and Douglass, absorbing the new slave-trade historiography to offer intricately woven Middle Passage narratives that tie the slave trade to 20th-century notions of greed and brutality.

In Unsworth's earlier novel, *Sugar and Rum* from 1988, the writer Clive Benson is ultimately overwhelmed by what he sees as the intimate connection between the Thatcherite '80s hunger for profit and casting aside of the underprivileged and the ideology of the slave trade.[38] Both D'Aguiar and Unsworth forge connections between the need for a collective memory of slavery and an understanding of how the sacred hunger for profit still drives human endeavour in the global economy.

At several points in *Sacred Hunger*, Unsworth makes analogies to contemporary society. He characterizes the 1750s as 'a time when the individual pursuit of wealth was regarded as inherently virtuous, on the grounds that it increased the wealth and well-being of the community' and calls this process 'wealth-creation'.[39] Later on, in the pidgin vernacular used by the members of the Florida maroon community, Unsworth offers yet another reference to the trickle-down theories that were a hallmark of the Reagan-Thatcher years. Kireku, one of the former slaves, tells Paris: 'Strong man get rich, him slave get rich. Strong man make everybody rich.'[40] Such connections are also implicit in Blackburn's work. Indeed, his argument that the slave system is part and parcel of what we know as modernity conceptualizes the slave trade as integral to the development of a global economy. Merchants like William Kemp determined that slave labour was the most efficient way to produce the sugar that fed the sacred hunger of European consumers. Jurists like the Lord Chief Justice Mansfield acquiesced to this system by maintaining the lawfulness of slavery. Excited by the prospect of his impending involvement in the slave trade, the elder Kemp gushes at the beginning of *Sacred Hunger*: 'I am talking about a commerce that will be worth millions. A lawful commerce - it is sanctioned by the law of the land.

Merchants trading to Africa can hold up their heads with the best.'[41] However, by equating piracy with the slave trade in the 1770s, Britain had acknowledged that the slave trade was illegal under international law.[42] Nevertheless, both the UK and the US refused to enter discussions about reparations for the slave trade at the August-September 2001 UN conference in Durban, South Africa on Racism, Intolerance, and Xenophobia.

As early as 1915 in *The Negro*, Du Bois expressed his outrage that '[f]or four hundred years, from 1450 to 1850, European civilization carried on a systematic trade in human beings of such tremendous proportions that the physical, economic, and moral effects are still plainly to be remarked throughout the world.'[43] Just as contemporary global perspectives have prompted scholars to see early American history from an Atlantic perspective, studies in Atlantic history can contextualize and illuminate the current era of globalization. Nowhere is this more apparent than in looking at the reappearance of slavery in recent years. The so-called new slavery has a double genesis: old colonialist patterns and the increasing integration of the global economy. The paradox of freedom and slavery has outlived the abolition of slavery in the late 1800s. By Kevin Bales' estimate, documented in his study of the new slavery, *Disposable People*, there are approximately 27 million slaves in the world today, more than the total of all the Africans forcibly taken from their homeland during the era of the transatlantic slave trade. The new slavery replicates the new globalization by the shift from ownership to control. The post-colonial age has industrialized nations and global financial institutions exerting control over so-called developing nations by various systems of coercion: capital investment and loans that have replaced the old costly system of maintaining colonies. The system of new slavery has likewise exchanged the cost of lifetime servitude for a looser relationship of disposability - new slaves are literally thrown away after use, like outdated computers - that in turn reaps high profits.[44] Some of these slaves are captives, who are smuggled to Europe and North America and within Africa on boats. The hidden history of the new slavery occasionally surfaces, as in the case of the *Eriteno* in April 2001. Forty-three children and young adults were rescued on their way to slave plantations in Gabon and the Ivory Coast. Their presence on the seas constitutes a new global underworld. The sea continues to be slavery. In *The Atlantic Sound*, his contemporary travelogue of the points of the trade, which interweaves narrative threads from the past and the present, Caryl Phillips expresses his relief upon leaving the old slave port of Liverpool: 'It is disquieting to be in a place where history is so physically present, yet so glaringly absent from people's consciousness. But where is it any different? Maybe this is the modern condition, and Liverpool is merely acting out this reality with an honest vigour.'[45] More often than not, at the dawn of the 21st century, there seems to be a willingness to forget the past and let the connections between the slave trade and the present global economy remain concealed.

Notes

1   Herbert S. Klein, *The Atlantic Slave Trade* (Cambridge: Cambridge University Press, 1999), xvii.

2   Barry Unsworth, 'Bristol Fashion' (review of Philippa Gregory, *A Respectable Trade*), *Sunday Times*, 9 April 1995.

3   Klein, *Atlantic Slave Trade*, 213.

4   Adam Potkay and Sandra Burr (eds), *Black Atlantic Writers of the 18th Century: Living the New Exodus in England and America* (New York: St Martin's Press, 1995) has excerpts from Cugoano and Equiano. Equiano's narrative is available in a number of editions. I might note that the veracity of Equiano's narrative has recently been called into question. See Vincent Carretta, 'Olaudah Equiano or Gustavus Vassa? New Light on an Eighteenth-Century Question of Identity', *Slavery and Abolition* 20, no. 3 (1999), 96-105. For Sancho, see *Letters of the Late Ignatius Sancho, An African* [1782], ed. Vincent Carretta (Harmondsworth: Penguin, 1998).

5   Maggie Monesinos Sale, *The Slumbering Volcano: American Slave Ship Revolts and the Production of Rebellious Masculinity* (Durham and London: Duke University Press, 1997), 146.

6   Edward Said, *Culture and Imperialism* (New York: Knopf, 1993), 94, 95.

7   Hugh Thomas, *The Slave Trade* (New York: Simon & Schuster, 1997), 819.

8   Robin D.G. Kelley, '"But a Local Phase of a World Problem": Black History's Global Vision, 1883-1950', *The Journal of American History* 86, no. 3 (1999), http://www.historycooperative.org/journals/jah/86.3/kelley.html (12 October 2001).

9   Ulrich Bonnell Phillips, *American Negro Slavery* [1918] (Baton Rouge: LSU Press, 1966), 37, 45.

10   Carter G. Woodson, *The Negro in Our History* (Washington: Associated Publishers, 1945), 67.

11   E. Franklin Frazier, *The Negro Family in the United States* [1939] (Chicago and London: The University of Chicago Press, 1966); and Melville Herskovits, *The Myth of the Negro Past* (New York and London: Harper and Bros., 1941).

12   Eric Williams, *Capitalism and Slavery* [1944] (Chapel Hill: University of North Carolina Press, 1994).

13   Philip Curtin, *The Atlantic Slave Trade* (Madison: University of Wisconsin Press, 1969); Alex Haley, *Roots* (Garden City, NY: Doubleday, 1976).

14   Haley was, of course, later accused of plagiarizing segments of Harold Courlander's 1967 novel *The African* and Margaret Walker's 1966 novel *Jubilee* for inclusion in *Roots*. A suit brought by Courlander was settled out of court. See Philip Nobile, 'Uncovering *Roots*', *The Village Voice*, 23 January 1993, 31-8.

15   David Eltis *et al.*, 'Introduction', *The Trans-Atlantic Slave Trade: A Database on CD-ROM* (Cambridge, MA: Harvard University Press, 1999), 1-38, 2.

16   Barbara Solow, 'The Transatlantic Slave Trade: A New Census', *The William and Mary Quarterly* 58, no. 1 (2001), 10-11.

2

202 *Carl Pedersen*

17 See Fernand Braudel, *The Mediterranean and the Mediterranean World in the Age of Phillip II* [1949], 2 vols (London: Collins, 1972-3).
18 Peter Linebaugh and Marcus Rediker, *The Many-Headed Hydra: Sailors, Slaves, Commoners, and the Hidden History of the Revolutionary Atlantic* (Boston: Beacon Press, 2000).
19 Jonathan Raban, 'Introduction', Raban (ed.), *The Oxford Book of the Sea* (Oxford: Oxford University Press, 1992), 1-34; and Marcus Rediker, *Between the Devil and the Deep Blue Sea: Merchant Seamen, Pirates, and the Anglo-American Maritime World, 1700-1750* (Cambridge: Cambridge University Press, 1987).
20 Fred D'Aguiar, 'Black Man's Burden', *Guardian*, 27 November 1997.
21 Robin Blackburn, *The Overthrow of Colonial Slavery* (London: Verso, 1988); and *The Making of New World Slavery* (London: Verso, 1997).
22 David Richardson, 'The British Empire and the Atlantic Slave Trade, 1660-1807', P.J. Marshal (ed.), *The Oxford History of the British Empire. Vol. 2: The Eighteenth Century* (Oxford: Oxford University Press, 1998), 440-64, 443.
23 Barry Unsworth, *Sacred Hunger* (New York: Norton, 1992), 15.
24 *Ibid.*, 130.
25 Peter Wood, 'Slave Labor Camps in Early America: Overcoming Denial and Discovering the Gulag', Carla Gardina Pestana and Sharon V. Salinger (eds), *Inequality in Early America* (Hanover: University Press of New England, 1999), 222-39.
26 Eltis *et al.*, 'Introduction', *The Trans-Atlantic Slave Trade Database*, 26.
27 Unsworth, *Sacred Hunger*, 130.
28 *Ibid.*, 455.
29 Ira Berlin, *Many Thousands Gone: The First Two Centuries of Slavery in North America* (Cambridge, MA: Harvard University Press, 1998), 64-5, 144.
30 Elizabeth Donnan, *Documents Illustrative of the History of the Slave Trade to America* [1931] (New York: Octagon Books, 1969), 555-7.
31 Paul Gilroy, 'Art of Darkness: Black Art and the Problem of Belonging to England', *Third Text* 10 (1990), 49.
32 Unsworth, *Sacred Hunger*, 459.
33 Fred D'Aguiar, *Feeding the Ghosts* (Hopewell, NJ: The Ecco Press, 1997), 11, 16.
34 Zora Neale Hurston, 'Cudjo's Own Story of the Last African Slaver', *Journal of Negro History* 27 (1927), 648-63.
35 D'Aguiar, *Feeding the Ghosts*, 113.
36 Olaudah Equiano, *The Interesting Narrative and Other Writings*, ed. Vincent Carretta (Harmondsworth: Penguin, 1995), 234.
37 Robert Rosenstone, *Visions of the Past: The Challenge of Film to Our Idea of History* (Cambridge, MA: Harvard University Press, 1996), 72.
38 Barry Unsworth, *Sugar and Rum* (New York: Norton, 1988).
39 Unsworth, *Sacred Hunger*, 158.
40 *Ibid.*, 581.
41 *Ibid.*, 16.
42 Geraldine Van Bueren, 'It's Britain's Guilty Secret', *Guardian*, 24 May 2001.
43 W.E.B. Du Bois, *The Negro* [1915] (Millwood, NY: Kraus-Thomson, 1975), 149.
44 Kevin Bales, *Disposable People: New Slavery in the Global Economy* (Berkeley: University of California Press, 1999).
45 Caryl Phillips, *The Atlantic Sound* (New York: Knopf, 2000), 117.

12 Cinematographic Seas: Metaphors of Crossing and Shipwreck on the Big Screen (1990-2001)

PATRIZIA A. MUSCOGIURI

Since the early 1990s, contemporary cinema has witnessed a dramatic increase in the use of the sea voyage and shipwreck as metaphors. Of particular note has been the revival of the classical understanding of the sea voyage as a transgressive crossing of 'natural' boundaries, which questions the pre-established order, and is therefore well worth the 'punishment' of a shipwreck (e.g., *The Truman Show*, 1998), set against the representation of the early modern view of the sea and shipwreck(s) as the true human condition (e.g., *Waterworld*, 1995; *Cast Away*, 2001). For the most part, however - with the notable exception of a dystopic film such as *The Beach* (2000) - in the cinematographic texts of the 1990s, sea-crossings and wrecks characteristically take on a disruptive and extremely subversive import. An instance of this can be traced even in apparently marginal (but in fact climacteric) uses of these metaphors, in films such as *Moll Flanders* (1996) - in which shipwreck is indeed a fortunate event for the protagonist, breaking and overthrowing a superimposed, highly oppressive and discriminating social order - or, as in *Shakespeare in Love* (1998), in the filmic rendition of the shipwreck metaphor and sea change as the locus of artistic creation reshaping the world. This radical significance of the shipwreck metaphor, which clearly derives from modern literary texts, emerges as the most consistent trend in its recent cinematic reworking, from the depiction of the 'shipwreck outside history', saving the shipwrecked, for instance, from the horrors of war and creating new unimaginable possibilities of life (e.g., *Mediterraneo*, 1991), to the latest adaptation of the historical crossing and foundering of the *Titanic*, occurring 'cinematographically' in parallel with the crossing of bounds - of class and gender - and the wreck of (social) identity of the fictional heroine (*Titanic*, 1997).

In this paper, I will explore some of the uses that directors and/or scriptwriters have made of the sea voyage involving shipwreck(s), and I will show how sophisticated modern transformations of this metaphor inform contemporary cinema. More specifically, I will focus on examples of films which engage with a radical understanding of metaphoric ship-wreck, and consciously use it in connection with questions of language, as well as with issues of gender and/or ideology - namely, James Cameron's *Titanic*, Gabriele Salvatores' *Mediterraneo* and Peter Weir's *The Truman Show*. It is my contention that all these films portray, in some way, breaks or escapes from a particular historical moment (including the present) and its social and cultural 'realities', and result in a subversive deconstruction of those 'realities' and the patriarchal, phallocratic and logocentric dis-course producing them. In my reading of these films, I will also address Kevin Reynold's *Waterworld* and Robert Zemeckis' *Cast Away*, as illustra-tive of a distinctive handling of shipwreck, based on a specific, early modern usage of this metaphor.

From Book to Screen

In view of my discussion of the bearing of this specific metaphor on con-temporary cinema, I will first engage with a necessarily brief outline of its development in writing through time, and the discontinuities in its percep-tion and construction. The 'cinematographic seas' of the 1990s draw on one of the most ancient and suggestive metaphors of all times, whose reworking and adaptations, like the ocean itself, seem indeed to be boundless. Usually imbued with ideological and cultural understandings, over almost two mil-lennia this very old metaphor has been used, in the first place, as a powerful instrument of the dominant discourse, with its implied 'meaning' changing according to the episteme and the historical moment.

Both within the classical and Christian traditions, the sea, with its charm, its mystery and its unpredictable character, was commonly identi-fied with evil and the demoniac. In so far as it is pure perpetual movement and a formless element, the sea was thought of as chaos undermining the fixity, order and stability built up by rationalist thought - which, as a con-sequence, were always identified with the land. The binary opposition sea versus land, together with the equation land = order/stability = rationalist thought, can be found, for instance - in a classical and influential writer such as Lucretius - explicitly linked to the metaphor of shipwreck. The second book of his *De Rerum Natura* opens in fact with a shipwreck 'gladly' watched by somebody who is safely ashore. The imperturbable on-looker is glad not because of the misadventure of the shipwrecked people, but about his safe status as spectator. His detachment comes precisely from his *doctrina sapientum* (Epicurean philosophy), from his standing on the 'solid ground' of reason and the logos and, last but not least, from the self-possession provided by his 'knowledge'. Lucretius conceives the universe as undergoing a continuous becoming and an eternal dissolution, and for him, the only way to oppose that dissolution is to build a solid, unchanging ground that can secure a 'protected' spectator position. He regards life essentially as a continuous shipwreck: only philosophy,

> By cunning craft, *out of such mighty waves*,
> Out of such mighty darkness, moored life
> In *havens* so serene, in light so clear.[1]

As Hans Blumenberg has pointed out,[2] the firm, self-assured position of Lucretius' spectator sums up a whole approach towards life, one that favours theoretical, 'objective' reasoning over individual exploration and praxis, external and detached observation over involvement and immersion in things, a secure status of spectator over the agency of the actor, fixity over fluidity. I will come back to this in my analysis of *The Truman Show*, a film that ingeniously reworks the opposition sea versus haven/land, as well as the one between actor and spectator.

Building on these implications, in his *Pensées* Blaise Pascal takes an essential theoretical step towards the modern notion of metaphorical shipwreck. After warning against the futility of 'look[ing] for certainty and stability', since '[o]ur reason is always deceived by fickle shadows',[3] Pascal intimates that there is not even such a thing as a choice between 'land' and 'sea': 'It is not optional. You are embarked',[4] he writes. The security of the 'land', in other words, is fictitious, and what is left to human beings is 'wager[ing]'[5] for the best possibility for them. This notion of being (even unwittingly) 'embarked' is suggestively outlined in a 'pensée' evoking an oceanic planet-like scenario, in which any attempt at phallogocentric constructions is inherently unstable:

> *We sail within a vast sphere, ever drifting* in uncertainty, driven from end to end. When we think to attach ourselves to any point and to fasten to it, it wavers and leaves us; and if we follow it, it eludes our grasp, slips past us, and vanishes forever. Nothing stays for us. This is our natural condition and yet most contrary to our inclination; we burn with desire to find *solid ground* and

> *an ultimate sure foundation whereon to build a tower* reaching to the Infinite.
> *But our whole groundwork cracks, and the earth opens to abysses.*[6]

This image of a watery 'sphere' over which people are 'ever drifting' is bodied forth in the basic concept of (a) Waterworld, in the film of that name, a place once known as planet Earth. It is Pascal's view that is reworked by the film's writers (Peter Rader and David Twothy) and director (Kevin Reynold). In a future era in which the greenhouse effect has melted the polar ice caps, the whole world - together with the certainties of civilization - has 'open[ed] to abysses', somehow 'shipwrecked' and 'foundered', having been completely submerged by water. Having lost their historical memory, the descendants of the survivors believe that the world was created in a deluge, and that human beings are destined to discover, sooner or later, the only piece of terra firma believed to exist in Waterworld, the mythic, utopic island of Dryland.

In line with the classical view, this oceanic world is a place where barbarism and violence reign among the survivors, although there are in fact groups of people who try to reinstate something like an orderly society, in the floating cities called 'atolls'. Nevertheless, besides individuals who, consistent with the foundering and erasure of socio-political apparatuses and logocentric convictions, live alone on their own vessels - nomads like the Mariner - a whole association of criminals living on plunder, the so-called Smokers, represent the most conspicuous, cohesive and best-organized floating congregation in *Waterworld*. Their leader Deacon binds them by the promise of being able to guide them to Dryland. Their pyramidal and phallocratic society is based on the consensual exploitation of a proletariat of rowers, whose labour allows this nightmarish and grotesque simulacrum of a 'ship of state' literally to go on. Caustically, the vessel of such a (distorted?) 'ship of state' is nothing but the restructured relic of the *Exxon Valdez*, the oil tanker responsible for one of the biggest environmental disasters of all times. Midway between a warship and a pirate ship, the liner emphatically functions as a spectre(ship) of the worst that humanity is capable of. However, there is indeed a lot of irony in the depiction of the Smokers - who also serve as the comic characters of the film. After all, in such an oceanic world logocentric categories and values are blurred: as a consequence, there is no such thing as a clear-cut opposition between 'good' and 'evil'. As an instance of this, consider the episode of the 'atollers' (supposedly 'good' people) who want to put to death the Mariner only because he is different:[7] a case of the mob versus the social outcast - outsider and physically different - in scenes clearly reminiscent of that widespread attitude (which borders on mass hysteria) associated with the practice of the death penalty in many American states. In the same way, the ecological disaster and the ensuing state of barbarism are not very different from what caused them. They sprang from a logic of domination and subjugation of nature based on the fundamental rationalist binary human/non-human, which led to the exploitation and disintegration of (almost) the entire non-human world. This is a logic that finds its core in that phallocentric cult of power inherently opposing the 'strong' to the 'weak' and harmless, and resulting in the annihilation of part of the human 'race' as well.

Subtly, the child that holds the key to a forgotten place and the prospect of (re)creating a human situation on new 'grounds', is a *little girl*, and she is named Enola.[8] The allusion is to the Enola Gay and the 'Little Boy' it carried, one of the most atrocious instruments of destruction devised by a phallocentric world[9] dominated by a merciless, hegemonic logic of power, which is here completely subverted. In fact, whereas the Enola Gay carried desolation and death, little Enola in *Waterworld* symbolically carries a map and the concrete possibility of (re)construction and (re)creation. Her association with (Dry)land and, more generally, with earth, points to a pre-rationalist world and to the reign of the Mother Goddess,[10] Gaia or the Earth, daughter of Chaos. The masculinist and male-dominated world that produced so much devastation (the atomic bomb, the greenhouse effect, pollution, and so on) is here submerged once and for all. After such global-scale destruction, the hope and utopia that this picture recounts is summed up in its tagline: 'Beyond the horizon lies a new beginning', where *new* signifies indeed a complete subversion of the politics of the current dominant discourse.

Whereas in *Waterworld* the entire Earth and 'civilization' have foundered, giving way to an aquatic world of chaos, in Robert Zemeckis' *Cast Away* shipwrecks mainly concern the individual and the submersion of his/her own certitudes. Here we move from Reynold's oceanic survivors to the predicament of one Chuck Noland (*No-land*); the key notion of the film, however, is again derived from Pascal. That is to say, each individual is essentially 'embarked', drifting on an open sea without certainties, and life takes him/her through a series of shipwrecks, in which each one can in fact count only on him/herself to survive, and on her/his own willpower, even at the risk of bordering on madness.[11] The Pascalian condition as a metaphor of existence (before the literal wreck, following the plane crash, shown in the film) is underscored and emphasized by the camera work in the first part of the film: the shots of the extremely hectic everyday life of worka-holic Chuck, 'immersed' in his work around the clock, are strobing, wavering, unstable, in a way that indeed suggests the sea - while giving the impression that the eye/I of the camera is 'embarked' as well. Chuck blindly lives by all the dogmas of the capitalist market and of globalization - work, profit, efficiency, productivity, worship of the clock.[12] All these 'values' and 'beliefs' shape and constitute Chuck Noland's identity. Suddenly, what seems unstoppable, i.e. this clock-regulated world, is stopped (as unequivocally symbolized by the breaking of his pocket watch). The crash and wreck on the island are an unexpected disruption that will eventually unfold to Chuck a fresh approach to life, one that can do without the useless, unstable, oppressing phallogocentric constructions that used to dominate his existence. The 'land' of certainties has foundered, and only the awareness of this enables a human being to save him/herself.

Shipwrecked on the island, Chuck Noland believed that there was at least one thing that he still had power to control, the decision over the manner and the exact moment of his death. However, he eventually cannot even take his life: the last certainty sinks and, suddenly, the *mad* idea of struggling to try and save himself emerges - 'mad' insofar as 'logic', as he explains later, tells him he will never make it. He discovers, on the contrary, that 'you never know what the tide will bring', and he is rescued, only to face another (metaphorical) shipwreck (his girlfriend got married during the four years he spent on the island, and now has a daughter). The difference is that now he has the 'instruments' to face this - no clocks, no certainties, just the willingness to trust himself *madly* to the tide.

Both *Waterworld* and *Cast Away*, therefore, exploit the (Pascalian) notion of shipwreck as a metaphor of existence. A collective and thoroughly man-produced shipwreck in *Waterworld*, is set against the unexpected wreck affecting the individual in *Cast Away*. This kind of sudden break, which obstructs the regular proceeding of the course of someone's (planned) life, is, however, dependent upon the contingent nature of the human condition. Yet in both cases shipwreck is conceived as a *fact* which is independent of the character's will and actions (not to mention that in *Cast Away* most of the film is based on the hope of rescue and return to the initial situation - although the latter will not exactly materialize in the terms of a restoration of the original *status quo*). The films that I am going to discuss in the next section take on different tenors of the shipwreck metaphor, which are explicitly subversive, and build upon uses of shipwreck in literary texts of the last two hundred years or so.

Escape and Revolt

Although, as we saw, discontinuities in the classical understanding of the sea can already be found after the Copernican revolution (e.g., Shakespeare and Pascal), the major epistemological change leading to a full exploitation of the revolutionary charge inherent in the classical notion of sea versus land takes place only toward the end of the 18th century, when the metaphor of shipwreck is increasingly developed in connection with questions of language and writing. Romantic and late modern developments in the handling of this metaphor find an important paradigm in an early work such as *The Rime of the Ancient Mariner* (1798). Here, as well as in later texts, the metaphor of shipwreck exploits the radical implications of an iconography of the sea which identifies the non-place (*u-topos*) of the deep with the primordial, the irrational, the unconscious, the unknown, the unthought. These texts emphasize and give a new, extremely positive value to the traditional conception of the abyss as the locus par excellence of the discovery of the 'other' - meaning by 'other' whatever is perceived as different and uncodified by the logos, anything that, by virtue of this difference, undermines the canons of the dominant discourse (e.g., the unconscious - with its drives, desires, the dream and its language).

As a consequence, in modernity shipwreck increasingly develops into a metaphor for the deepest immersion in those depths, a sinking that brings about (just like in Ariel's song, in Shakespeare's *The Tempest*) a disruptive 'sea-change': more specifically, a sea-change that constitutes the psychic death of (social) identity, of the 'I' with all its logocentric constructions (language, in the first place), coincident with the birth of writing and of a distinctive language (poetic language) that always bears traces of those deep waters. As an unexpected break and deviation from the pre-established path, shipwreck can be read metaphorically as the threshold to a different, individual, pragmatic kind of (non-monologic) cognition, as the locus of creativity and (re)invention of the self. Hence, it represents a heuristic and/or epiphanic moment - epiphanic in the sense of a secular revelation or realization - which, by virtue of producing valuable insights, ultimately takes on an epistemological as well as a disruptively utopic value.

It is this significance of the metaphorical shipwreck which informs three major films of the 1990s, James Cameron's *Titanic*, Gabriele Salvatores' *Mediterraneo*, and the latest masterpiece of Peter Weir, *The Truman Show*. Both *Titanic* and *Mediterraneo* are based on historical events associated with the sea - the former scrupulously faithful to historical detail, and the latter a rather free adaptation. However, it is my contention that in these two films we are given reconfigurations of history or readings of it which are, in the end, metaphorical - in the sense that they create a perspectival dimension exceeding the temporal and national boundaries in which the actual events are inscribed, so that more far-reaching and topical issues are emphasized. History, that is, becomes a background for metahistorical metaphors that question the present, aimed at radically deconstructing the dominant discourse - an objective also shared by *The Truman Show*.

Directed and written by James Cameron, *Titanic* is probably remembered, in the first instance, as a huge commercial operation. However, on the whole the film offers much more than that. Building on the historical, tragic events related to the transnational phenomenon of the RMS *Titanic*, Cameron creates a few fictional characters, whose addition to his narration of history works as a sort of gigantic magnifier. That is to say, their function is to reveal and emphasize the nature of the discourses underlying and producing the actual events that the film recounts. Crucially, as I will demonstrate, this allows Cameron to forge a radically divergent cinematic rendition of those events in respect to previous *Titanic* films, in the sense that, while all the other subject-related films focused on *fatality* (the iceberg), Cameron succeeds in effectively stressing the *agency* behind the tragedy.

The history of the *Titanic* is well known. At the dawn of the 20th century, the prestige of the British Empire meant, in the first instance, Great Britain ruling the seas. Nationalism and economy fuelled tough rivalry and strong competition, particularly with Germany, for the domination of the transatlantic travel industry which was booming at the turn of the century. The White Star Line, leader in passenger lines and pride of Britain, planned to launch the biggest, most comfortable and luxurious ocean liner ever built, completed in such a short time (two years, which then became three) that safety measures were almost completely disregarded, bringing over fifteen hundred people to their death.

Cameron's *Titanic* focuses upon life on board a ship which was indeed a floating social microcosm, reproducing the rigid structure of Edwardian society: a huge pleasure steamer, for the wealthy Anglo-American high society, and, at the same time, an emigrant ship of hope, for its hundreds of steerage passengers travelling with all they owned. For all those third-class men, women, children and entire families the sea was an immense borderline between different national and economic 'realities', a threshold towards the realization of new (material) possibilities of life: for them, the *Titanic* was indeed - as it was called - 'the ship of dreams'.

In a way, it was 'the ship of dreams' also for the upper-class passengers crossing the sea just for pleasure: in so far as it embodied all the comfort and luxury that status and money could buy even at sea, it was another sought-after emblem of their wealth. It represented the highest achievement of the technology of the time, what was thought to be the 'triumph' of 'man' and reason over nature. As the film reveals, however, the notion of 'mastery over nature' is for Cameron a very complex and multifarious one, which exceeds the concept of progress as a linear, always-increasing development of material human conditions. Indeed, for Cameron, 'mastery over nature' seems to embrace every logocentric construction aimed at controlling and repressing 'nature' in the broadest sense of the word, including 'human nature': feelings, (unconscious) drives, inborn characteristics, and so on. The allusion is to the hegemony of the logos, to the domination of reason over 'chaos' which characterizes Western thought and which - through language as a system of classification and categorization, made up of differences and binary oppositions (e.g., rational versus irrational, feelings and drives) - brought about the conceptualization of 'reality' in the constant endeavour to superimpose order over 'chaos'.

The constitution of a social pyramid divided into classes represents only the most apparent result and further instrument of that domination. James Cameron makes the critique of the Edwardian class system extremely explicit. Through the introduction of the fictional characters of Rose, Ruth, Cal and Jack he emphasizes the degree to which every logocentric fabrication bringing about repression and discrimination of the 'individual' as well as of whole social groups is to be traced back, in the first instance, to the patriarchal family (which Ruth, Rose's mother represents), to phallocentrism (embodied especially by Cal, Rose's fiancé) and, even more, to language itself. In this film, Cameron perceives language as a comprehensive system of 'signs' which exceeds words and speech and encompasses other equally significant semiotic phenomena - such as, for instance, (socio-historically and class-determined conventions of) clothing, comportment, as well as body language. Cameron demonstrates how language (in this broad sense) is in fact a repository of pre-established concepts, as well as a restrictive/prescriptive code of behaviour, inculcated in the subject since his/her early childhood. This radical critique of language is artistically re-created, for instance, in the scene of the upper-class little girl rehearsing with her elegant mother how to sit properly for tea, like 'a real lady'. Etiquette is but one aspect of the fabrications and the constraints of the logos that the film shows and, yet, a crucial one. To conform to formalities and rules was vital for the upper classes, and it is interesting that Ruth tries to force her daughter to marry a man whom she does not love (for the sake of status and money) while she is lacing tightly Rose's corset - the most stiffening and constrictive undergarment of the time, a symbol of the obliteration of the body and everything that is 'inside', 'within'.

Seventeen-year-old Rose feels trapped by the repressive conformism of her class: she belongs to a modern generation of women who want to break free from patriarchy. She reads Freud and is keen on art, especially Picasso, whose paintings she finds 'fascinating, like being in a dream or something: there's truth, but no logic.' 'Logic' is a key word both in *Titanic* and *Mediterraneo*. Logic - as 'reason' and 'ambition' - made it possible to build the huge ship of dreams that the *Titanic* was. Logic - as presumption, arrogance, discrimination and repression (all products of phallogocentrism) - led, at the same time, to the death of fifteen hundred people in the icy cold waters of the Atlantic. For them, there was no second chance, no metaphorical sea-change.

Set against that logic, shipwreck for Rose emerges as the death of her (social) identity, of the 'I' with all its logocentric fabrications, coincident with the birth of a new 'individuality', with a creative redefinition of 'identity'. This rebirth is reflected in Rose's change of name soon after she is rescued. After the wreck, she never looks for her mother again, letting the world believe she is dead, and giving herself the possibility, in this way, to create her own (new) life. Rose's shipwreck brings about a radical breakthrough, giving her access to an existence free from the rule of somebody else's authority, as well as from constraints of class and gender. Her mother's relinquished and submissive 'We're women' speech, stating the lack of alternatives and the necessity for women to conform to the expectations of a phallogocentric system, is disruptively subverted. Hence, the historical shipwreck of the *Titanic* is both linked to, and also reread in the light of, the shipwreck metaphor and its most subversive imports.

This use of the metaphor of shipwreck also informs another film that moves between fiction and history, the Italian *Mediterraneo* - directed by Gabriele Salvatores and written by Vincenzo Monteleone. Set during the Second World War at the time of the Nazi occupation of Greece, the film opens with a warship crossing the Mediterranean sea to reach a small Greek island, which eight Italian soldiers have been sent to garrison. They have been called back to the army because of the war, and are rather clumsy as soldiers: they shoot their donkey thinking it is the enemy (it is dark and it would not say the password), and even break their radio, so that, when their ship is sunk by the Allies, they are completely cut out of history and time. Little by little, the island seems to charm the eight Italians, who soon forget about - just as they are forgotten by - their native country, about war and the phallogocentric discourse producing it. As a consequence, they are far from behaving like enemies with the small native population of women, children and old men (the younger men having been taken away by the Germans). 'Italians, Greeks: my face, my race ... one face, one race',[13] is a sort of refrain in this film, just like the phrase 'we're friends'. A small Greek-Italian community is soon formed, and the discourse of the nation, of race and war is easily splintered and invalidated.

The sea, from functioning geographically as *discrimen*, that is, as separation and difference, between similar cultures, not only becomes a bridge between them, but also acts as a threshold towards a brand new conception of life, which was unimaginable before. Once again, shipwreck takes on the value of a break, which brings about the (psychic) death of (social and national) identity, as well as of all the phallogocentric discriminations emphasized by fascism, a death coincident with a rebirth and an invaluable sea-change. To that effect, the allusion to 'origins' and 'roots' points to a sort of primordial dimension, through reference to the island - formerly a dwelling place of gods and goddesses - as the locus of an ancient, mythic 'civilization' cultivating the arts, living in harmony, writing poetry 'seven centuries before Christ', as the learned Lieutenant Montini remarks. All that the Italians do on the island is read poetry, paint, dance, (make) love and, why not, play football. Inevitably, any sense of time is lost: 'like in the Odyssey ... We're staying in the island of oblivion.' Allusions to the *Odyssey* abound throughout *Mediterraneo*, a film proposing oblivion (in the etymological sense of forgetfulness) together with escape and desertion, as the only way to preserve the 'individual' from the repression and violence inherent in the dominant discourse. The notion of oblivion is embodied, it could be said, by the character of the Turk, who comes from the sea, from places where there is no war, and who just answers 'dunno' whenever he is asked his name. Significantly, when the Italians get stoned on the Turkish hashish he provides, he steals from them their weapons, watches and wallets - very likely symbols for violence, time, and identity, the three major foundations of phallogocentrism. The Italians' initial disappointment is replaced by a crucial realization: 'If things were always this way ... if they took your weapons and left this stuff [hashish] ... we'd live better, right?'

Far away and out of time, most of them discover desires never manifest before: Strazzabosco, for instance, discloses his homosexual feeling for Sergeant Lo Russo - whose name ironically means 'the Russian', or 'the Red', an epithet not very appropriate for somebody fighting for Mussolini. Vassilissa, herself in a way 'shipwrecked' on the island, as she was brought and left there by the Germans, recognizes that she is a prostitute because her mother was one, and before her mother, her grandmother was a prostitute too: 'Logic, isn't it?', she remarks. Against that social determinism, she eventually succeeds in realizing her dream and opens a restaurant. Shipwreck unravels some-thing 'new' about themselves to most of them, letting emerge what is 'deep down inside' without rational censure and fears of repression.

Unfortunately, this state of oblivion does not last forever: 'the one jarring note comes when a small plane arrives with the news that now Italians are fighting alongside the Allies. This passage of three years comes unexpectedly, since the audience is still thinking in terms of elapsed months.'[14] Their presence on the island is communicated to the authorities and, hence, their 'recovery' arranged.

The scene of the arrival of the British, who intend to 'rescue' the eight 'soldiers' and bring them back to 'civilization', is particularly fascinating: the shots of the perfectly white shoes, white socks and white uniforms of the officers of the Navy - the restorers of order, disgustedly facing a bunch of savage-looking grown-ups - is a clear intertextual reference to Peter Brook's 1963 cinematic version of *Lord of the Flies*.[15] Unequivocally, that dystopia is deliberately subverted and deconstructed in *Mediterraneo*, which shows how violence and dystopic contents are inherent in phallogo-centrism, which brought about war and decided who is friend and who is to be brutally killed (according to the convenience of the moment), a system of which armies and glittering national politics, symbolized here by the immaculately dressed Navy officers, are a structuring and essential part.

However, the news of the civil war in Italy, of the 'great ideals at stake', calls for action. While Farina (in love with Vassilissa) decides never to leave the island and Noventa, after several attempts, finally succeeds in escaping - desertion is the most immediate individual form of subversion of the dominant discourse that the film emphasizes - Lo Russo thinks that the time has come to be *engagé*, to try and change things on a wider scale, to fight for those great ideals. But he ends up crossing over the sea again, reaching for the island: 'They didn't let us change anything. So ... so I told them: "You win, but don't consider me your accomplice."'

Such a position, which the film recreates for one of the characters, derives, in fact, from the bitter disillusionment with the 'idealist', radical battles of the late 1960s and the 1970s in Italy, which are transposed in the film as (frustrated) ideals of re-creation of a new Italy in the post-war period. Salvatores and Monteleone seem to suggest that, against any form of fascism, both as a 'manifest' regime and a more subtle kind of politics inherent in the dominant discourse and informed by phallogocentrism, only the 'individual' has a way out. The epigraph by Henri Laborit, which introduces the film, clearly sets the tone for such a reading of *Mediterraneo*: 'In times like these, escape is the only way to stay alive and to continue dreaming.' In his *Éloge de la fuite*, Laborit claims that escape allows one to discover unknown shores emerging on the horizon of waters newly becalmed. Unknown shores which will be forever ignored by those who have the illusory fortune of being able to follow the course of the freighters and the tankers, the course without unexpected events *imposed* by the shipping companies.[16]

That is to say, a course without shipwrecks, as well as freedom. This is the subversive sense of a simple, and yet intensely poetic, film which is 'dedicated to all those who are running away', a film pointing at the concrete possibility of (individual) sea-changes - as an endless process of (re)creation of the self - which indeed have the value of an ultimate, radical challenge to the pre-established order.

Intriguingly, Laborit's excerpt, together with his disruptive notion of escape, is not only apposite to Cameron's fictional heroine, but also applies perfectly to that immense metaphor which *The Truman Show* is - a film regarded by many as the greatest achievement in the brilliant career of Australian director Peter Weir. In *The Truman Show*, Weir engages with that 'disturbance to our perception of reality'[17] induced by the media - 'to the point where you can't differentiate anymore'[18] - as a metaphor for the 'fabrication' and control of 'personality' and individual drives by the entire social environment surrounding the individual (his/her family, in the first place). In other words, 'what could easily have been a mere satire about the nature of TV media and the role it plays in our society, or about corporate greed, or about the voyeurism of American audiences, becomes instead a much deeper, more compelling drama about the conflicting fear of, and desire for, individual free-will, with all its incumbent risks'.[19] As I will show, it is exactly through an informed and skilful use of the shipwreck metaphor that Weir achieves this.

The film opens with a series of TV interviews with the fictional director and actors of the most popular and longest running television show (i.e., 'The Truman Show'), mixed with images of Truman Burbank's 'real' life (the unwitting star of the production), and followed by an alternation of scenes from the show - midway between a soap opera and a real-life documentary - and shots of the fictional audiences watching it. In this way, Weir deliberately confuses his own film audience, leaving us for some time to figure out by ourselves what is 'really' going on. In fact, the film focuses on Truman himself trying to unravel precisely 'what is really going on' in his life. The whole world knows that he is the unknowing protagonist of a 'watched-by-millions' show running twenty-four hours a day for thirty years, from the time when he was legally adopted by the TV network Omnicam Corporation - whose name already suggests the kind of global, totalitarian control of minds, emotions and lives through cameras and TV screens à la *1984*. Since his birth, Truman has been placed on a gigantic television set (in fact a whole town) and surrounded exclusively by paid actors, from his parents, to his wife and friends, down to every single passer-by in the street: he is the only genuine person (true-man) in the huge, picture-perfect city-set. He was still in the womb when his life began to be controlled and directed by the creator of the show, Christof, who claims that, by doing so, he gave Truman 'a chance to live a normal life' in a protected albeit counterfeited world, in which he has 'nothing to fear'.[20] 'Normality' is thus perceived as an idealized 'value', firmly anchored in the security, stability and conformism of a phony world, which is in fact a golden cage.

It is revealing that while scriptwriter Andrew Niccol originally set his story in New York, Weir changed the setting into an idyllic *island*-town, significantly named Seahaven. Ironically, unlike a real *haven*, this town is no place of 'exchange', and rather recalls Lucretius' notion of the haven as a safe (closed) space, opposed to the sea. In fact, apart from working actors, nobody truly arrives from outside the city-set and, more importantly, nobody leaves - at least Truman does not, being prevented at all times from doing so. Seahaven, that is, embodies the fixity classically associated with the land. Christof, the creator-father-director, had to envisage several ways to keep Truman (who, as a child, not surprisingly dreamt of being an explorer) within its borders. Besides the local travel agency discouraging potential clients to travel[21] - echoed by 'Radio Land' and its subtle news of the airplane 'shedding parts' in flight, luckily without victims - the most effective strategy proves to be the deliberate inculcation in young Truman of an insurmountable, paralysing fear of water. After sundry attempts, Christof attained this by staging the death of Truman's (fictional) father, Kirk, as a terrible boat accident during a sudden storm, which broke while young Truman and the actor he believes to be his dad are sailing. The connection of Truman's phobia of the sea to a (procured) sense of guilt for the death of the father bears a tremendous significance, as this adds more emphasis to the ancient import of the sea metaphors that the film exploits. More specifically, the sea crossing is perceived as a transgression of the (rational) law of the father/Father, hence echoing also original sin. In its subversive metaphorical association with the adventitious, unforeseeable 'other', setting out to sea implies a disavowal of pre-established codes and precepts, i.e. the 'death' of patriarchal phallogocentrism.

As the film progresses, the collision between 'otherness' versus the codified manifestly substantiates the conflict between Truman and Christof. After a series of production gaffes, Truman grows tremendously suspicious and begins to comprehend the warning of his lost love Sylvia, a former member of the cast who decided to *break* from the *script* - and therefore was hastily removed from the production. He suddenly begins to change his normal, 'scheduled' behaviour and improvises: 'Somebody help me! I'm being *spontaneous*!', he merrily yells in defiance. His destabilizing conduct sends the production haywire, beginning with Christof: 'Why wasn't I told? Any *unpredictable* behaviour has to be reported!' On top of his 'unpredictable actions' is his final decision to confront his phobia and sail on his boat, symbolically named the *Santa Maria* - like Columbus' own discovery ship - while singing, to take heart, 'What should we do with a drunken sailor?' When Christof ultimately realizes it, he does not hesitate to access 'the weather program' and send a storm over the huge water-tank, reproducing the sea in the gigantic studio. Almost drowned, Truman perseveres and, eventually, shipwrecks on the horizon, i.e. against the sky-painted scenery, limit of his faked world. Truman's disruptive crossing gets him ashore (metaphorically) in a new world, in which he presumably will be free to *act* according to his own drives and inclination, to explore new possibilities, to perform a fresh, creative approach to life against a superimposed one. This notion of 'acting', in the sense of (subversively) *taking action*, surely constitutes a reinstatement of Blumenberg's theory of actor (as 'doer' or *agent*) versus spectator (the one who prefers not to take risks, and to conform to safe, pre-established, fixed rational norms). However, the conception informing *The Truman Show* is in fact more complex.

It is my contention that Weir disrupts the notion of 'actor', and renders it more problematic, by introducing a splintered, manifold idea of 'actor'. Instead of simply re-establishing Blumenberg's binary (actor versus spectator), Weir propounds several intermediate positions, which draw on the polysemy of the word 'actor' itself, i.e.: the conscious impersonator (either artist or liar) and the oblivious performer. That is to say, the alternative to the position of spectator (who would rather contemplate other people's active, venturesome lives) is not just, straightforwardly, the one of the 'actor' (or 'doer') as agent-transgressor, the daring individual who creatively takes action (like Truman in the second half of the film). Subtly, 'actor' is also the impersonator, like all the paid actors of the show, who voluntarily 'play by the script' *and* also deliberately lie to Truman. In addition, ominously indeed as he is unaware of it, 'actor' is also Truman himself in the first thirty years of his life, before he realizes it and 'takes action'. In other words, in so far as he behaves according to the *expectations* of the dominant, hegemonic discourse, Truman is himself a performer, i.e. plays a part, an expected, pre-fabricated role, behaving in a way that is not genuine, but is alien to his authentic nature and desires - being in fact a prisoner. His unawareness not only makes him a victim, but also an *accomplice*, and this lines him up with the spectators of the show, and the (unconscious) structuring power they indirectly exert on it. On the other hand, the numb dependence of the viewers on the TV screen and their morbid interest in the linear, conventional plot of someone else's counterfeited life, body forth the notion of an audience which constitutes a counterpoint of Lucretius' image of the onlooker. While the latter willingly adopts his own conservative and firm views, they seem to be utterly incognizant of their position, undiscerning and apathetic toward their own lives. Alienated and entranced, they watch as if hypnotized by the TV screen. Significantly, the shots of the five thousand hidden cameras spying on Truman are mostly *eye*-shaped. Many of them, however, especially towards the end, are round and similar to *portholes*, so as to suggest that a specific kind of informed, artistic film can indeed be conceived, just like writing has been for centuries, as a metaphorical ship, a contemporary *bouteille à la mer*, bringing the precious shipment of its message through the sea of its audience, to those willing to receive it.

Epilogue

> *Interviewer*: Christof, may I ask you, why do you think that, uh, Truman has never come close to discovering the true nature of his world until now?
> *Christof*: We accept the reality of the world with which we're presented. It's as simple as that.

Set against the passive spectator, or the performer who conforms and accepts unquestioningly, (semi)unconsciously acting according to society's expectations, the 'drunken sailor' (Truman) proves the God-like creator-father-director (Christof) wrong, just like Cameron's female protagonist and some of the characters of *Mediterraneo* do. As all the films discussed above demonstrate, contemporary cinema is more and more informed by a radical and disruptive use of metaphoric seas and shipwrecks. In both literary and film texts, the forbidden boundary of the sea increasingly changes into a threshold, a gateway to an alternative, non-conventional, ex-centric kind of cognition, which resists any logocentric codification. Accordingly, whereas in ancient times shipwreck was thought of as a punishment for the transgressors, within the modern discourse of the sea not only is it conceived as a necessary risk, as 'the price to escape closure, torpidity'[22] and the *status quo*, but it also takes on new epiphanic and subversive connotations. Sea voyage and shipwreck, that is, become an extremely significant metaphor for the potentiality of creating sites of resistance, as well as the concrete possibility for an (emancipated) individual to forge authentic counter-hegemonic discourses.

Notes

1   Lucretius, *On the Nature of Things*, book 5, trans. William Ellery Leonard, The Internet Classics Archive. http://classics.mit.edu//Carus/nature_things.html (21 January 2000) (my italics).
2   Hans Blumenberg, *Schiffbruch mit Zuschauer. Paradigma einer Daseinsmetapher* (Frankfurt am Main: Suhrkamp, 1979). English edition: *Shipwreck with Spectator. Paradigm of a Metaphor for Existence*, trans. Steven Rendall (Cambridge, MA, and London: MIT Press, 1996).
3   Blaise Pascal, *Pensées* [1660], II: 72, trans. W.F. Trotter, The English Server, *Collections in the Arts and Humanities*, 6 June 1994. http://eserver.org/philosophy/pascal-pensees.txt (3 February 2000).
4   *Ibid.*, III: 233.
5   *Ibid.*
6   *Ibid.*, II: 72 (my italics).
7   After centuries of drifting in Waterworld, some humans undergo a genetic mutation. The Mariner has developed gills and webbed feet. His different anatomy allows him to fathom the deep, to see the submerged cities, and to understand what really happened. The significance of his mutation (feared by most) is the adaptation to the 'new' reality, to the lack of certainties, which is reflected in his resistance to the reconstruction of socio-political structures, of a pre-established, ordered system of communal life. Such an attitude is condemned by those who still believe that such 'stability' is possible even in the middle of an ocean (and who, in turn, resist the acknowledgement of their real situation). The mutant Mariner has no name, i.e. no social identity. His position toward social life is reiterated in his choice not to join his new friends at the end of the film.
8   An orphan with a strange tattoo on her back, believed to be the map to Dryland. Entrusted to the waters when she was a small child, in a dinghy and with a small pot containing earth, she was found and adopted by the atoller Helen. Enola's 'visions', as old Gregor calls her drawings, are in fact subconscious memories of her past life on the only fertile piece of earth left (the mythic Dryland, her 'home'). She sketches trees and animals, something nobody has ever seen. Not only is she associated with painting, but also with music (she continuously hums) and, more generally, with (fertile) creativity.
9   As Susan Stanford Friedman points out, 'the pervasive use of the birth metaphor at Los Alamos to describe the creation of the first atomic bomb (known as "Oppenheimer's baby", christened informally as "Little Boy", and dropped from a plane named Enola Gay, after the pilot's mother) serves to obscure the bomb's destructiveness and implicate women in its birth'. S. Stanford Friedman, 'Creativity and the Childbirth Metaphor: Gender Difference in Literary Discourse', *Feminist Studies* 13, no. 1 (Spring 1987), 49-82, 63.
10 Dryland is, in fact, a miniature reign of Gaia. Everything on the island is consistent with many of the mythological symbols of the Goddess: the mountain, the waterfalls, the horses, the teeming vegetation. The very vase found when Enola was rescued, and containing earth, is another image of fertility associated with Gaia, just like the tree

Enola often draws, another of her epiphanies. Cf. G.C. Benelli, *Il Mito e l'Uomo* (Milan: Mondadori, 1992), 78-82, 86.

11   The volleyball found on the shore and baptized Wilson - 'will-son' - after his manufacturer, and given human features by painting it in blood, becomes the silent interlocutor of Chuck on the desert island and a symbol of that willpower.

12   It must be said that, somehow, *Cast Away* shares some of these views, as it can indeed be seen as a film-length advertisement for a leading courier company.

13   All the citations from *Mediterraneo* are taken from the English subtitles included in the English release of the film.

14   Edwin Jahiel, 'Mediterraneo', *Movie Reviews by Edwin Jahiel*, http://www.prairienet. org/ejahiel (30 June 2000).

15   I am indebted to Ulrich Kinzel for bringing this to my attention.

16   Henri Laborit, Preface to *Éloge de la fuite*, 1976; *Elogio della Fuga* (Milan: Mondadori, 1982). My translation and italics.

17   Peter Weir, from an interview by Jenny Peters, 'The Man Behind Truman', *Mr. Showbiz Interview*, 2001, http://mrshowbiz.go.com/interviews/415_2.html (20 March 2001).

18   *Ibid.*

19   Derek Neff, 'The Truman Show', *The Bliss Point Film Review*, June 1998. http://www2.apex.net/users/neffd/truman.html (27 March 2001).

20   In this respect, *The Truman Show* reveals a strong analogy with *Brave New World*. The counterfeited but 'comfortable' world that Christof created for Truman surely recalls Mustafa Mond's idea of a 'perfect' world without wars and passions, while the entranced spectators of the show, in a way 'drugged' by the screen and addict to television, evoke the drowsy dwellers of Mond's world.

21   Posters with warnings such as 'Travellers Beware: terrorists, disease, wild animals, street gangs', or the picture of a plane struck by thunder complete with the slogan 'It could happen to you', wittily substitute the attractive exotic images normally displayed by real agencies.

22   Patrizio Tucci, 'Introduzione', L. Sannia Nowé and M. Virdis (eds), *Naufragi* (Rome: Bulzoni Editure, 1993), xxxii. My translation.

Select Bibliography

Albion, Robert Greenhalgh, *Five Centuries of Famous Ships. From the Santa Maria to the Glomar Explorer* (New York et al.: McGraw-Hill, 1978).

Andrews, Kenneth R., *The Elizabethan Seaman* (London: National Maritime Museum, 1982).

Astro, Richard (ed.), *Literature and the Sea* (Corvallis: Oregon State University Press, 1976).

Auden, W.H., *The Enchafèd Flood, or The Romantic Iconography of the Sea* (London: Faber and Faber, 1951).

Babcock, F. Lawrence, *Spanning the Atlantic* (New York: Knopf, 1931).

Bachelard, Gaston, *Water and Dreams: An Essay on the Imagination of Matter* [French original 1942], trans. Edith Farrell (Dallas: The Dallas Institute of Humanities and Culture Publications, 1983).

Bass, George F. (ed.), *History of Seafaring* (London: Thames and Hudson, 1972).

Behrman, Cynthia Fansler, *Victorian Myths of the Sea* (Athens, OH: Ohio University Press, 1977).

Beil, Steve, *Down with the Old Canoe: A Cultural History of the Titanic Disaster* (New York: W.W. Norton, 1996).

Bender, Bert, *Sea-Brothers. The Tradition of American Sea Fiction from Moby Dick to the Present* (Philadelphia: University of Pennsylvania Press, 1988).

Bennett, Tom, *Shipwrecks Around Anglesey* (Holmws: Happy Fish, 1995).

Blumenberg, Hans, *Shipwreck with Spectator. Paradigm of a Metaphor for Existence* [German original 1979], trans. Steven Rendall (Cambridge, MA, and London: MIT Press, 1996).

Böhme, Hartmut (ed.), *Kulturgeschichte des Wassers* (Frankfurt am Main: Suhrkamp, 1988).

Bolster, Jeffrey, *Black Jacks. African American Seamen in the Age of Sail* (Cambridge, MA: Harvard University Press, 1997).

Bourke, John, *The Sea as a Symbol in English Poetry* (Eton: Alden & Blackwell, 1954).

Bowen, Frank C., *A Century of Atlantic Travel, 1830-1930* (London: Sampson Low, Marston and Co., 1932[?]).

Braudel, Fernand, *The Mediterranean and the Mediterranean World in the Age of Philipp II*, trans. Siân Reynolds, 2 vols (London: Fontana, 1975).

Broecheler, Kirsten, *Seereisen in der englischsprachigen Romanliteratur vom 18. bis 20. Jahrhundert* (Frankfurt am Main et al.: Lang, 1998).

Bromley, J.S., *The Manning of the Royal Navy: Selected Published Pamphlets, 1693-1873* (London: Navy Records Society, 1974).

Brown, E.D., *The International Law of the Sea*, 2 vols (Aldershot, Hants.; Brookfield, VT: Dartmouth, 1994).

221

Burg, B.R., *Sodomy and the Pirate Tradition* (New York: New York University Press, 1995).

Burton, Valerie, 'Counting Seafarers: the Published Records of the Registrar of Merchant Seamen, 1849-1913', *Mariner's Mirror* 71 (1985), 305-20.

Burton, Valerie, 'The Making of a Nineteenth-Century Profession: Shipmasters and the British Shipping Industry', *Journal of the Canadian Historical Association* 1 (1990), 97-118.

Burton, Valerie, 'Household and Labour Market Interactions in the Late Nineteenth Century British Shipping Industry: Breadwinning and Seafaring Families', T.W Guiannane and P. Johnson (eds), *The Microeconomic Analysis of the Household and the Labour Market, 1880-1939* (Seville: Universidad de Sevilla, 1998), 99-109.

Burton, Valerie, '"Whoring, Drinking Sailors": Reflections on Masculinity from the Labour History of Nineteenth-Century British Shipping', Margaret Walsh (ed.), *Working Out Gender* (Aldershot *et al.*: Ashgate, 1999), 84-101.

Capper, Charles, *The Port and Trade of London: Historical, Statistical, Local and General* (London: Smith, Elder and Co., 1862).

Carlson, Patricia Ann (ed.), *Literature and Lore of the Sea* (Amsterdam: Rodopi, 1986).

Carson, Rachel, *The Sea Around Us* [1951] (New York: Mentor, 1989).

Chappell, David, *Double Ghosts: Oceanian Voyagers on Euroamerican Ships* (Armonk, NY: M.E. Sharpe, 1997).

Clowes, William Laird, *The Royal Navy. A History from the Earliest Times to 1900* [1897-1903], 7 vols, facs. ed. (London: Chatham Publishing, 1996-97).

Cockcroft, Robert, *The Voyages of Life: Ship Imagery in Art, Literature and Life* (Nottingham: Nottingham University Art Gallery, 1982).

Cohen, Daniel A. (ed.), *The Female Marine and Related Works: Narratives of Cross-Dressing and Urban Vice in America's Early Republic* (Amherst: University of Massachusetts Press, 1997).

Cohn, Michael, and Michael Platzer, *Black Men of the Sea* (New York: Dodd, Mead, 1978).

Connery, Christopher L., 'The Oceanic Feeling and the Regional Imaginary', Rob Wilson and Wimal Dissanayake (eds), *Global/Local. Cultural Production and the Transnational Imaginary* (Durham: Duke University Press, 1996), 284-311.

Coote, John (ed.), *The Faber Book of the Sea* (London: Faber, 1989).

Coote, John (ed.), *The Faber Book of Tales of the Sea* (London: Faber, 1991).

Corbin, Alain, *The Lure of the Sea. The Discovery of the Seaside in the Western World, 1750-1840* [French original 1988], trans. Jocelyn Phelps (Cambridge: Polity Press, 1994).

Creighton, Margaret, and Lisa Norling (eds), *Iron Men, Wooden Women. Gender and Seafaring in the Atlantic World, 1700-1920* (Baltimore: Johns Hopkins University Press, 1996).

Dening, Greg, *Islands and Beaches. Discourses on a Silent Land: Marquesas 1774-1880* (Chicago: The Dorsey Press, 1980).

Dening, Greg, *Mr Bligh's Bad Language. Passion, Power and Theatre on the Bounty* (Cambridge: Cambridge University Press, 1992).

Diedrich, Maria, *et al.* (eds), *Black Imagination and the Middle Passage* (Oxford: Oxford University Press, 1999).

Doerflinger, William Main, *Shantymen and Shantyboys* (New York: Macmillan, 1951).

Döring, Tobias, and Bernhard Klein, 'Of Bogs and Oceans. Alternative Histories in the Poetry of Seamus Heaney and Derek Walcott', Bernhard Klein and Jürgen Kramer (eds), *Common Ground? Crossovers between Cultural Studies and Postcolonial Studies* (Trier: Wissenschaftlicher Verlag, 2001), 113-36.

Edmond, Rod, *Representing the South Pacific. Colonial Discourse from Cook to Gauguin* (Cambridge: Cambridge University Press, 1997).

Edwards, Philip, *The Story of the Voyage. Sea-Narratives in 18th Century England* (Cambridge: Cambridge University Press, 1994).

Edwards, Philip, *Sea-Marks. The Metaphorical Voyage, Spenser to Milton* (Liverpool: Liverpool University Press, 1997).

Falconer, Alexander Frederick, *Shakespeare and the Sea* (London: Constable, 1964).

Fisher, Stephen (ed.), *British Shipping and Seamen, 1630-1960* (Exeter: University of Exeter Press, 1984).

Foster, John Wilson, *The Titanic Complex* (Vancouver: Belcouver Press, 1997).

Foster, John Wilson (ed.), *Titanic* (Harmondsworth: Penguin, 1999).

Foulke, R.D., 'Life in the Dying World of Sail', *The Journal of British Studies* 3, no. 1 (1963), 105-36.

Fricke, Peter H. (ed.), *Seafarer and Community: Towards a Social Understanding of Seafaring* (London: Croom Helm, 1973).

Froude, James Anthony, *Oceana; or, England and Her Colonies* (London: Longman, Green & Co., 1886).

Froude, James Anthony, *The English in the West Indies, or The Bow of Ulysses* [1887] (London: Longman, Green & Co., 1909).

Froude, James Anthony, *English Seamen in the Sixteenth Century* [1893] (London: Longman, Green & Co., 1897).

Fry, Henry, *The History of the North Atlantic Steam Navigation - with Some Account of Early Ships and Shipowners* [1896] (London: Cornmarket Press, 1969).

Gilroy, Paul, *The Black Atlantic. Modernity and Double Consciousness* (Cambridge, MA: Harvard University Press, 1993).

Gordon, Paul, and Danny Reilly, 'Guest Workers of the Sea: Racism in British Shipping', *Race & Class* 28, no. 2 (Autumn 1986), 73-82.

Grant de Pauw, Linda, *Seafaring Women* (Boston: Houghton Mifflin, 1982).

Hamilton-Paterson, James, *Seven Tenths. The Sea and Its Thresholds* (London: Hutchinson, 1992).

Hanson, Neil, *The Custom of the Sea* (London: Doubleday, 1997).

Hattendorf, John (ed.), *Maritime History*, 2 vols (Malabar, FL: Krieger, 1996).

Hau'ofa, Epeli, 'The Ocean in Us', *The Contemporary Pacific* 10 (1998), 391-410.

Henningsen, Henning, *Crossing the Equator: Sailor's Baptisms and Other Initiation Rites* (Copenhagen: Munksgaard, 1961).

Howell, Colin, and Richard Twomey (eds), *Jack Tar in History. Essays in the History of Maritime Life and Labour* (Fredricton, New Brunswick: Acadiensis Press, 1991).

Hugill, Stan, *Shanties from the Seven Seas* (London: Routledge and Kegan Paul, 1961).

Hugill, Stan, *Shanties and Sailors' Songs* (New York: Praeger, 1969).

Hugill, Stan, *Sailortown* (London: Routledge and Kegan Paul, 1976).

Hugill, Stan, *Sea Shanties* (London: Barrie and Jenkins, 1977).

Hulme, Peter, *Colonial Encounters. Europe and the Native Caribbean, 1492-1797* (London: Methuen, 1992).

Hulme, Peter, and William H. Sherman (eds), *'The Tempest' and Its Travels* (London: Reaktion, 2000).

Hyde, Francis, *Cunard and the North Atlantic, 1840-1973: A History of Shipping and Financial Management* (London: Macmillan, 1975).

Jenkin, A.K., *Cornish Seafarers: The Smuggling, Wrecking & Fishing Life of Cornwall* (London and Toronto: Dent, 1932).

Kinsey, Terry L., *Songs of the Sea* (London: Robert Hale, 1989).

Klausmann, Ulrike, *et al.* (eds), *Women Pirates and the Politics of the Jolly Roger* (Montreal and London: Black Rose, 1997).

Klein, Bernhard, and Gesa Mackenthun (eds), *Oceans and Voyagers. Historicizing the Sea as a Transnational Contact Zone* (forthcoming).

Klein, Bernhard, and Gesa Mackenthun (eds), *Das Meer als kulturelle Kontaktzone: Räume, Reisende, Repräsentationen* (Konstanz: Universitätsverlag Konstanz, forthcoming).

Krahé, Peter, *Literarische Seestücke: Darstellungen von Meer und Seefahrt in der englischen Literatur des 18.-20. Jahrhunderts* (Hamburg: Kabel, 1992).

Kramer, Jürgen, 'The Sea Is Culture', Bernhard Klein and Jürgen Kramer (eds), *Common Ground? Crossovers between Cultural Studies and Postcolonial Studies* (Trier: Wissenschaftlicher Verlag, 2001), 101-112.

Kunzig, Robert, *The Restless Sea. Exploring the World Beneath the Waves* (New York: W.W. Norton, 1999).

Kyselka, Will, *An Ocean in Mind* (Honolulu: University of Hawai'i Press, 1987).

Lemisch, Jesse, 'Jack Tar in the Streets: Merchant Seamen in the Politics of Revolutionary America', *William and Mary Quarterly* 25, no. 3 (1968), 371-407.

Leslie, Edward E., *Desperate Journeys, Abandoned Souls: True Stories of Castaways and Other Survivors* (Boston: Mariner Books, 1988).

Lincoln, Margarette, 'Shipwreck Narratives of the Eighteenth and Early Nineteenth Century', *British Journal for Eighteenth-Century Studies* 20 (1997), 155-72.

Lindsay, W.S., *History of Merchant Shipping and Ancient Commerce*, 4 vols (London: Sampson Low, Marston, Low, and Searle, 1874-6).

Linebaugh, Peter, 'All the Atlantic Mountains Shook', *Labour/Le Travailleur* 10 (1982), 87-121.

Linebaugh, Peter, and Marcus Rediker, *The Many-Headed Hydra. Sailors, Slaves, Commoners, and the Hidden History of the Revolutionary Atlantic* (Boston: Beacon Press, 2000).

Lloyd, Christopher, *The British Seaman, 1200-1860. A Social Survey* (London: Collins, 1968).

Lochbaum, Iris, *Fathoming Metaphors. Meeresbilder in viktorianischer Lyrik* (Trier: Wissenschaftlicher Verlag, 2001).

Louis, W. Roger (gen. ed.), *The Oxford History of the British Empire*, 5 vols (Oxford: Oxford University Press, 1998).

Lydenberg, Harry Miller, *Crossing the Line* (New York: New York Public Library, 1957).

Marsh, Arthur, and Victoria Ryan, *The Seamen: A History of the National Union of Seamen* (Oxford: Malthouse Press, 1989).

Mason, Michael, *et al.*, *The British Seafarer* (London: Hutchinson / BBC / The National Maritime Museum, 1980).

McPherson, Kenneth, *The Indian Ocean: A History of People and the Sea* (Delhi: Oxford University Press, 1993).

Michelet, Jules, *The Sea* [1861], trans. W.H.D. Adams (London: n.p., 1875).

Milne, Gordon, *Ports of Call. A Study of the American Nautical Novel* (Lanham and London: University Press of America, 1986).

Morton, Lena Beatrice, *The Influence of the Sea upon English Poetry from the Anglo-Saxon to the Victorian Period* (New York: Revisionist Press, 1976).

Nowé, L. Sannia, and M. Virdis (eds), *Naufragi* (Rome: Bulzoni Editure, 1993).

Parkhurst, P.G., *Ships of Peace: A Record of Some of the Problems Which Came Before the Board of Trade in Connection with the Mercantile Marine* (New Malden: P.G. Parkhurst, 1962).

Parry, J.H., *The Discovery of the Sea* (London: Weidenfeld and Nicolson, 1974).

Peck, John, *Maritime Fiction. Sailors and the Sea in British and American Novels, 1719-1917* (Basingstoke: Palgrave, 2001).

Pettinger, Alasdair (ed.), *Always Elsewhere: Travels of the Black Atlantic* (London: Cassell, 1998).

Philbrick, Thomas, *James Fenimore Cooper and the Development of American Sea Fiction* (Cambridge, MA: Harvard University Press, 1961).

Phillips, Caryl, *The Atlantic Sound* (New York: Knopf, 2000).

Prager, Ellen J., *The Oceans* (New York: McGraw Hill, 2000).

Raban, Jonathan (ed.), *The Oxford Book of the Sea* (Oxford: Oxford University Press, 1991).

Rankin, Hugh F., *The Golden Age of Piracy* (Williamsburg, VA: Colonial Williamsburg; New York: Holt, Rinehart and Winston, 1969).

Rediker, Marcus, *Between the Devil and the Deep Blue Sea: Merchant Seamen, Pirates, and the Anglo-American Maritime World, 1700-1750* (Cambridge: Cambridge University Press, 1987).

Rennie, Neil, *Far Fetched Facts: The Literature of Travel and the Idea of the South Seas* (Oxford: Oxford University Press, 1995).

Rice, E.E. (ed.), *The Sea and History* (Stround: Sutton Publishing, 1996).

Ritchie, Robert, *Captain Kidd and the War Against the Pirates* (Cambridge, MA: Harvard University Press, 1986).

Roncière, Monique de la, and Michel Mollat du Jourdin, *Portulane. Seekarten vom 13. bis zum 17. Jahrhundert* (München: Hirmer, 1984).

Ross, Ernest Carson, *The Development of the English Sea Novel from Defoe to Conrad* (Ann Arbor: Edwards Bros., 1925).

Rowe, Richard, *Jack Afloat and Jack Ashore* (London: Smith, Elder, 1875).

Rule, John, 'Wrecking and Coastal Plunder', Douglas Hay *et al.*, *Albion's Fatal Tree: Crime and Society in Eighteenth-Century England* (New York: Pantheon, 1975), 167-88.

Sager, Eric W., *Seafaring Labour: The Merchant Marine of Atlantic Canada, 1820-1914* (Kingston: McGill Queen's University Press, 1989).

Sauer, Albrecht, *Das 'Seebuch'. Das älteste erhaltene Seehandbuch und die spätmittelalterliche Navigation in Nordwesteuropa* (Hamburg: Ernst Kabel, 1997).

Scammell, G.V., *Ships, Oceans, and Empire. Studies in European Maritime and Colonial History, 1400-1750*, Variorum Collected Studies Series (Aldershot *et al.*: Ashgate, 1995).

Schmitt, Carl, *Land and Sea* [German original 1944], trans. Simona Draghici (Washington, DC: Plutarch Press, 1997).

Scott, Julius Sherrard III, 'The Common Wind: Circuits of Afro-American Communication in the Era of the Haitian Revolution', Ph.D. dissertation, Duke University, 1986.

Skallerup, Harry R., *Books Afloat and Ashore. A History of Books, Libraries, and Reading Among Seamen During the Age of Sail* (Hamden, CT: Archon, 1974).

Smetherton, Bobbie B., and Robert M. Smetherton, *Territorial Seas and Inter-American Relations* (New York: Praeger, 1974).

Smith, C. Fox, *Sailor Town Days* (London: Methuen, sec. ed. 1924).

Smith, Roger C., *Vanguard of Empire. Ships of Exploration in the Age of Columbus* (New York and Oxford: Oxford University Press, 1993).

Smith, Vanessa, *Literary Culture and the Pacific: Nineteenth-Century Textual Encounters* (Cambridge: Cambridge University Press, 1998).

Spratt, H. Philip, *Transatlantic Paddle Steamers* (Glasgow: Brown, Son and Ferguson, 1961).

Springer, Haskell (ed.), *America and the Sea* (Athens: University of Georgia Press, 1995).

Spufford, Francis, *I May Be Some Time: Ice and the English Imagination* (London: Faber and Faber, 1996).

Stark, Suzanne, *Female Tars. Women Aboard Ship in the Age of Sail* (London: Pimlico, 1998).

Stilgoe, John, *Alongshore* (New Haven: Yale University Press, 1994).

Tanner, Tony (ed.), *The Oxford Book of Sea Stories* (Oxford: Oxford University Press, 1994).

Treneer, Anne, *The Sea in English Literature. From Beowulf to Donne* (Liverpool: The University Press of Liverpool; London: Hodder and Stoughton, 1926).

Warner, Oliver, *English Maritime Writing: Hakluyt to Cook* (London: Longmans, 1958).

Waters, David W., *The Rutters of the Sea* (New Haven, CT, and London: Yale University Press, 1967).

Waters, David W., *The Art of Navigation in England in Elizabethan and Early Stuart Times*, 3 vols (Greenwich: National Maritime Museum, sec. ed. 1978).

Watson, Harold Francis, *The Sailor in English Fiction and Drama, 1550-1800* (New York: Columbia University Press, 1931).

Weibust, Knut, *Deep Sea Sailors: A Study in Maritime Ethnology* (Stockholm: Nordiska Museet, 1969).

Whall, W.B., *Sea Songs and Shanties* (Glasgow: Brown, and Ferguson, 6th ed. 1948).

Index

abolitionism, 68, 91, 188-9
Ackroyd, Peter, 53, 69-71
Act of Union, 96
Adams, John, 86
Admiralty, 80-81, 122, 124, 145
Africa Delivered (Grahame), 68
African, The (Courlander), 201n14
Alexander VI, 16, 17, 19, 20, 26n21
Allen, Jerry, 170
American Negro Slavery (Phillips, Ulrich B.), 189
Amistad (film by Spielberg), 199
Amistad (ship), 189
Anglesey Association for the Preservation of Life from Shipwreck, 110
Annus Mirabilis (Dryden), 55, 61, 74n34
Anson, George Lord, 66, 71, 76n60
Aristotle, 18
Armitage, David, 2
Arte de Navegar (Cortez), 33
astrolabe, 33
Atlantic Slave Trade: A Census, The (Curtin), 190
Atlantic Sound, The (Phillips, Caryl), 200
Atlas, or a geographicke description of the world (Mercator, Hondius, Janssonius), 59, Figure 3.3
Auden, W.H., 77
Augustine, 72n2
Austen, Jane, 183, 189

Bacon, Francis, 55

Bakhtin, Michail, 43
Bales, Kevin, 200
Ball, Alexander, 77
Barron, Joseph, 160
'Battle of the Sommer Islands' (Waller), 56
Battle Pieces and Aspects of War (Melville), 125-6
Bayley, John, 183, 187
Beach, The (film), 203
Behrendt, Stephen D., 191
Beloved (Morrison), 198
Benito Cereno (Melville), 189
Bennett, Tom, 110
Bentley, Richard, 51, 58-60, 74n32, 74n36
Berlin, Ira, 195
'Bermudas' (Marvell), 56, 58
Bestiarum (Anon.), 53-4, Figure 3.2
Black Atlantic, The (Gilroy), 191
Black Jacobins, The (James), 193
'Black Legend', 76n66
Blackburn, Robin, 191, 193, 199
Blackstone, Sir William, 96
Blackwood, William, 160, 169
Blackwood's Edinburgh Magazine, 163-4
Bligh, William, 81, 82, 84
Blue at the Mizzen (O'Brian), 183, 185
Blumenberg, Hans, 47n57, 48n64, 105-6, 107, 108, 115, 205, 217
Boccalini, Traiano, 41
Bodleian Library, 53
Bolshevik Revolution, 192

227